NINJA FOODI COOKBOOK

Easy - to - Make

550

Delicious Ninja Foodi Recipes

Jordan Roman

Legal & Disclaimer

Table of Content

Chapter 1 Breakfast Recipes

Cauliflower Hash browns

Servings: 6, **Prep Time:** 5 minutes, **Cooking Time:** 30 minutes

Ingredients:

- 6 eggs
- 4 cups riced cauliflower
- ¼ cup milk
- 1 onion, chopped
- 3 Tbsp butter
- 1 ½ cups chopped, cooked ham
- ½ cup shredded cheese

Directions:

1. Press the saute button on your Ninja Foodi and add the butter and the onions. Cook, stirring occasionally until the onions are soft, about 5 minutes.
2. Add the iced cauliflower to the pot and stir. Turn on the air crisper for 15 minutes, turning the cauliflower halfway through.
3. In a small bowl, mix the eggs and milk together then pour over the browned cauliflower.
4. Sprinkle the ham over the top of the egg mix.
5. Press the air crisp button again and set the timer for 10 minutes.
6. Sprinkle the cheddar cheese on top and close the lid of the Ninja Foodi for one minute to just melt the cheese. Serve while hot

Nutritional Info:

Calories: 166g, Carbohydrates: 3g, Protein: 9g, Fat: 14 g, Sugar: 1g, Sodium: 278 g

Raspberry Breakfast Cake

Servings: 6, **Prep Time:** 15 minutes, **Cooking Time:** 25 minutes

Ingredients:

- 8 Tbsp butter
- ½ cup Baking Stevia
- 1 egg
- 1 tsp vanilla
- 2 cups almond flour
- 2 tsp baking powder
- 1 tsp salt
- 1 cup fresh raspberries
- ½ cup buttermilk

Directions:

1. Use an electric mixer to cream the butter and stevia together until they are light and fluffy.
2. Mix the vanilla and eggs in a small bowl then add to the mixer with the butter blend. Ix until just combined

3. In a separate bowl, toss the raspberries and ¼ cup almond flour to coat the berries.
4. Add the remaining dry ingredients to the mixer and fold together by hand. Add the buttermilk and mix until smooth.
5. Add the raspberries to the batter and mix briefly.
6. Pour the cake batter into your Ninja Foodi and place the lid on.
7. Press the air crisp button and set the temperature to 350 degrees and program the timer to 25 minutes.
8. Once cooked, a toothpick should come out of the center of the cake cleanly. Allow to cool and serve.

Nutritional Info:
Calories: 183 g, Carbohydrates: 8g, Protein: 3g, Fat: 16 g, Sugar: 3g, Sodium: 464 g

Pumpkin Spice Breakfast Cake

Servings: 6, **Prep Time:** 15 minutes, **Cooking Time:** 25 minutes

Ingredients:
- 8 Tbsp butter
- ½ cup Baking Stevia
- 1 egg
- 1 tsp vanilla
- 2 cups almond flour
- 2 tsp baking powder
- 1 tsp salt
- 1 tsp cinnamon
- ¼ tsp nutmeg
- ¼ tsp ginger
- 1 cup pumpkin puree

Directions:
1. Use an electric mixer to cream the butter and stevia together until they are light and fluffy.
2. Mix the vanilla and eggs in a small bowl then add to the mixer with the butter blend. Ix until just combined
3. Add the remaining dry ingredients to the mixer and fold together by hand. Add the pumpkin puree and mix until smooth.
4. Pour the cake batter into your Ninja Foodi and place the lid on.
5. Press the air crisp button and set the temperature to 350 degrees and program the timer to 25 minutes.
6. Once cooked, a toothpick should come out of the center of the cake cleanly. Allow to cool and serve.

Nutritional Info:
Calories: 176g, Carbohydrates: 8g, Protein: 3g, Fat: 16 g, Sugar: 2g, Sodium: 127 g

Bacon and Egg Bites

Servings: 6, **Prep Time:** 10 minutes, **Cooking Time:** 20 minutes

Ingredients:

- 5 slices bacon
- ½ cup milk
- 1 cup chopped spinach
- 6 eggs

Directions:

1. Place the bacon strips in the Ninja Foodi air crisper basket and use the air crisp function, set for 10 minutes to cook the bacon. Remove the basket and the strips and pour the bacon grease into a separate small bowl.
2. Add the eggs to the bacon grease along with the spinach, crumbled cooked bacon and milk.
3. Spray an egg bite mold and pour the egg mix evenly into each mold. Place the mold on top of the metal trivet inside the Ninja Foodi. Lower the crisper lid and set the temperature for 375 for 17 minutes.
4. Once cooked, remove the egg mold from the Ninja Foodi and let cool. Pop the egg bites out of the mold and serve hot or cold.

Nutritional Info:

Calories: 118g, Carbohydrates: 2g , Protein: 9g, Fat: 8 g, Sugar: 2g, Sodium: 216 g

Veggie Egg Casserole

Servings: 4, **Prep Time:** 5 minutes, **Cooking Time:** 7 minutes

Ingredients:

- 4 eggs
- 1 Tbsp milk
- 1 tomato, diced
- ½ cup spinach
- ¼ tsp salt
- ¼ tsp ground black pepper

Directions:

1. Prepare a baking pan that fits in your Ninja Foodi bowl by greasing the pan with butter. Set aside
2. In a medium bowl, whisk together the eggs, milk, salt and pepper and then add the veggies to the bowl and stir briefly.
3. Pour the egg mix into the prepared baking pan and lower the pan into the Ninja Foodi.
4. Set the Ninja Foodi to air crisp at 325 for 7 minutes.
5. Remove the pan of eggs from the Ninja Foodi and enjoy while hot!

Nutritional Info:

Calories: 78g, Carbohydrates: 1g , Protein: 7g, Fat: 5g, Sugar: 2g, Sodium: 660 g

Ham and Eggs Casserole

Servings: 4, **Prep Time:** 5 minutes, **Cooking Time:** 7 minutes

Ingredients:

- 4 eggs
- 1 Tbsp milk
- 1 cup cooked, chopped ham
- ½ cup Shredded cheddar cheese
- ¼ tsp salt
- ¼ tsp ground black pepper

Directions:

1. Prepare a baking pan that fits in your Ninja Foodi bowl by greasing the pan with butter. Set aside
2. In a medium bowl, whisk together the eggs, milk, salt and pepper and then add the ham and cheese to the bowl and stir briefly.
3. Pour the egg mix into the prepared baking pan and lower the pan into the Ninja Foodi.
4. Set the Ninja Foodi to air crisp at 325 for 7 minutes.
5. Remove the pan of eggs from the Ninja Foodi and enjoy while hot!

Nutritional Info:

Calories: 169g, Carbohydrates: 1g , Protein: 12g, Fat: 13g, Sugar: 1g, Sodium: 455 g

Bacon, Broccoli and Cheddar Frittata

Servings: 4, **Prep Time:** 5 minutes, **Cooking Time:** 7 minutes

Ingredients:

- 6 eggs
- 2 Tbsp milk
- ½ cup chopped, cooked bacon
- 1 cup cooked broccoli
- ½ cup shredded cheddar cheese
- ¼ tsp salt
- ¼ tsp ground black pepper

Directions:

1. Prepare a baking pan that fits in your Ninja Foodi bowl by greasing the pan with butter. Set aside
2. In a medium bowl, whisk together the eggs, milk, salt and pepper and then add the bacon, broccoli and cheese to the bowl and stir briefly.
3. Pour the egg mix into the prepared baking pan and lower the pan into the Ninja Foodi.
4. Set the Ninja Foodi to air crisp at 325 for 7 minutes.
5. Remove the pan of eggs from the Ninja Foodi and enjoy while hot!

Nutritional Info:

Calories: 269g, Carbohydrates: 3g, Protein: 19g, Fat: 20g, Sugar: 2g, Sodium: 370 g

Blackberry Muffins

Servings: 6, **Prep Time:** 15 minutes, **Cooking Time:** 25 minutes

Ingredients:

- 8 Tbsp butter
- ½ cup Baking Stevia
- 1 egg
- 1 tsp vanilla
- 2 cups coconut flour
- 2 tsp baking powder
- 1 tsp salt
- 1 cup fresh blackberries
- ½ cup buttermilk

Directions:

1. Use an electric mixer to cream the butter and stevia together until they are light and fluffy.
2. Mix the vanilla and eggs in a small bowl then add to the mixer with the butter blend. Mix until just combined
3. In a separate bowl, toss the blackberries and ¼ cup almond flour to coat the berries.
4. Add the remaining dry ingredients to the mixer and fold together by hand. Add the buttermilk and mix until smooth.
5. Add the blackberries to the batter and mix briefly.
6. Pour the muffin batter into eight silicone muffin cups. Place the muffin cups inside the Ninja Foodi on top of a metal trivet.
7. Press the air crisp button and set the temperature to 350 degrees and program the timer to 25 minutes.
8. Once cooked, a toothpick should come out of the center of the cake cleanly. Allow to cool and serve.

Nutritional Info:

Calories: 285g, Carbohydrates: 2g , Protein: 6g, Fat: 17g, Sugar: 3g, Sodium: 590 g

Coconut Oatmeal

Servings:6, **Prep Time:** 5 minutes, **Cooking Time:** 10 minutes

Ingredients:

- 1 cup shredded dried coconut flakes
- 3 cups coconut milk
- 3 cups water
- ¼ cup psyllium husks
- ½ cup coconut flour
- 1 ½ tsp vanilla extract
- ½ tsp cinnamon
- ½ cup granulated stevia

Directions:

1. Add all of the ingredients into the Ninja Foodi and stir together briefly
2. Place the lid on and set the steamer valve to seal. Set the pressure cooker

function to 1 minute (it will take about 10 minutes to come to pressure).

3. When the oatmeal is done, do a quick pressure release by opening the steamer valve carefully. Serve while hot

Nutritional Info:
Calories: 202g, Carbohydrates: 6g , Protein: 3g, Fat: 16g, Sugar: 2g, Sodium: 52 g

Almond Spice Oatmeal

Servings: 6, **Prep Time:** 5 minutes, **Cooking Time:** 10 minutes

Ingredients:

- 1 ½ cups chopped almonds
- 3 cups almond milk
- 2 cups water
- ½ cup psyllium husks
- 1 ½ tsp vanilla extract
- ½ tsp cinnamon
- ¼ tsp nutmeg
- ½ cup granulated stevia

Directions:

1. Add all of the ingredients into the Ninja Foodi and stir together briefly

2. Place the lid on and set the steamer valve to seal. Set the pressure cooker function to 1 minute (it will take about 10 minutes to come to pressure).

3. When the oatmeal is done, do a quick pressure release by opening the steamer valve carefully. Serve while hot

Nutritional Info:
Calories: 136g, Carbohydrates: 3g, Protein: 4g, Fat: 9g, Sugar: 1g, Sodium: 66 g

Almond Muffins

Servings: 6, **Prep Time:** 15 minutes, **Cooking Time:** 25 minutes

Ingredients:

- 8 Tbsp butter
- ½ cup Baking Stevia
- 1 egg
- 1 tsp vanilla
- 2 cups coconut flour
- 2 tsp baking powder
- 1 tsp salt
- ½ cup chopped almonds
- ½ cup buttermilk

Directions:

1. Use an electric mixer to cream the butter and stevia together until they are light and fluffy.

2. Mix the vanilla and eggs in a small bowl then add to the mixer with the butter blend. Mix until just combined

3. Add the remaining dry ingredients to the mixer and fold together by hand. Add the buttermilk and mix until smooth.
4. Add the almonds to the batter and mix briefly.
5. Pour the muffin batter into eight silicone muffin cups. Place the muffin cups inside the Ninja Foodi on top of a metal trivet.
6. Press the air crisp button and set the temperature to 350 degrees and program the timer to 25 minutes.
7. Once cooked, a toothpick should come out of the center of the cake cleanly. Allow to cool and serve.

Nutritional Info:
Calories: 2386g, Carbohydrates: 29g, Protein: 6g, Fat: 26g, Sugar: 5g, Sodium: 699 g

Three Cheese Eggs

Servings: 4, **Prep Time:** 5 minutes, **Cooking Time:** 7 minutes

Ingredients:
- 4 eggs
- 1 Tbsp milk
- ¼ cup Shredded cheddar cheese
- ¼ cup swiss cheese
- ¼ cup American cheese
- ¼ tsp salt
- ¼ tsp ground black pepper

Directions:
1. Prepare a baking pan that fits in your Ninja Foodi bowl by greasing the pan with butter. Set aside
2. In a medium bowl, whisk together the eggs, milk, salt and pepper and then add the ham and cheese to the bowl and stir briefly.
3. Pour the egg mix into the prepared baking pan and lower the pan into the Ninja Foodi.
4. Set the Ninja Foodi to air crisp at 325 for 7 minutes.
5. Remove the pan of eggs from the Ninja Foodi and enjoy while hot!

Nutritional Info:
Calories: 138g, Carbohydrates: 1g , Protein: 11g, Fat: 10g, Sugar: 2g, Sodium: 711 g

Bacon, Tomato and Eggs

Servings: 4, **Prep Time:** 5 minutes, **Cooking Time:** 7 minutes

Ingredients:

- 4 eggs
- 1 Tbsp milk
- ½ cup crumbled bacon
- 1 tomato, diced
- ¼ tsp salt
- ¼ tsp ground black pepper

Directions:

1. Prepare a baking pan that fits in your Ninja Foodi bowl by greasing the pan with butter. Set aside
2. In a medium bowl, whisk together the eggs, milk, salt and pepper and then add the ham and cheese to the bowl and stir briefly.
3. Pour the egg mix into the prepared baking pan and lower the pan into the Ninja Foodi.
4. Set the Ninja Foodi to air crisp at 325 for 7 minutes.
5. Remove the pan of eggs from the Ninja Foodi and enjoy while hot!

Nutritional Info:

Calories: 157g, Carbohydrates: 2g , Protein: 11g, Fat: 12g, Sugar: 3g, Sodium: 957 g

Avocado Eggs

Servings: 4, **Prep Time:** 5 minutes, **Cooking Time:** 7 minutes

Ingredients:

- 4 eggs
- 2 Avocados, sliced
- ¼ tsp salt
- ¼ tsp ground black pepper

Directions:

1. Prepare a baking pan that fits in your Ninja Foodi bowl by greasing the pan with butter. Set aside
2. Crack the eggs into the prepared baking pan and sprinkle with the salt and pepper. Lower the pan into the Ninja Foodi.
3. Set the Ninja Foodi to air crisp at 325 for 7 minutes.
4. Remove the pan of eggs from the Ninja Foodi and place the sliced avocado on top. Enjoy while hot!

Nutritional Info:

Calories: 190g, Carbohydrates: 7g , Protein: 8g, Fat: 15g, Sugar: 2g, Sodium: 657 g

Bacon, Avocado and Cheese

Servings: 4, **Prep Time:** 5 minutes, **Cooking Time:** 7 minutes

Ingredients:

- 8 slices bacon
- 2 Avocados, sliced
- ½ cup cheddar cheese
- ¼ tsp ground black pepper

Directions:

1. Prepare a baking pan that fits in your Ninja Foodi bowl by greasing the pan with butter. Set aside
2. Lay the bacon strips inside the Ninja Foodi, trying not to layer them on top of each other.
3. Set the Ninja Foodi to air crisp at 325 for 7 minutes.
4. Remove the pan of bacon from the Ninja Foodi and place the sliced avocado on top. Sprinkle the top with the cheese and with the ground black pepper. Return to the Foodi and cook for another 2 minutes to melt the cheese. Remove and enjoy while hot!

Nutritional Info:

Calories: 265g, Carbohydrates: 8g , Protein: 10g, Fat: 23g, Sugar: 2g, Sodium: 431 g

Cheesy Hash

Servings: 6, **Prep Time:** 5 minutes, **Cooking Time:** 30 minutes

Ingredients:

- 6 eggs
- 4 cups riced cauliflower
- ¼ cup milk
- 1 onion, chopped
- 3 Tbsp butter
- 1 ½ cups cheddar cheese

Directions:

1. Press the saute button on your Ninja Foodi and add the butter and the onions. Cook, stirring occasionally until the onions are soft, about 5 minutes.
2. Add the iced cauliflower to the pot and stir. Turn on the air crisper for 15 minutes, turning the cauliflower halfway through.
3. In a small bowl, mix the eggs and milk together then pour over the browned cauliflower.
4. Sprinkle the cheddar cheese on top and close the lid of the Ninja Foodi for one minute to just melt the cheese. Serve while hot

Nutritional Info:

Calories: 291g, Carbohydrates: 8g, Protein: 18g, Fat: 22 g, Sugar: 1g, Sodium: 729g

Bacon and Egg Hash

Servings: 6, **Prep Time:** 5 minutes, **Cooking Time:** 30 minutes

Ingredients:

- 6 eggs
- 4 cups riced cauliflower
- ¼ cup milk
- 1 cup crumbled, cooked bacon
- 1 onion, chopped
- 3 Tbsp butter
- ½ cups cheddar cheese

Directions:

1. Press the saute button on your Ninja Foodi and add the butter and the onions. Cook, stirring occasionally until the onions are soft, about 5 minutes.
2. Add the riced cauliflower to the pot and stir. Turn on the air crisper for 15 minutes, turning the cauliflower halfway through.
3. In a small bowl, mix the eggs and milk together then pour over the browned cauliflower.
4. Sprinkle the cheddar cheese on top and close the lid of the Ninja Foodi for one minute to just melt the cheese. Serve while hot

Nutritional Info:

Calories: 301g, Carbohydrates: 3g, Protein: 18g, Fat: 26 g, Sugar: 1g, Sodium: 595g

Sweet and Savory Oatmeal

Servings: 6   **Prep Time:** 5 minutes   **Cooking Time:** 10 minutes

Ingredients:

- 3 cups almond milk
- 2 cups water
- ½ cup psyllium husks
- 1 ½ tsp vanilla extract
- ½ tsp cinnamon
- ¼ tsp nutmeg
- ½ cup granulated stevia
- ½ cup crumbled, cooked bacon

Directions:

1. Add all of the ingredients into the Ninja Foodi and stir together briefly
2. Place the lid on and set the steamer valve to seal. Set the pressure cooker function to 1 minute (it will take about 10 minutes to come to pressure).
3. When the oatmeal is done, do a quick pressure release by opening the steamer valve carefully. Serve while hot

Nutritional Info:

Calories: 65g, Carbohydrates: 4g , Protein: 1g, Fat: 8g, Sugar: 0g, Sodium: 316 g

Almond French Toast

Servings: 4   **Prep Time:** 5 minutes   **Cooking Time:** 7 minutes

Ingredients:
- 6 eggs
- 1 cup milk
- 4 cups keto almond bread, cut in cubes
- ¼ tsp salt
- 1 tsp vanilla extract
- ½ tsp cinnamon

Directions:
1. Prepare a baking pan that fits in your Ninja Foodi bowl by greasing the pan with butter. Set aside
2. In a medium bowl, whisk together the eggs, milk, salt, vanilla and cinnamon and then add the almond bread to the bowl and stir briefly. Let sit for one hour
3. Pour the egg mix into the prepared baking pan and lower the pan into the Ninja Foodi.
4. Set the Ninja Foodi to air crisp at 325 for 18 minutes.
5. Remove the pan of French toast from the Ninja Foodi and enjoy while hot!

Nutritional Info:
Calories: 220g, Carbohydrates: 8g , Protein: 22g, Fat: 11g, Sugar: 5g, Sodium:708 g

Almond French Toast

Servings: 4   **Prep Time:** 5 minutes   **Cooking Time:** 7 minutes

Ingredients:
- 6 eggs
- 1 cup milk
- 4 cups keto almond bread, cut in cubes
- ¼ tsp salt
- 1 tsp vanilla extract
- ½ tsp cinnamon
- 1 cup fresh raspberries

Directions:
1. Prepare a baking pan that fits in your Ninja Foodi bowl by greasing the pan with butter. Set aside
2. In a medium bowl, whisk together the eggs, milk, salt, vanilla and cinnamon and then add the almond bread to the bowl and stir briefly. Let sit for one hour
3. Fold raspberries into mix.
4. Pour the egg mix into the prepared baking pan and lower the pan into the Ninja Foodi.
5. Set the Ninja Foodi to air crisp at 325 for 18 minutes.
6. Remove the pan of French toast from the Ninja Foodi and enjoy while hot!

Nutritional Info:
Calories: 228g, Carbohydrates: 11g , Protein: 22g, Fat: 11g, Sugar: 6g, Sodium:708 mg

Spinach Quiche

Serves: 6, Cooking Time: 45 minutes

Ingredients:

- 1 tbsp. melted butter
- 10 oz. frozen and thawed spinach
- 5 beaten eggs
- Salt and black pepper
- 3 c. shredded Monterey Jack cheese

Directions:

1. Press "Sauté" on Ninja Foodi and add butter and spinach.
2. Sauté for about 3 minutes and dish out in a bowl.
3. Add eggs, Monterey Jack cheese, salt and black pepper to a bowl and transfer into greased molds.
4. Place the molds inside the pot of Ninja Foodi and press "Bake/Roast".
5. Set the timer to 30 minutes at 360 degrees F and press "Start".
6. Remove from the Ninja Foodi after 30 minutes and cut into equal sized wedges to serve.

Nutritional Info:
349 calories, 27.8g fat, 3.2g carbs, 23g protein

Tofu with Mushrooms

Serves: 6, Cooking Time: 10 minutes

Ingredients:

- 8 tbsps. shredded Parmesan cheese
- 2 c. freshly chopped mushrooms
- 2 blocks tofu, cubed
- Salt and black pepper
- 8 tbsps. butter

Directions:

1. Mix together tofu, salt and black pepper in a bowl.
2. Press "Sauté" on Ninja Foodi and add butter and seasoned tofu.
3. Sauté for about 5 minutes and add mushrooms and Parmesan cheese.
4. Sauté for about 3 minutes and press "Air Crisp".
5. Cook for about 2 minutes at 350 degrees F and dish out in a serving plate.

Nutritional Info: 211 calories, 18.5g fat, 2g carbs, 11.5g protein

Bacon Veggies Combo

Serves: 4, Cooking Time: 25 minutes

Ingredients:

- 1 chopped green bell pepper, seeded
- 4 bacon slices
- ½ c. Parmesan Cheese
- 1 tbsp. avocado mayonnaise
- 2 chopped scallions

Directions:

1. Arrange bacon slices in the pot of Ninja Foodi and top with avocado mayonnaise, bell peppers, scallions and Parmesan Cheese.
2. Press "Bake/Roast" and set the timer to 25 minutes at 365 degrees F.
3. Remove from the Ninja Foodi after 25 minutes and dish out to serve.

Nutritional Info: 197 calories, 13.8g fat, 4.7g carbs, 14.3g protein

Onion Tofu Scramble

(Cooking Time: 8 minutes | Serves: 4)

Ingredients:

- 4 tbsps. butter
- 2 blocks tofu, cubed
- Salt and black pepper
- 1 c. grated cheddar cheese
- 2 medium sliced onions

Directions:

1. Mix together tofu, salt and black pepper in a bowl.
2. Press "Sauté" on Ninja Foodi and add butter and onions.
3. Sauté for about 3 minutes and add seasoned tofu.
4. Cook for about 2 minutes and add cheddar cheese.
5. Lock the lid and set the Ninja Foodi on "Air Crisp" for about 3 minutes at 340 degrees F.
6. Dish out in a serving plate and serve hot.

Nutritional Info: 184 calories, 12.7g fat, 6.3g carbs, 12.2g protein

Pepperoni Omelet

(Cooking Time: 5 minutes | Serves: 4)

Ingredients:
- 4 tbsps. heavy cream
- 15 pepperoni slices
- 2 tbsps. butter
- Salt and black pepper
- 6 eggs

Directions:
1. Whisk together the eggs, heavy cream, pepperoni slices, salt and black pepper in a bowl.
2. Press "Sauté" on Ninja Foodi and add butter and egg mixture.
3. Sauté for about 3 minutes and flip the side of the omelette.
4. Lock the lid and set the Ninja Foodi on "Air Crisp" for about 2 minutes at 350 degrees F.
5. Dish out in a serving plate and serve with low carb bread.

Nutritional Info: 141 calories, 11.3g fat, 0.6g carbs, 8.9g protein

Ham Spinach Ballet

(Cooking Time: 35 minutes | Serves: 8)

Ingredients:
- 3 lbs. fresh baby spinach
- ½ c. cream
- 28 oz. sliced ham
- 4 tbsps. melted butter
- Salt and freshly ground black pepper

Directions:
1. Press "Sauté" on Ninja Foodi and add butter and spinach.
2. Sauté for about 3 minutes and top with cream, ham slices, salt and black pepper.
3. Lock the lid and set the Ninja Foodi to "Bake/Roast" for about 8 minutes at 360 degrees F.
4. Remove from the Ninja Foodi after 8 minutes and dish out to serve.

Nutritional Info: 188 calories, 12.5g fat, 4.9g carbs, 14.6g protein

Sausage Solo

(Cooking Time: 35 minutes | Serves: 4)

Ingredients:

- 4 eggs
- 4 cooked and sliced sausages
- 2 tbsps. butter
- ½ c. grated mozzarella cheese
- ½ c. cream

Directions:

1. Mix together eggs and cream in a bowl and beat well.
2. Put the egg mixture in the pot of Ninja Foodi and top evenly with cheese and sausage slices.
3. Press "Bake/Roast" and set the timer to 20 minutes at 345 degrees F.
4. Dish out after 20 minutes and serve immediately.

Nutritional Info: 180 calories, 12.7g fat, 3.9g carbs, 12.4g protein

Mini Frittatas

(Cooking Time: 10 minutes | Serves: 5)

Ingredients:

- 5 eggs
- Splash of almond milk
- Salt and pepper
- Desired mix in's: cheese, veggies, meats, the options are endless!

Directions:

1. Preparing the ingredients, Mix eggs, milk, and mix-in's in a dish. Pour mixture into individual baking molds. Place molds on rack in Ninja Foodi with 1 cup of water.
2. High pressure for 5 minutes. Close the lid and the pressure valve and then cook for 5 minutes. To get 5-minutes cook time, press "Pressure" button and use the TIME ADJUSTMENT button to adjust the cook time to 5 minutes.
3. Pressure Release Use the quick-release method when the timer goes off and cooking is done.
4. Enjoy!

Nutritional Info: 342.5 calories, 23.7g fat, 8.2g carbs, 25g protein

Chapter 2 Vegetable Recipes

Chive 'n Parsnips Chowder

Serving: 2, Cooking time: 10 minutes

Ingredients:

- 10-oz parsnips, trimmed and peeled
- 1 clove garlic, minced
- 1 tbsp raw cashews
- 1 1/4 cup vegetable broth
- ¼ lemon, juiced, freshly squeezed
- 2 tbsp fresh chives, chopped
- Salt and pepper to taste

Directions:

1. Place all ingredients in the Ninja Foodi
2. Install pressure lid. Close Ninja Foodi, press the pressure button, choose high settings, and set time to 10 minutes.
3. Once done cooking, do a quick release.
4. Open the lid and use an immersion blender to pulse everything until smooth.
5. Serve and enjoy.

Nutrition information:
Calories: 199; carbohydrates: 29.9g; protein: 3.5g; fat: 7.2g

Vegetable Masala Indian Style

Serving: 2, Cooking time: 25 minutes

Ingredients:

- 1 tablespoon olive oil
- 3 black whole peppercorns
- 2 green cardamoms
- 2 whole cloves
- 1 bay leave
- 1/4 cup tomato puree
- 1 teaspoon coriander powder
- 1/2 teaspoon garam masala
- ¼ teaspoon red chili powder
- 1/4 teaspoon turmeric powder
- 1/4 cup water
- 1/2 cup coconut milk
- ½ teaspoon sugar
- 1 small potato, peeled and chopped
- Salt and pepper to taste
- ¼ lemon, juiced
- 1 tablespoon chopped cilantro

Directions:

1. Press the sauté button on the Ninja Foodi and heat the oil.

2. Stir in the whole peppercorns, cardamoms, cloves, and bay leaf until fragrant.

3. Add in the tomato puree, coriander powder, garam masala, chili powder, and turmeric powder.

4. Stir in water, coconut milk, sugar and potatoes. Season with salt and pepper to taste.

5. Install pressure lid. Close Ninja Foodi, press the button, choose high settings, and set time to 20 minutes. Once done cooking, do a quick release.

6. Open the lid and stir in the lemon juice and cilantro. Serve and enjoy.

Nutrition information:
Calories: 261; carbohydrates: 14g; protein: 4g; fat: 21g

Parmesan 'n Garlic Fries

Servings: 2, Cooking time:15 minutes

Ingredients:
- 2 russet potatoes, scrubbed and julienned into thick strips
- 1 tablespoon olive oil
- 1 tablespoon salt
- ¼ cup parmesan cheese, grated
- ½ teaspoon garlic powder
- 2 tablespoons chopped parsley

Directions:
1. Place the potatoes in a bowl and add the rest of the ingredients.

2. Toss to combine all ingredients.

3. Add ingredients to the Cook & Crisp basket.

4. Close the Ninja Foodi and cook for 15 minutes.

5. Halfway through the cooking time, give a good shake.

Nutrition information:
Calories: 417; carbs: 69g; protein: 11.7g; fat: 10.5g

Crispy Sweet Potato Fries

Servings: 2, Cooking time:15 minutes

Ingredients:

- 2 large sweet orange sweet potatoes, peeled and cut into thick strips
- 2 tablespoons olive oil
- 1 teaspoon paprika
- 1 teaspoon garlic powder
- Salt and pepper to taste
- 1 ripe avocado, flesh scooped
- 2 tablespoons sour cream
- 2 tablespoons fresh cilantro, chopped
- Juice from ½ lime
- ½ teaspoon garlic, minced

Directions:

1. Place the sweet potatoes in a bowl and season with oil, paprika, garlic powder, salt, and pepper.
2. Toss to coat.
3. Add ingredients to the Cook & Crisp basket.
4. Close the Ninja Foodi and cook for 15 minutes at 330°F.
5. Halfway through the cooking time, give the basket a shake.
6. Meanwhile, prepare the avocado dip by combining the rest of the ingredient in a food processor.
7. Dip the sweet potatoes in the avocado dressing.

Nutrition information:
Calories: 506; carbs: 52g; protein: 7.1g; fat:30 g

Southwest' s Chickpea Gumbo

Serving: 2, Cooking time: 12 minutes

Ingredients:

- 1/2 tablespoon olive oil
- 1 teaspoon minced garlic
- 3/4 cup chopped onion
- 1 celery rib, chopped
- 1 tsp oregano
- ½ teaspoon cayenne pepper
- 1/3 cup cooked chickpeas
- 1 1/2 cups vegetable broth
- 1/2 cup frozen okra
- 1/2 red bell pepper, chopped
- 1/2 can diced tomatoes, drained
- 1 tablespoon apple cider vinegar
- ½ cups tomato sauce
- 1/2 cup cauliflower, cut into florets

- Salt and pepper to taste

Directions:

1. Press the sauté button on the Ninja Foodi and heat the oil. Sauté the garlic, onions, and celery until fragrant.
2. Stir in the rest of the ingredients.
3. Install pressure lid. Close Ninja Foodi, press the manual button, choose high settings, and set time to 10 minutes.
4. Once done cooking, do a quick release.
5. Serve and enjoy.

Nutrition information:
Calories: 227; carbohydrates: 29.2g; protein: 13.2g; fat: 6.3g

Tasty 'n Easy To Make Baked Potatoes

Servings: 2, Cooking time: 35 minutes

Ingredients:

- 2 medium russet potato
- 2 teaspoon canola oil
- 1/2 teaspoon onion powder
- Salt and pepper to taste
- 2 tablespoons cream cheese
- 2 tablespoons chopped chives

Directions:

1. Brush the potatoes until clean.
2. Place the Cook & Crisp basket in the Ninja Foodi and add potatoes.
3. Brush with oil on all surface and season with onion powder, salt, and pepper.
4. Close the Ninja Foodi and cook for 35 minutes at 350^0F.
5. Once cooked, slice through the potato and serve with cream cheese and chives.

Nutrition information:
Calories: 413; carbs: 72.3g; protein:10.2 g; fat: 9.2g

Crispy Fried Green Tomatoes

Servings: 2, Cooking time:7 minutes

Ingredients:
- 1 cup panko bread crumbs
- 6 tablespoons cornstarch
- 1 teaspoon dried basil, ground
- 1 teaspoon dried oregano, ground
- 1 teaspoon granulated onion
- Salt and pepper to taste
- 2 medium-sized green tomato, sliced
- 1 teaspoon cooking oil

Directions:
1. In a mixing bowl, combine the panko bread crumbs, cornstarch, basil, oregano, onion, salt and pepper.
2. Dredge the tomato slices in the bread crumb mixture.
3. Brush with oil and arrange on the Cook & Crisp basket.
4. Place the Cook & Crisp basket in the Ninja Foodi.
5. Close the lid and cook for 7 minutes at 330^0F.

Nutrition information:
Calories: 269; carbs: 54.1g; protein: 5.4g; fat: 3.4g

Crispy Kale Chips in Ninja Foodi

Servings: 2, Cooking time: 7 minutes

Ingredients:
- 3 cups kale leaves, stem removed
- 1 tablespoon olive oil
- Salt and pepper to taste

Directions:
1) In a bowl, combine all of the ingredients: and toss to coat the kale leaves with oil, salt and pepper.
2) Arrange kale leaves on the double layer rack and insert inside the Ninja Foodi.
3) Close the Ninja Foodi and cook it to 7 minutes at 370^0f.
4) Allow to cool before serving.

Nutrition information:
Calories: 85; carbs: 4.2g; protein: 1.35g; fat: 6.9g

Quinoa 'n Lime-Cilantro Salad

Serving: 2, Cooking time: 15 minutes

Ingredients:
- 1 cup quinoa, rinsed and drained
- 1 ¼ cups vegetable broth
- 2 tablespoons lime juice
- Zest from one lime, grated
- ½ cup chopped cilantro
- Salt to taste

Directions:
1. In the Ninja Foodi, place the quinoa and vegetable broth.
2. Install pressure lid. Close Ninja Foodi, press the pressure button, choose high settings, and set time to 15 minutes.
3. Once done cooking, do a quick release.
4. Open the lid and fluff the quinoa using fork. Transfer to a bowl and let it cool.
5. Assemble the salad by adding into the quinoa the remaining ingredients.
6. Serve and enjoy.

Nutrition information:
Calories: 101; carbohydrates: 19g; protein: 4g; fat: 1g

Tomato 'n Eggplant Pasta

Serving: 3, Cooking time: 25 minutes

Ingredients:
- 1 tablespoon olive oil
- 1 red onion, chopped
- 2 cloves of garlic, chopped
- 1 eggplant, chopped
- 1 can chopped tomatoes
- 1-pound pasta
- Enough vegetable broth to cover the pasta
- ¼ cup black olives, pitted and sliced
- Salt and pepper to taste

Directions:
1. Press the sauté button on the Ninja Foodi and heat the oil. Sauté the onions and garlic until fragrant before adding the eggplants. Allow the eggplants to wilt before adding the rest of the ingredients.
2. Install pressure lid. Close Ninja Foodi, press the pressure button, choose high settings, and set time to 20 minutes.
3. Once done cooking, do a quick release.
4. Serve and enjoy.

Nutrition information:
Calories: 394; carbohydrates: 73g; protein: 12g; fat: 6g

Creamy Tomato-Basil soup

Serving: 2, Cooking time: 9 minutes

Ingredients:
- 1 tablespoon olive oil
- 1 onion, chopped
- 2 medium carrots, peeled and chopped
- 1 can fire roasted tomatoes
- ¾ cup vegetable broth
- 2 teaspoons dried basil
- 1 teaspoon salt
- 2 teaspoons sugar
- 1/2 cup cashew nuts, soaked

Directions:
1. Press the sauté button on the Ninja Foodi and heat the oil.
2. Stir in the onions and carrots for 3 minutes
3. Add the rest of the ingredients.
4. Install pressure lid. Close Ninja Foodi, press the pressure button, choose high settings, and set time to 6 minutes.
5. Once done cooking, do a quick release.
6. Open the lid and transfer the contents into a blender. Pulse until smooth.
7. Serve and enjoy.

Nutrition information:
Calories: 415; carbohydrates: 27.7g; protein: 8.8g; fat: 29.9g

Vegan-Approved Fajita Pasta

Serving: 2, Cooking time: 9 minutes

Ingredients:
- 1 teaspoon oil
- 2 cloves of garlic, minced
- 1/3 cup chopped bell peppers
- 1/3 cup black beans, cooked
- 1/2 teaspoon taco seasoning mix
- 1 1/3 cups pasta, cooked according to package instruction
- 2/3 cup commercial enchilada sauce
- Salt and pepper to taste

Directions:
1. Press the sauté button on the Ninja Foodi and heat the oil. Stir in the garlic and bell peppers and allow to wilt for 3 minutes.
2. Add the rest of the ingredients.
3. Install pressure lid. Close Ninja Foodi, press the manual button, choose high settings, and set time to 6 minutes.
4. Once done cooking, do a quick release.
5. Serve and enjoy.

Nutrition information:
Calories: 282; carbohydrates: 52.1g; protein: 10.4g; fat: 3.5g

Tasty Mushroom Ala Bourguignon

Serving: 2, Cooking time: 10 minutes

Ingredients:

- 1 teaspoon oil
- 1 onion, chopped
- 3 cloves of garlic, minced
- 2 carrots, cut into thick strips
- 5 cups mushrooms, halved
- 1 cup red wine
- 4 tablespoons tomato paste
- 1 teaspoon dried marjoram
- 1 cup vegetable broth
- 3 teaspoons italian herbs
- Salt and pepper to taste
- 1 tablespoon cornstarch + 2 tablespoons water

Directions:

1. Press the sauté button on the Ninja Foodi and heat the oil. Stir in the onion and garlic until fragrant.
2. Add the carrots and mushrooms and allow to sweat. Stir in the rest of the ingredients except for the cornstarch slurry.
3. Install pressure lid. Close Ninja Foodi, press the manual button, choose high settings, and set time to 5 minutes.
4. Once done cooking, do a quick release.
5. Open the lid and press the sauté button. Stir in the cornstarch slurry and allow to simmer until the sauce thickens.
6. Serve and enjoy.

Nutrition information:
Calories: 171; carbohydrates: 25.1g; protein: 10.2g; fat: 3.3g

Vegetarian-Approved Meatballs in BBQ Sauce

Serving: 2, Cooking time: 10 minutes

Ingredients:

- ¼ cup water
- 1-pound frozen vegan meatballs
- 3/4 cup barbecue sauce
- 1/2 can cranberry sauce
- Salt and pepper to taste

Directions:

1. Place all ingredients in the Ninja Foodi and give a good stir.
2. Install pressure lid. Close Ninja Foodi, press the manual button, choose high settings, and set time to 10 minutes.
3. Once done cooking, do a quick release.
4. Serve and enjoy.

Nutrition information:
Calories: 357; carbohydrates: 68.1g; protein: 17.1g; fat: 1.8g

Chili Tomatoes 'n Black Beans

Serving: 2, Cooking time: 13 minutes

Ingredients:

- 1 teaspoon olive oil
- 1/2 onion, diced
- 1/2 bell pepper, diced
- 1/2 teaspoon dried oregano
- 1 clove garlic, minced
- 1 tablespoon chili powder
- 1 teaspoon ground cumin
- 1 can cooked black beans, drained
- 1/2 can tomatoes
- 1/2 jalapeno pepper, minced
- Salt and pepper to taste
- 1/2 cup water

Directions:

1. Press the sauté button on the Ninja Foodi and heat the olive oil.
2. Once hot, stir in the onion, bell pepper, oregano, and garlic until fragrant.
3. Stir in the rest of the ingredients.
4. Install pressure lid. Close Ninja Foodi, press the manual button, choose high settings, and set time to 10 minutes.
5. Once done cooking, do a quick release.
6. Serve and enjoy.

Nutrition information:
Calories: 309; carbohydrates: 50.4g; protein: 17.2g; fat: 4.3g

Root Veggie Mix

Servings: 6 servings, **Prep Time:** 3 minutes, **Cooking Time:** 15 minutes

Ingredients:

- 1 tsp kosher salt
- ½ tsp ground black pepper
- 2 Tbsp olive oil
- 3 cloves garlic
- 1 Tbsp thyme, fresh, minced
- 3 large carrots, peeled and chopped
- 3 large parsnips, peeled, chopped
- 1 cup pearl onions

Directions:

1. Toss all the ingredients together in a medium sized bowl.
2. Place the veggies in the crisper bowl and lower them into the Ninja Foodi. Close the crisper lid and set the temperature to 350 degrees for 15 minutes.
3. Open the lid and serve the veggies warm.

Nutritional Info:
Calories: 84, Carbohydrates: 9g, Protein: 1g, Fat: 5g, Sugar: 4g, Sodium: 248g

Cauliflower Gratin

Servings: 4 servings, **Prep Time:** 10 minutes, **Cooking Time:** 15 minutes

Ingredients:
- 1 cup water
- 1 large cauliflower head, cup into florets
- 2 tsp salt
- ¼ tsp ground nutmeg
- ½ cup grated parmesan cheese
- ½ cup heavy cream
- 1 Tbsp coconut flour

Directions:
1. Add the water, cauliflower, salt and nutmeg to the bowl and place the lid on the machine, setting the steamer valve to seal. Use the pressure cooker function to cook the cauliflower on high pressure for 2 minutes. Do a quick pressure release and remove the lid once the timer is done.
2. In a separate bowl, mix together the cream and coconut flour. Add this mix to the pot and stir Press the saute button and bring the mix to a boil.
3. Sprinkle the cheese over the top and lower the air crisper lid. Set the temperature to 400 degrees and set the timer for 10 minutes. Cook until browned and then serve hot.

Nutritional Info:
Calories: 357g, Carbohydrates: 11g, Protein: 23g, Fat: 26g, Sugar: 7g, Sodium: 2071 mg

Crispy Brussel Sprouts

Servings: 4 servings, **Prep Time:** 5 minutes, **Cooking Time:** 14 minutes

Ingredients:
- 4 cups Brussel sprouts
- 2 Tablespoons olive oil
- 1 tsp salt
- ½ tsp pepper

Directions:
1. Cut the Brussel sprouts in half and toss together with the olive oil, salt and pepper.
2. Place the cook and crisp pot inside the Ninja Foodi. Close the crisper lid and set the pot to 400 degrees F using the air crisp function.
3. Add the Brussel Sprouts to the basket and set the timer for 6 minutes.
4. Open the lid, mix the Brussel sprouts inside the pot and then cook for another 8 minutes to get nice and crispy.

Nutritional Info:
Calories: 62g, Carbohydrates: 0g, Protein: 0g, Fat: 7g, Sugar: 0g, Sodium: 35g

Coconut Carrots

Servings: 4 servings, **Prep Time:** 5 minutes, **Cooking Time:** 16 minutes

Ingredients:
- 4 cups sliced carrots
- 2 Tablespoons coconut oil
- 1 tsp salt
- ½ tsp pepper

Directions:
1. Cut the carrots in half and toss together with the coconut oil, salt and pepper.
2. Place the cook and crisp pot inside the Ninja Foodi. Close the crisper lid and set the pot to 400 degrees F using the air crisp function.
3. Add the carrots to the basket and set the timer for 8 minutes.
4. Open the lid, mix the carrots inside the pot and then cook for another 8 minutes to get nice and crispy.

Nutritional Info:
Calories: 113g, Carbohydrates: 12g, Protein: 1g, Fat: 7g, Sugar: 6g, Sodium: 122mg

Zucchini Fries

Servings: 4 servings, **Prep Time:** 10 minutes, **Cooking Time:** 25 minutes

Ingredients:
- 2 Zucchinis
- 2 tsp salt
- ½ tsp ground black pepper
- 2 cups almond flour
- 3 eggs
- 1 cup grated parmesan cheese
- 1 Tbsp garlic powder
- 2 tsp onion powder

Directions:
1. Cut the zucchini into strips about ¼ inch wide and 3 inches long. Sprinkle with the salt and let sit for about 20 minutes then pat dry to take any extra moisture off of the fries.
2. Add the almond flour and ground black pepper to a bowl and put the eggs in a separate small bowl and whisk briefly.
3. In a third small bowl, mix the parmesan, garlic powder and onion powder together.
4. Dip the fries one at a time in the flour then in the egg mix and finally in the cheese mix and set coated fries aside on a plate. Dip all the fries.
5. Place the fries in the cook and crisp basket and then put the basket inside the pot. Lose the crisper lid and set the temperature to 375 degrees F and set the timer for 12 minutes.
6. After 12 minutes has passed, open the Ninja Foodi, flip the fries and continue to crisp for another 12 minutes. Serve fries while hot.

Nutritional Info:
Calories: 575g, Carbohydrates: 12g, Protein: 47g, Fat: 38g, Sugar: 6g, Sodium: 2916 mg

Eggplant Parmesan

Servings: 4 servings, **Prep Time:** 5 minutes, **Cooking Time:** 11 minutes

Ingredients:
- 1 medium eggplant, sliced about ¼ inch thick
- 2 cups Keto Tomato Sauce
- 1½ cup water
- 1/2 cup shredded mozzarella cheese
- ¼ tsp red pepper flakes

Directions:
1. Place one cup of water in the bottom of the Ninja Foodi and then layer the eggplant slices inside the pot. Spread some of the tomato sauce across the eggplant when you are halfway through and continue layering

2. Pour the remaining sauce over the eggplant once it is all in the pot and sprinkle with the cheese and red pepper flakes. 'Place the lid on the Foodi and use the pressure cooking function, set on high pressure for eleven minutes.
3. Once the timer is done, use the quick pressure release, open the lid and serve.

Nutritional Info:
Calories: 132g, Carbohydrates: 13g, Protein: 6g, Fat: 4g, Sugar: 8g, Sodium: 134mg

Roasted Beets

Servings: 4 servings, **Prep Time:** 2 minutes, **Cooking Time:** 15 minutes

Ingredients:
- 1 cup water
- 4 whole beets
- ½ tsp salt
- 1/8 tsp black pepper
- 1 tbsp olive oil

Directions:
1. Add the water to the Ninja Foodi Pot and place the metal trivet inside as well.
2. Rinse the beets and then place in the pot on top of the trivet.

3. Close the lid and seal then use the pressure cooker function set at high heat for 15 minutes.
4. Once the timer has gone off, let the steam release naturally.
5. Open the lid and remove the beets and peel with your hand, the skin should come right off.
6. Slice and toss in a bowl with the olive oil, salt and black pepper

Nutritional Info:
Calories: 65g, Carbohydrates: 8g, Protein: 1g, Fat: 4g, Sugar: 7g, Sodium: 645mg

Bacon and Cabbage

Servings: 4 servings, **Prep Time:** 5 minutes, **Cooking Time:** 11 minutes

Ingredients:
- 1 head of cabbage, core removed
- 3 sliced bacon
- 4 Tbsp butter
- 2 cups chicken broth
- 1 tsp salt
- ½ tsp black pepper

Directions:
1. Use the saute function to cook the bacon strips for about 8 minutes, flipping halfway through. Add the butter to the pot and stir to melt.
2. Chopp the cabbage and place it into the pot with the cooked bacon.
3. Add the chicken broth, salt and pepper to the bowl and stir to combine everything.
4. Place the pressure cooker lid on the Ninja Foodie and set the steamer valve to seal. Pressure cook for three minutes on high heat then quickly release the steam by opening the steamer valve carefully.
5. Serve the bacon cabbage while hot.

Nutritional Info:
Calories: 236g, Carbohydrates: 1g, Protein: 5g, Fat: 14g, Sugar: 2g, Sodium: 801 mg

Spicy Green Beans

Servings: 4 servings, **Prep Time:** 10 minutes, **Cooking Time:** 10 minutes

Ingredients:
- 1 pound green beans, ends trimmed
- 1 Tbsp coconut oil
- 1 tsp coconut aminos
- 1 tsp rice wine vinegar
- 1 garlic clove, chopped
- ¾ tsp red pepper flakes

Directions:
1. Toss all the ingredients together in a bowl and let sit for 10 minutes to marinate.
2. Add the green beans into the crisp and cook basket and set the air crisper to 400 degrees F for 10 minutes.
3. Remove the green beans and serve hot

Nutritional Info:
Calories: 69g, Carbohydrates: 9g, Protein: 2g, Fat: 4g, Sugar: 4g, Sodium: 30 mg

Kale Chips

Servings: 4 servings, **Prep Time:** 5 minutes, **Cooking Time:** 10 minutes

Ingredients:

- 1 bunch curly leaf kale, chopped, stems removed
- ¼ tsp garlic powder
- ¼ tsp baking stevia
- 1 ½ tsp salt
- 3 Tbsp olive oil

Directions:

1. Toss the kale leaves in the olive oil and then add the dry seasonings and toss again.
2. Place the kale on a dehydrating rack inside the Ninja Foodi, being careful not to overlap the leaves too much.
3. Place the lid on the Foodi and set the dehydrator function to 135 degrees for 7 hours.
4. Remove the lid once the time has completed and allow the chips to cool. Store in an air tight container.

Nutritional Info:

Calories: 108g, Carbohydrates: 2g, Protein: 1g, Fat: 10g, Sugar: 1g, Sodium: 618 mg

Mediterranean Spinach with Cheese

(Cooking Time: 20 minutes | Serves: 6)

Ingredients:

- 4 tbsps. butter
- 2 lbs. boiled and chopped spinach
- Salt and black pepper
- 2/3 c. pitted Kalamata olives, halved
- 1½ c. grated feta cheese
- 4 tsps. Freshly grated lemon zest

Directions:

1- Mix together spinach, butter, salt and black pepper in a bowl.
2- Place the basket in the Ninja Foodi and add seasoned spinach.
3- Press "Air Crisp" and set the timer to 15 minutes at 340 degrees F.
4- Dish out from the Ninja Foodi and stir in the olives, lemon zest and feta cheese to serve.

Nutritional Info: 247 calories, 18.7g fat, 7.2g carbs, 9.9g protein

Stunning Broccoli Florets

(Cooking Time: 16 minutes | Serves: 6)

Ingredients:
- 4 tbsps. butter
- Salt and black pepper
- 2 lbs. broccoli florets
- 1 c. whipping cream

Directions:
1- Arrange the basket in the bottom of Ninja Foodi and add water.
2- Place the broccoli florets on top of the basket and lock the lid.
3- Press "Pressure" and cook for about 5 minutes.
4- Release the pressure quickly and replace the pot with the basket.
5- Transfer the broccoli florets in the pot and top with salt, black pepper and butter.
6- Press "Air Crisp" and cook for about 3 minutes at 360 degrees F.
7- Dish out to serve immediately.

Nutritional Info: 178 calories, 14.4g fat, 9.6g carbs, 4.7g protein

Cauliflower Mash

(Cooking Time: 15 minutes | Serves: 6)

Ingredients:
- 1 tbsp. softened butter
- ½ c. feta cheese
- Salt and black pepper
- 1 large head cauliflower, chopped
- 1 minced garlic clove
- 2 tsps. freshly minced chives

Directions:
1- Arrange the basket in the bottom of Ninja Foodi and add water.
2- Place the cauliflower pieces on top of the basket and lock the lid.
3- Press "Pressure" and cook for about 5 minutes.
4- Release the pressure quickly and dish out in a bowl.
5- Transfer the cauliflower in an immersion hand blender along with rest of the ingredients.
6- Blend until desired texture is achieved and dish out to serve.

Nutritional Info: 124 calories, 9.3g fat, 6.1g carbs, 5.4g protein

Nutty Brussels Sprouts

(Cooking Time: 16 minutes | Serves: 8)

Ingredients:

- 2 lbs. trimmed Brussels sprouts, halved
- 1 c. chopped almonds
- 1 tbsp. melted butter, unsalted

Directions:

1- Arrange the basket in the bottom of Ninja Foodi and add water.
2- Place the Brussels sprout on top of the basket and lock the lid.
3- Press "Pressure" and cook for about 3 minutes.
4- Release the pressure quickly and replace the pot with the basket.
5- Transfer the Brussels sprout in the pot and top with almonds and butter.
6- Press "Air Crisp" and cook for about 3 minutes at 350 degrees F.
7- Dish out to serve.

Nutritional Info: 130 calories, 7.8g fat, 8.9g carbs, 6.4g protein

Luncheon Green Beans

(Cooking Time: 15 minutes | Serves: 4)

Ingredients:

- 1 lb. fresh green beans
- 2 tbsps. butter
- 1 minced garlic clove
- Salt and freshly ground black pepper
- 1½ c. water

Directions:

1. Put all the ingredients in the pot of Ninja Foodi and lock the lid.
2. Press "Pressure" and cook for about 5 minutes.
3. Release the pressure quickly and dish out to serve hot.

Nutritional Info: 87 calories, 5.9g fat, 8.4g carbs, 2.2g protein

Cheesy Cauliflower

(Cooking Time: 35 minutes | Serves: 5)

Ingredients:

- 1 tbsp. prepared mustard
- 1 head cauliflower
- 1 tsp. avocado mayonnaise
- ½ c. grated Parmesan cheese
- ¼ c. butter, chopped

Directions:

1. Press "Sauté" on Ninja Foodi and add butter and cauliflower.

2. Sauté for about 3 minutes and add rest of the ingredients.

3. Lock the lid and set the Ninja Foodi to "Pressure" for about 30 minutes.

4. Release the pressure naturally and dish out to serve hot.

Nutritional Info: 155 calories, 13.3g fat, 3.8g carbs, 6.7g protein

Sugar-Glazed Carrots

(Cooking Time: 8 minutes | Serves: 6)

Ingredients:

- 8 large carrots, peeled and chopped
- 2 tbsps. butter, unsalted
- 1 tbsp. sugar
- 1 tbsp. rice vinegar, unseasoned

Directions:

1. Preparing the ingredients.
2. Put the carrots in the Ninja Foodi; add enough cool tap water that they're submerged by 2 inches.
3. High pressure for 3 minutes. Lock the lid onto the pot.
4. Pressure release. Use the quick-release method to return the pot's pressure to normal.
5. Finish the dish. Unlock and open the pot. Drain the carrots. Turn the Ninja Foodi to its "browning" function. Add the butter; when it has melted, stir in the sugar and cook until it melts and becomes bubbly, stirring all the while, less than 1 minute.
6. Add the carrots and vinegar; toss over the heat for 1 minute to glaze the carrots evenly and thoroughly.

Nutritional Info: 83 calories, 3g fat, 14g carbs, 1g protein

Simple Roasted Veggie Stock

(Cooking Time: 110 minutes | Serves: 1 quart)

Ingredients

- 1 quartered onion
- 2 large carrots, peeled and chopped
- 1 tbsp. vegetable oil
- 12 oz. sliced mushroom
- ¼ tsp. salt
- 3½ c. water

Directions:

1. Take cook and crisp basket out of the inner pot, close crisping lid and let it pre-heat for 3 minutes at 400 degrees F on Bake/Roast settings
2. While the pot heats up, add onion, carrot chunks in the Cook and Crisp basket and drizzle vegetable oil, toss well
3. Place basket back into the inner pot, close crisping lid and cook for 15 minutes at 400 degrees F on Bake/Roast mode
4. Make sure to shake the basket halfway through
5. Remove basket from pot and add onions, carrots, mushrooms, water and season with salt
6. Lock pressure lid and seal the valves, cook on HIGH pressure for 60 minutes
7. Release the pressure naturally over 10 minutes
8. Line a cheesecloth on a colander and place it over a large bowl, pour vegetables and stock into the colander
9. Strain the stock and discard veggies
10. Enjoy and use as needed!

Nutritional Info: 45 calories, 4g fat, 3g carbs, 0g protein

Heart-Felt Caramelized Onions

(Cooking Time: 65 minutes | Serves: 4)

Ingredients

- 2 tbsps. butter, unsalted
- 3 sliced onions
- 2 tbsps. water
- 1 tsp. salt

Directions:

1. Set your pot to Sauté mode and adjust the heat to Medium, pre-heat the inner pot for 5 minutes
2. Add butter and melt, add water, salt, onions, and stir well
3. Lock pressure lid into place, making sure that the pressure valve is locked
4. Cook on HIGH pressure for 30 minutes
5. Quick release the pressure once done
6. Remove the lid and set the pot to Sauté mode, let it sear in the Medium-HIGH mode for about 15 minutes until the liquid is almost gone Enjoy!

Nutritional Info: 110 calories, 6g fat, 14g carbs, 2g protein

Tastiest Cauliflower

Serves: 4, Prep Time: 15 minutes, Cooking Time: 13 minutes

Ingredients:
- 1 medium head cauliflower
- ¼ C. olive oil
- 4 garlic cloves, minced
- 2 tbsp. capers, minced
- ½ C. Parmesan cheese, grated

Directions:
1) With a knife, cut an X into the cauliflower head, slicing about halfway down.
2) In the pot of Ninja Foodi, place ½ C. of water. Place the cauliflower head into "Cook & Crisp Basket". Arrange the "Cook & Crisp Basket" in the pot. Cover the Ninja Foodi with the pressure lid and place the pressure valve to "Seal" position.
3) Select "Pressure" and set to "Low" for about 3 minutes.
4) Press "Start/Stop" to begin. Switch the valve to "Vent" and do a "Quick" release.
5) Meanwhile, in a small bowl, add the oil, garlic and capers and mix well.
6) Once all the pressure is released, open the lid.
7) Place the oil mixture over the cauliflower evenly and sprinkle with the Parmesan cheese, close the Ninja Foodi with crisping lid and select "Air Crisp".
8) Set the temperature to 390 degrees F for 10 minutes.
9) Press "Start/Stop" to begin. Open the lid and serve warm.

Nutrition Information:
Calories: 172; Carbohydrates: 5.1g; Protein: 5.4g; Fat: 15.5g; Sugar: 1.6g; Sodium: 317mg; Fiber: 1.9g

Authentic French Potato Gratin

Serves: 4, Prep Time: 15 minutes, Cooking Time: 20 minutes

Ingredients:
- 2 large potatoes, sliced thinly
- 5½ tbsp. cream
- 2 eggs
- 1 tbsp. plain flour
- ½ C. cheddar cheese, grated

Directions:
1) Arrange the "Cook & Crisp Basket" in the pot of Ninja Foodi. Close the Ninja Foodi with crisping lid and select "Air Crisp". Press "Start/Stop" to begin and set the temperature to 355 degrees F. Set the time for 5 minutes to preheat.
2) Now, place the potatoes into "Cook & Crisp Basket". Arrange the "Cook &

Crisp Basket" in the pot. Close the Ninja Foodi with crisping lid and select "Air Crisp".

3) Set the temperature to 355 degrees F for 10 minutes.

4) Press "Start/Stop" to begin. Meanwhile, in a bowl, add cream, eggs and flour and mix until a thick sauce forms. Remove the potatoes from the basket.

5) Now, divide the potato slices in 4 ramekins evenly and top with the egg mixture evenly, followed by the cheese.

6) Arrange the ramekins into the "Cook & Crisp Basket".

7) Close the Ninja Foodi with crisping lid and select "Air Crisp".

8) Set the temperature to 390 degrees F for 10 minutes.

9) Press "Start/Stop" to begin. Open the lid and serve warm.

Nutrition Information:
Calories: 233; Carbohydrates: 31.3g; Protein: 9.7g; Fat: 8g; Sugar: 2.7g; Sodium: 135mg; Fiber: 4.5g__

Cheesy Spinach Bake

Serves: 6, Prep Time: 15 minutes, Cooking Time: 15 minutes

Ingredients:
- 2 lb. fresh spinach, chopped
- 4 tbsp. butter, melted
- Salt and freshly ground black pepper, to taste
- 1 C. feta cheese, crumbled
- 1 tsp. fresh lemon zest, grated

Directions:
1) In a bowl, add the spinach, butter, salt and black pepper and mix well.

2) Arrange the "Cook & Crisp Basket" in the pot of Ninja Foodi. Close the Ninja Foodi with crisping lid and select "Air Crisp". Press "Start/Stop" to begin and set the temperature to

340 degrees F. Set the time for 5 minutes to preheat.

3) Now, place the spinach mixture into "Cook & Crisp Basket".

4) Close the Ninja Foodi with crisping lid and select "Air Crisp".

5) Set the temperature to 340 degrees F for 15 minutes.

6) Press "Start/Stop" to begin. Open the lid and immediately, stir in the cheese and lemon zest. Serve hot.

Nutrition Information:
Calories: 169; Carbohydrates: 6.6g; Protein: 8g; Fat: 13.6g; Sugar: 1.7g; Sodium: 480mg; Fiber: 3.4g__

Delicate Stuffed Tomatoes

Serves: 2 , Prep Time: 15 minutes, Cooking Time: 15 minutes

Ingredients:
- 2 large tomatoes
- ½ C. broccoli, chopped finely
- ½ C. cheddar cheese, shredded
- 1 tbsp. unsalted butter, melted
- ½ tsp. dried thyme, crushed

Directions:
1) Carefully, cut the top of each tomato and scoop out pulp and seeds.
2) In a bowl, mix together chopped broccoli and cheese.
3) Stuff each tomato with broccoli mixture evenly.
4) Arrange the "Cook & Crisp Basket" in the pot of Ninja Foodi.
5) Close the Ninja Foodi with crisping lid and select "Air Crisp".
6) Press "Start/Stop" to begin and set the temperature to 355 degrees F.
7) Set the time for 5 minutes to preheat.
8) Now, place the stuffed tomatoes into "Cook & Crisp Basket" and drizzle with the butter. Close the Ninja Foodi with crisping lid and select "Air Crisp".
9) Set the temperature to 355 degrees F for 15 minutes.
10) Press "Start/Stop" to begin. Open the lid and serve with the garnishing of thyme.

Nutrition Information:
Calories: 206; Carbohydrates: 9.1g; Protein: 9.4g; Fat: 15.6g; Sugar: 5.3g; Sodium: 233mg; Fiber: 2.9g

Light Luncheon Meal

Serves: 4, Prep Time: 15 minutes, Cooking Time: 12 minutes

Ingredients:
- 1 lb. green beans, washed and trimmed
- 1 tsp. butter, melted
- 1 tbsp. fresh lemon juice
- ¼ tsp. garlic powder
- Salt and freshly ground black pepper, to taste

Directions:
1) In a large bowl, add all ingredients and toss to coat well.
2) Arrange the "Cook & Crisp Basket" in the pot of Ninja Foodi.
3) Close the Ninja Foodi with crisping lid and select "Air Crisp".
4) Press "Start/Stop" to begin and set the temperature to 400 degrees F.
5) Set the time for 5 minutes to preheat.
6) Now, place the green beans mixture into "Cook & Crisp Basket".
7) Close the Ninja Foodi with crisping lid and select "Air Crisp".
8) Set the temperature to 400 degrees F for 12 minutes.

9) Press "Start/Stop" to begin.
10) Open the lid and serve warm.

Nutrition Information:

Calories: 45; Carbohydrates: 8.3g; Protein: 2.1g; Fat: 1.1g; Sugar: 1.7g; Sodium: 53mg; Fiber: 3.9g___

Wonderful Side Dish

Serves: 2, Prep Time: 15 minutes, Cooking Time: 12 minutes

Ingredients:
- 1 lb. Brussels sprouts, cut in half
- 2 tbsp. olive oil
- 2 garlic cloves, minced
- Salt and freshly ground black pepper, to taste

Directions:
1) In a bowl, add all the ingredients and toss to coat well.
2) Arrange the "Cook & Crisp Basket" in the pot of Ninja Foodi.
3) Close the Ninja Foodi with crisping lid and select "Air Crisp".
4) Press "Start/Stop" to begin and set the temperature to 390 degrees F.
5) Set the time for 5 minutes to preheat.
6) Now, place the Brussels sprout into "Cook & Crisp Basket".
7) Close the Ninja Foodi with crisping lid and select "Air Crisp".
8) Set the temperature to 390 degrees F for 12 minutes, shaking once after 6 minutes.
9) Press "Start/Stop" to begin. Open the lid and serve

Nutrition Information:
Calories: 111; Carbohydrates: 10.8g; Protein: 4g; Fat: 7.4g; Sugar: 2.5g; Sodium: 67mg; Fiber: 4.3g

Fall-Time Vegetarian Dish

Serves: 8, Prep Time: 15 minutes, Cooking Time: 4 hours

Ingredients:
- 1 (3 lb.) butternut squash, peeled, seeded and cut into cubes
- 3 apples, peeled, cored and chopped
- ½ C. dried cranberries
- ½ white onion, chopped
- 1 tbsp. ground cinnamon

Directions:
1) Grease the pot of Ninja Foodi generously.
2) In the prepared pot, add all the ingredients and stir to combine.
3) Close the crisping lid and select "Slow Cooker".
4) Set on "High" for about 4 hours.

5) Press "Start/Stop" to begin.

6) Open the lid and serve.

Nutrition Information:

Calories: 129; Carbohydrates: 33.4g; Protein: 2g; Fat: 0.3g; Sugar: 13g; Sodium: 8mg; Fiber: 6.3g

Garden Fresh Veggie Combo

Serves: 5, Prep Time: 15 minutes, Cooking Time: 35 minutes

Ingredients:
- 6 tsp. olive oil, divided
- ½ lb. carrots, peeled and sliced
- 2 lb. zucchini, sliced
- 1 tbsp. fresh basil, chopped
- Salt and freshly ground black pepper, to taste

Directions:
1) In a bowl, mix together 2 tsp. of oil and carrots.
2) Arrange the "Cook & Crisp Basket" in the pot of Ninja Foodi.
3) Close the Ninja Foodi with crisping lid and select "Air Crisp".
4) Press "Start/Stop" to begin and set the temperature to 400 degrees F.
5) Set the time for 5 minutes to preheat.
6) Now, place the carrots into "Cook & Crisp Basket".
7) Close the Ninja Foodi with crisping lid and select "Air Crisp".
8) Set the temperature to 400 degrees F for 5 minutes. Press "Start/Stop" to begin.
9) Meanwhile, in a large bowl, mix together remaining oil, zucchini, basil, salt and black pepper.
10) Open the lid and place the zucchini mixture into basket with carrots.
11) Close the Ninja Foodi with crisping lid and set the time for 30 minutes.
12) Press "Start/Stop" to begin. Toss the vegetable mixture 2-3 times during the coking. Open the lid and serve.

Nutrition Information:

Calories: 96; Carbohydrates: 10.6g; Protein: 2.6g; Fat: 5.9g; Sugar: 5.4g; Sodium: 80mg; Fiber: 3.1g

Marinated Tofu

Serves: 4, Prep Time: 15 minutes, Cooking Time: 25 minutes

Ingredients:
- 2 tbsp. low-sodium soy sauce
- 2 tbsp. fish sauce
- 1 tsp. sesame oil
- 12-oz. extra-firm tofu, drained and cubed into 1-inch size
- 1 tsp. butter, melted

Directions:
1) In a large bowl, add soy sauce, fish sauce and sesame oil and mix until well combined.
2) Add tofu cubes and toss to coat well.
3) Set aside to marinate for about 30 minutes, tossing occasionally.
4) Arrange the "Cook & Crisp Basket" in the pot of Ninja Foodi.
5) Close the Ninja Foodi with crisping lid and select "Air Crisp".
6) Press "Start/Stop" to begin and set the temperature to 355 degrees F.
7) Set the time for 5 minutes to preheat.
8) Now, place the tofu cubes into "Cook & Crisp Basket" and drizzle with the butter.
9) Close the Ninja Foodi with crisping lid and select "Air Crisp".
10) Set the temperature to 355 degrees F for 25 minutes.
11) Press "Start/Stop" to begin. Flip the tofu after every 10 minutes during the cooking. Open the lid and serve

Nutrition Information:
Calories: 102; Carbohydrates: 2.5g; Protein: 9.4g; Fat: 7.1g; Sugar: 1.3g; Sodium: 1100mg; Fiber: 0.3g__

Kids Favorite Pasta

Serves: 6, Prep Time: 10 minutes, Cooking Time: 2 hours

Ingredients:
- 2 egg whites
- 1½ C. milk
- 2 tsp. tapioca starch
- 2 C. whole wheat penne pasta
- 4-oz. cheddar cheese, shredded

Directions:
1) In a bowl, add egg whites, milk and tapioca starch and beat until well combined.
2) Add remaining ingredients and stir to combine.
3) In the pot of Ninja Foodi, place the pasta mixture
4) Close the crisping lid and select "Slow Cooker".
5) Set on "Low" for about 1½-2 hours.
6) Press "Start/Stop" to begin.
7) Open the lid and serve warm.

Nutrition Information:
Calories: 395; Carbohydrates: 60g; Protein: 17.2g; Fat: 9.6g; Sugar: 5.6g; Sodium: 170mg; Fiber: 6.7g__

Chapter 3 Pasta & Grains Recipe

Beef, Veggie 'N Barley Stew

Servings: 2, Cooking time: 30 minutes

Ingredients:

- ¾-lb stew beef, cut into 1-inch cubes
- 2 tsp olive oil
- 1/2 tsp salt
- 1/2 tsp ground pepper
- 1/4 cup red wine
- 1 cup beef broth
- 1 clove garlic, finely diced
- 1/4 cup onion, diced
- 1 tbsp tomato paste
- 1/2 tsp dried thyme
- 1 bay leaf
- 1/2 tsp Italian seasoning
- 1 tomato, chopped
- 1/2 cup carrots, 1/2" pieces
- 1/2 cup potatoes, diced 1/2" pieces
- 2 tbsp barley

Directions:

1. Press sear button and heat oil. Once hot, add beef and season with pepper and salt. Cook until browned, around 8 minutes.
2. Add wine and deglaze pot.
3. Stir in broth, garlic, onion, tomato paste, thyme, bay leaf, Italian seasoning, diced tomatoes, carrots, potatoes and barley. Mix well.
4. Install pressure lid. Close Ninja Foodi, press pressure button, set on high for 20 minutes.
5. Once done cooking, do a quick release.
6. Mix well and discard bay leaf.
7. Serve and enjoy.

Nutrition information:
Calories: 379; carbohydrates: 26.9g; protein: 41.2g; fat: 11.8g

Capers 'n Olives on Red Sauce Pasta

Servings: 2, Cooking time: 7 minutes

Ingredients:

- 2 cloves garlic minced
- 2 cups pasta sauce
- 1 ½ cups water
- 1 1/2 cups pasta such as penne or fusilli
- 1/4 teaspoon crushed red pepper flakes
- 1 tablespoon capers
- 1/4 cup kalamata olives sliced
- Salt to taste
- Pepper to taste

Directions:

1. Press sauté and add a splash of water. Add garlic and sauté for 30 seconds. Press stop.

2. Stir in olives, capers, crushed red pepper flakes, pasta, water, and pasta sauce. Mix well.
3. Install pressure lid. Close Ninja Foodi, press pressure button, choose high settings, and set time to 5 minutes.
4. Once done cooking, do a quick release.

5. Mix well and adjust seasoning to taste
6. Serve and enjoy.

Nutrition information:
Calories: 450; carbohydrates: 85.9g; protein: 10.0g; fat: 7.3g

Veggie 'n Shrimp Fried Rice

Servings: 2, Cooking time: 30 minutes

Ingredients:
- 1 tablespoon oil, divided
- 1 small onion, peeled and diced
- 2 tablespoons of garlic
- 2 eggs, whisked
- 1/2 cup uncooked basmati rice
- 2 teaspoons of soy sauce
- 1 cup of chicken broth
- ½ cup of mixed frozen vegetables
- 1/2-pound frozen shrimp
- 1/2 cup of water

Directions:
1. Add rice, water, and stock in Ninja Foodi.
2. Install pressure lid and place valve to vent position.
3. Close Ninja Foodi, press steam button and set timer to 8 minutes.
4. Once done cooking, do a 5-minute natural release and then a quick release. Transfer rice to a bowl.

5. Press stop, press sauté button and add 1/2 tbsp oil.
6. Once hot, scramble eggs for 4 minutes. Transfer to a bowl and cut into small pieces.
7. Add remaining oil and once hot sauté garlic for a minute. Stir in onions and cook for another 3 minutes.
8. Add shrimps and cook until opaque, around 5 minutes.
9. Stir in frozen vegetables and cook until heated through around 3 minutes.
10. Stir in rice. Add soy sauce. Mix well and cook for 2 minutes.
11. Serve and enjoy.

Nutrition information:
Calories: 463; carbohydrates: 47.2g; protein: 39.1g; fat: 13.1g

Asparagus, Shrooms 'n Shrimp Risotto

Servings: 4, Cooking time: 20 minutes

Ingredients:

- 2 tsp olive oil
- 1 small onion, diced
- 3/4 cup arborio rice
- 1 cup sliced cremini or white button mushrooms
- 1/4 cup dry white wine
- 1 1/2 cups chicken broth
- 1 tbsp butter
- 1/2 cup chopped asparagus
- 1/4 lb shrimp, defrosted if frozen, peeled and deveined
- 1/4 cup grated parmigiano-reggiano cheese
- 1/2 tsp fresh black pepper

Directions:

1. Press sear button and heat oil. Sauté onions for 3 minutes.
2. Stir in mushrooms and rice. Cook for 5 minutes.
3. Add wine and deglaze pot for a minute.
4. Add chicken broth. Press stop.
5. Install pressure lid and place valve to vent position.
6. Close Ninja Foodi, press steam button, and set time to 6 minutes.
7. Once done cooking, do a 5-minute natural release and then a quick release.
8. Press stop, press sear button, stir in asparagus and butter. Cook for a minute.
9. Add shrimps and stirring frequently, cook for 3 minutes.
10. Stir in cheese. Serve and enjoy.

Nutrition information:
Calories: 430; carbohydrates: 30.3g; protein: 23.2g; fat: 24.0g

Chicken-Parm Fettucine Alfredo

Servings: 2, Cooking time: 10 minutes

Ingredients:

- 1 1/2 tbsp butter, cut in a few small pieces
- 2 cloves garlic, pressed/minced
- 1 cup chicken broth
- 4 oz fettuccine noodles, broken in half
- 1/2-lb small chicken breasts, uncooked cut larger breasts in half
- 1/2 cup heavy cream
- 1/2 tsp salt (or more to taste)
- 1/2 tsp pepper
- 1/4 cup parmesan cheese, grated

Directions:

1. Place the butter and garlic in the pot. Pour chicken broth.
2. Sprinkle in the fettuccine noodles, in a random pattern, and gently press them down.

3. If adding chicken: add the chicken breasts, and space evenly over the noodles. Pour the cream over them, then sprinkle with the salt and pepper.
4. Install pressure lid. Close Ninja Foodi, press pressure button, choose high settings, and set time to 5 minutes.

5. Once done cooking, do a quick release.
6. Stir in parmesan and mix well. Let it rest for 5 minutes.
7. Serve and enjoy.

Nutrition information:
Calories: 726; carbohydrates: 50.8g; protein: 42.7g; fat: 39.1g

Breakfast Oats with Apricots 'n Nuts

Servings: 2, Cooking time: 6 minutes

Ingredients:
- 1 ½ cups water
- 1 cup chopped strawberries, for topping
- 1 cup freshly squeezed orange juice
- 1 cup steel cut oats
- 1 tbsp chopped dried apricots
- 1 tbsp dried cranberries
- 1 tbsp raisins
- 1/4 tsp ground cinnamon
- 1/8 tsp salt
- 2 tbsp butter
- 2 tbsp pure maple syrup
- 3 tbsp chopped pecans, for topping

Directions:

1. Lightly grease Ninja Foodi insert with cooking spray and then add all ingredients except for pecans. Mix well.
2. Install pressure lid.
3. Close Ninja Foodi, press pressure button, choose high settings, and set time to 6 minutes.
4. Once done cooking, do a quick release.
5. Transfer to two bowl and evenly divide toppings on bowl.
6. Serve and enjoy.

Nutrition information:
Calories: 507; carbohydrates: 72.4g; protein: 11.1g; fat: 19.2g

Brekky Bacon 'n Egg Risotto

Servings: 2, Cooking time: 10 minutes

Ingredients:

- 1 1/2 cups chicken broth
- 1/3 cup chopped onion
- 2 eggs
- 2 tablespoons grated parmesan cheese
- 3 slices center cut bacon, chopped
- 3 tablespoons dry white wine
- 3/4 cup arborio rice
- Chives, for garnish
- Salt and pepper, to taste

Directions:

1. Press sauté button and cook bacon to a crisp, around 6 minutes.
2. Stir in onion and sauté for 3 minutes. Add rice and sauté for a minute.
3. Pour in wine and deglaze pot. Continue sautéing until wine is completely absorbed by rice, around 5 minutes.
4. Stir in chicken broth.
5. Install pressure lid. Close Ninja Foodi, press pressure button, choose high settings, and set time to 5 minutes.
6. Meanwhile, cook eggs sunny side up to desired doneness.
7. Once done cooking, do a quick release. Stir in pepper, salt, and parmesan.
8. Divide risotto evenly on to two plates, add egg, and sprinkle with chives.
9. Serve and enjoy.

Nutrition information:
Calories: 211; carbohydrates: 16.0g; protein: 12.0g; fat: 11.0g

Seafood with Chorizo 'n Chicken Spanish Rice

Servings: 2, Cooking time: 30 minutes

Ingredients:

- 1/4-lb chicken breast, diced
- 2 oz. Spicy chorizo
- 1 tbsp olive oil
- ½ onion, diced
- 1/4 tsp marjoram
- 1/4 tsp cumin
- 1/8 tsp whole saffron
- 1/2 cup long-grain rice, uncooked
- 1 1/2 cups chicken stock
- 2 cloves garlic, minced
- 1/4-lb whole shrimp
- ¼-lb clams, in the shell, drained
- ¼ cup green peas; frozen
- Salt
- 1/2 lemon, wedged

Directions:

1. Press sauté and heat oil.
2. Sauté saffron, cumin, marjoram, and onions for a minute.

3. Stir in chorizo and chopped chicken, cook for 8 minutes.
4. Stir in rice and cook for a minute. Add water and chicken stock. Deglaze pot.
5. Install pressure lid and place valve to vent position.
6. Close Ninja Foodi, press steam button, and set time to 10 minutes.
7. Once done cooking, do a quick release.

8. Press stop, press sauté button. Stir in salt, garlic, clams, green peas and shrimp. Cook for 3 minutes.
9. Press stop and let it sit for 5 more minutes to continue cooking.
10. Serve and enjoy with lemon wedges.

Nutrition information:
Calories: 563; carbohydrates: 49.9g; protein: 40.8g; fat: 22.2g

Vanilla-Espresso Flavored Oats

Servings: 2, Cooking time: 20 minutes

Ingredients:
- 1/2 cup milk
- 1/2 cup steel cut oats
- 1 teaspoon espresso powder
- 1/4 teaspoon salt
- 1 1/4 cups water
- 1 tablespoon sugar
- 1 teaspoon vanilla extract
- Finely grated chocolate

Directions:
1. Mix well salt, espresso powder, sugar, oats, milk, and water in Ninja Foodi.
2. Install pressure lid and place valve to vent position.
3. Close Ninja Foodi, press steam button, and set time to 2 minutes.
4. Once done cooking, do a natural release for 10-minutes and then do a quick release.
5. Uncover pot and stir in vanilla extract. Spoon into bowls.
6. Garnish with grated chocolate.
7. Serve and enjoy.

Nutrition information:
Calories: 198; carbohydrates: 27.6g; protein: 6.5g; fat: 6.8g

Easy Chow Mein Topped with Green Onions

Servings: 2 , Cooking time: 15 minutes

Ingredients:
- 4 oz chow mein noodles
- 2 tablespoons peanut oil
- 4 green onions, chopped, white and green parts separated
- 3 cloves garlic, minced
- 1 teaspoon ginger , minced
- 1 small bell pepper, thinly sliced

Sauce ingredients:
- 1/4 cup chicken broth
- 2 tablespoons shaoxing wine , or dry sherry
- 2 tablespoons oyster sauce
- 1 tablespoon soy sauce
- 1/2 teaspoon sesame oil

Directions:
1. In a small bowl, whisk well all sauce ingredients.
2. Boil noodles according to package instructions. Pour into colander and run under tap water to stop the cooking process. Drain well.
3. In Ninja Foodi, press sauté button and heat 3 tbsps oil. Heat for 4 minutes. Once hot add noodles and cook for a minute.
4. Stir in ginger and garlic. Cook for a minute until fragrant.
5. Stir in bell pepper and cook for 2 minutes.
6. Add sauce and toss noodles to coat well. Serve and enjoy.

Nutrition information:
Calories: 441; carbohydrates: 49.9g; protein: 6.6g; fat: 23.8g

Chapter 4 Poultry Recipes

Chili Rubbed Chicken

Servings: 2 servings, **Prep Time:** 5 minutes, **Cooking Time:** 10 minutes

Ingredients:
- 2 tsp salt
- 1 Tbsp paprika
- 1 tbsp chili powder
- T tsp ground black pepper
- 1 tsp onion powder
- 1 tsp garlic powder
- 1 tsp ground cumin
- 2 chicken thighs, bone in
- 1 tbsp olive oil

Directions:
1. Mix all of the spices together in a bowl and then set aside.
2. Rub the chicken thighs with the olive oil and then coat in the spice seasoning.
3. Place the spiced chicken in the cook and crisp basket and turn the Ninja Foodi to 375 degrees. Place the basket in the Foodi and set the timer for 30 minutes. Serve while hot straight out of the pot.

Nutritional Info:
Calories: 230g, Carbohydrates: 7g, Protein: 15g, Fat: 16g, Sugar: 1g, Sodium: 473 mg

Chicken Jerky

Servings: 6 servings, **Prep Time:** 5 minutes, **Cooking Time:** 7 hours

Ingredients:
- ½ pound Chicken breast, sliced into 1/8" Thick strips
- ½ cup coconut aminos
- 2 Tbsp Worcestershire sauce
- 2 tsp ground black pepper
- 1 tsp liquid smoke
- 1 tsp onion powders
- ½ tsp garlic powder
- 1 tsp kosher salt

Directions:
1. Place all the ingredients in a large Ziploc bag and seal shut. Shake to mix. Leave in the fridge overnight.
2. Lay the strips on the dehydrator trays, being careful not to overlap them.
3. Place the cook and crisp lid on and set the temperature for 135 degrees for 7 hours. Once done, store in an airtight container.

Nutritional Info:
Calories: 67g, Carbohydrates: 9g, Protein: 4g, Fat: 1g, Sugar: 7g, Sodium: 938 mg

Pulled BBQ Chicken

Servings: 6 servings, **Prep Time:** 10 minutes, **Cooking Time:** 15 minutes

Ingredients:

- 1 ½ pounds boneless, skinless chicken thighs
- 1 Tbsp olive oil
- 1 tsp ground paprika
- ¼ tsp salt
- ¼ tsp ground black pepper
- 1 onion, chopped
- ¼ cup hot sauce
- ¼ cup water
- 2 Tbsp vinegar

Directions:

1. Turn the Ninja Foodi on to saute and add the olive oil. Once hot, add the chicken thighs and sear on each side for 2 minutes.
2. Sprinkle the salt and pepper on the chicken and then add all the remaining ingredients to the pot.
3. Cover the Foodi and use the pressure cooker function to cook the chicken for 15 minutes under high heat pressure.
4. Release the pressure using a natural steam release and then use two forks to pull he chicken apart. Serve warm or chilled

Nutritional Info:

Calories: 215g, Carbohydrates: 1g, Protein: 17g, Fat: 16g, Sugar: 1g, Sodium: 1672 mg

Spicy Chicken Jerky

Servings: 6 servings, **Prep Time:** 5 minutes, **Cooking Time:** 10 minutes

Ingredients:

- ½ pound Chicken breast, sliced into 1/8" Thick strips
- ½ cup soy sauce
- 2 Tbsp Worcestershire sauce
- 2 tsp ground black pepper
- 1 tsp liquid smoke
- 1 tsp onion powder
- 1 tsp cayenne pepper
- ½ tsp garlic powder
- 1 tsp kosher salt

Directions:

1. Place all the ingredients in a large Ziploc bag and seal shut. Shake to mix. Leave in the fridge overnight.
2. Lay the strips on the dehydrator trays, being careful not to overlap them.
3. Place the cook and crisp lid on and set the temperature for 135 degrees for 7 hours. Once done, store in an airtight container.

Nutritional Info:

Calories: 42g, Carbohydrates: 2g, Protein: 4g, Fat: 1g, Sugar: 1g, Sodium: 1493 mg

Chili Chicken Wings

Servings: 4 servings, **Prep Time:** 10 minutes, **Cooking Time:** 28 minutes

Ingredients:
- ½ cup water
- ½ cup hot sauce
- 2 Tbsp butter
- 1 ½ tbsp. apple cider vinegar
- 32 ounces frozen chicken wings
- ½ tsp paprika

Directions:
1. Add all the ingredients into the cook and crisp basket and place the basket inside the Ninja Foodi.
2. Place the pressure cooker lid on top of the pot and close the pressure valve to the seal position. Set the pressure cooker function to high heat and set the timer for 5 minutes.
3. Once the coking cycle is complete, release the pressure quickly by carefully opening the steamer valve. Enjoy while hot

Nutritional Info:
Calories: 311g , Carbohydrates: 0g, Protein: 24g, Fat: 23g, Sugar: 0g, Sodium: 2657 mg

Whole Roasted Chicken

Servings: 6 servings, **Prep Time:** 5 minutes, **Cooking Time:** 40 minutes

Ingredients:
- Whole 5 pounds Chicken
- 2 Tbsp salt
- ¼ cup lemon juice
- ¼ cup water
- 1 Tbsp stevia powder
- 1 tsp salt
- ½ tsp ground black pepper
- 1 Tbsp dried thyme
- 4 garlic cloves, minced
- 1 Tbsp olive oil

Directions:
1. Add the salt, lemon juice, water, stevia, black pepper, thyme and garlic to the Ninja Foodi Pot.
2. Place the chicken inside the pot as well and brush with the seasoning mix.
3. Move the chicken to the air crisper basket and place back into the pot.
4. Put the pressure cooker lid on the Foodi and seal. Set the pressure cooker function to high for 15 minutes. Once the cooking cycle is complete, do a quick pressure release and open the top.
5. Coat the chicken with the olive oil and put the crisper lid on and sue the air crisper function set to 400 degrees for 15 minutes.
6. Check the chicken after 15 minutes and make sure the internal temperature is 165. Slice and serve while hot.

Nutritional Info:
Calories: 235 g, Carbohydrates: 4g, Protein: 18g, Fat: 17g, Sugar: 2g, Sodium: 592 mg

Lemon Drumsticks

Servings: 2 servings, **Prep Time:** 10 minutes, **Cooking Time:** 28 minutes

Ingredients:

- ½ cup water
- ½ cup hot sauce
- 2 Tbsp butter
- 1/3 cup lemon juice
- 1 pound drumsticks
- ½ tsp paprika

Directions:

1. Add all the ingredients into the cook and crisp basket and place the basket inside the Ninja Foodi.
2. Place the pressure cooker lid on top of the pot and close the pressure valve to the seal position. Set the pressure cooker function to high heat and set the timer for 5 minutes.
3. Once the coking cycle is complete, release the pressure quickly by carefully opening the steamer valve. Enjoy while hot

Nutritional Info:

Calories: 414g, Carbohydrates: 3g, Protein: 42g, Fat: 26g, Sugar: 1g, Sodium: 4571 mg

Everyday Chicken Breast

Servings: 4 servings, **Prep Time:** 2 minutes, **Cooking Time:** 8 minutes

Ingredients:

- 4 boneless skinless chicken breasts
- ½ cup water

Directions:

1. Place the chicken breast in the Ninja Foodi pot and add the water.
2. Close the pressure seal lid and set the steamer valve to seal.
3. Cook on high pressure for 8 minutes then do a quick pressure release. Serve the chicken while hot.

Nutritional Info:

Calories: 249g, Carbohydrates: 0g, Protein: 52g, Fat: 2g, Sugar: 0g, Sodium: 149mg

Salsa Chicken Breast

Servings: 4 servings, **Prep Time:**   2 minutes, **Cooking Time:** 8 minutes

Ingredients:
- 4 boneless skinless chicken breasts
- ½ cup water
- 1 cup chopped tomatoes
- ½ cup chopped onion
- 1 tbsp lemon juice
- ½ tsp salt
- ¼ tsp ground black pepper

Directions:

1. Place the chicken breast in the Ninja Foodi pot and add all the ingredients to the bowl.
2. Close the pressure seal lid and set the steamer valve to seal.
3. Cook on high pressure for 8 minutes then do a quick pressure release. Serve the chicken while hot.

Nutritional Info:
Calories: 271g, Carbohydrates: 5g, Protein: 53g, Fat: 2g, Sugar: 4g, Sodium: 731 mg

Mexican Style Chicken Breast

Servings: 4 servings, **Prep Time:**   2 minutes, **Cooking Time:** 8 minutes

Ingredients:
- 4 boneless skinless chicken breasts
- ½ cup water
- 1 cup chopped tomatoes
- ½ cup chopped onion
- 1 jalapeno, seeds removed, minced
- 1 tbsp lime juice
- ½ tsp salt
- ¼ tsp ground black pepper

Directions:

1. Place the chicken breast in the Ninja Foodi pot and add all the ingredients to the bowl.
2. Close the pressure seal lid and set the steamer valve to seal.
3. Cook on high pressure for 8 minutes then do a quick pressure release. Serve the chicken while hot.

Nutritional Info:
Calories: 242g, Carbohydrates: 10g, Protein: 42g, Fat: 5g, Sugar: 6g, Sodium: 655mg

Cheesy Chicken Breast

Servings: 4 servings, **Prep Time:**   2 minutes, **Cooking Time:** 8 minutes

Ingredients:

- 4 boneless skinless chicken breasts
- ½ cup water
- 1 cup chopped tomatoes
- ½ cup chopped onion
- 1 tbsp lemon juice
- ½ tsp salt
- ¼ tsp ground black pepper
- 1 cup Mexican Blend shredded cheese

Directions:

1. Place the chicken breast in the Ninja Foodi pot and add all the ingredients to the bowl.
2. Close the pressure seal lid and set the steamer valve to seal.
3. Cook on high pressure for 8 minutes then do a quick pressure release.
4. Sprinkle the cheese on top of the hot chicken and place the air crisper lid on. Set to broil and the timer for 5 minutes. The cheese should be melted and beginning to brown. Serve the chicken while hot.

Nutritional Info:

Calories: 301g, Carbohydrates: 6g, Protein: 46g, Fat: 11g, Sugar: 4g, Sodium: 788mg

Keto Chicken Chili

Servings: 4 servings, **Prep Time:**   2 minutes, **Cooking Time:** 8 minutes

Ingredients:

- 1 pound chicken breast
- 1 ½ cup chicken broth
- 2 cloves of garlic, chopped
- 1 jalapeno, seeds removed, diced
- 1 bell pepper, chopped
- ½ white onion, chopped
- ¼ cup heavy cream
- 4 oz cream cheese
- 1 tsp dried oregano
- ¼ tsp cayenne pepper
- ¼ tsp salt
- 1/8 tsp ground black pepper
- ¼ cup shredded cheddar cheese

Directions:

1. Place the chicken breast in the Ninja Foodi pot and sprinkle with the oregano, salt, cayenne and ground black pepper.
2. Add the broth, garlic, jalapeno, bell pepper and onion to the pot and close the pressure cooker lid.
3. Cook on high pressure for 10 minutes. Do a quick steam release and remove the lid. Add the cream cheese and heavy cream and stir to blend.
4. Sprinkle the cheese on top of the chili and put the air crisper top on. Use the broil function to brown the cheese for 2 minutes.

Nutritional Info:

Calories: 448g, Carbohydrates: 9g, Protein: 38g, Fat: 31g, Sugar: 6g, Sodium: 1171 mg

Chicken Soup

Servings: 4 servings, **Prep Time:** 2 minutes, **Cooking Time:** 8 minutes

Ingredients:

- 1 pound chicken breast
- 4 cups chicken broth
- 2 cloves of garlic, chopped
- 1 carrot, chopped
- 2 celery stalks, chopped
- ½ white onion, chopped
- ¼ tsp salt
- 1/8 tsp ground black pepper
- ¼ cup shredded cheddar cheese

Directions:

1. Add all the ingredients to the pot and place the pressure cooker lid on the Ninja Foodi.
2. Cook on high pressure for 10 minutes. Do a quick steam release and remove the lid.
3. Shred the chicken using two forks.
4. Serve while hot or freeze to use at a later date.

Nutritional Info:

Calories: 217g, Carbohydrates: 2g, Protein: 33g, Fat: 4g, Sugar: 2g, Sodium: 755 mg

Veggie Chicken Soup

Servings: 4 servings, **Prep Time:** 2 minutes, **Cooking Time:** 12 minutes

Ingredients:

- 1 pound chicken breast
- 6 cups chicken broth
- 2 cloves of garlic, chopped
- 1 carrot, chopped
- 1 Bell pepper, chopped
- 1 sweet potato, peeled, diced
- 2 celery stalks, chopped
- ½ white onion, chopped
- ¼ tsp salt
- 1/8 tsp ground black pepper
- ¼ cup shredded cheddar cheese

Directions:

1. Add all the ingredients to the pot and place the pressure cooker lid on the Ninja Foodi.
2. Cook on high pressure for 12 minutes. Do a quick steam release and remove the lid.
3. Remove the chicken from the pot and shred the chicken using two forks.
4. Serve while hot or freeze to use at a later date.

Nutritional Info:

Calories: 310g, Carbohydrates: 14g, Protein: 37g, Fat: 6g, Sugar: 5g, Sodium: 376 mg

Sweet and Sour Chicken Wings

Servings: 4 servings, **Prep Time:** 10 minutes, **Cooking Time:** 28 minutes

Ingredients:

- ½ cup water
- 2 Tbsp baking stevia
- 2 Tbsp butter
- 2 Tbsp lemon juice
- 32 ounces frozen chicken wings
- ½ tsp salt
- ½ tsp ground black pepper

Directions:

1. Add all the ingredients into the cook and crisp basket and place the basket inside the Ninja Foodi.
2. Place the pressure cooker lid on top of the pot and close the pressure valve to the seal position. Set the pressure cooker function to high heat and set the timer for 5 minutes.
3. Once the coking cycle is complete, release the pressure quickly by carefully opening the steamer valve. Enjoy while hot

Nutritional Info:
Calories: 312g, Carbohydrates: 2g, Protein: 24g, Fat: 23g, Sugar: 2g, Sodium: 985 mg

Ninja Foodi salsa verde chicken

Serving: 2, Cooking time: 20 minutes

Ingredients:

- 1-pound boneless chicken breasts
- 1/4 teaspoon salt
- 1 cup commercial salsa verde

Directions:

1. Place all ingredients in the Ninja Foodi.
2. Install pressure lid. Close Ninja Foodi, press the manual button, choose high settings, and set time to 20 minutes.
3. Once done cooking, do a quick release.
4. Serve and enjoy.

Nutrition information:
Calories: 273; carbohydrates: 2.5g; protein: 51.4g; fat: 6.3g

Garlicky-Ginger drumsticks

Serving: 2, Cooking time: 20 minutes

Ingredients:

- 4 chicken drumsticks
- ¼ cup water
- ½ cup soy sauce
- 2 tablespoons honey
- 2 tablespoons sear button sugar
- 2 tablespoons rice wine vinegar
- 2 cloves of garlic, minced
- 1 teaspoon minced ginger
- 1 onion, chopped

Directions:

1. Place all ingredients in the Ninja Foodi.
2. Install pressure lid. Close Ninja Foodi, press the manual button, choose high settings, and set time to 20 minutes.
3. Once done cooking, do a quick release.
4. Serve and enjoy.

Nutrition information:

Calories: 277; carbohydrates: 12.3g; protein: 24.8g; fat: 14.6g

Easy Kung Pao Chicken

Serving: 2, Cooking time: 20 minutes

Ingredients:

- 1 tablespoon olive oil
- 1 clove garlic, minced
- 1/2 teaspoon grated ginger
- 1/2 teaspoon crushed red pepper
- 1/2 onion, chopped
- 1-pound chicken breasts, cut into bite-sized pieces
- 1/4 cup soy sauce
- 2 tbsp honey
- 2 tbsp hoisin sauce
- 1/2 zucchini, diced
- 1/2 red bell pepper, chopped

Directions:

1. Press the sauté button on the Ninja Foodi and heat the oil. Sauté the garlic, ginger, red pepper, and onion until fragrant.
2. Add the chicken breasts and stir for 3 minutes until lightly golden.
3. Stir in the soy sauce, honey, and hoisin sauce.
4. Close Ninja Foodi, press bake button, set temperature to 350°F, and set time to 20 minutes. Halfway through cooking time, stir and continue cooking.
5. Open the lid and press the sauté button. Stir in the zucchini and bell pepper. Allow to simmer until the vegetables are cooked.
6. Serve and enjoy.

Nutrition information:

Calories: 501; carbohydrates: 29.4g; protein: 40.7g; fat: 24.5g

Quick Shredded Buffalo Chicken

Serving: 2, Cooking time: 20 minutes

Ingredients:

- 2 chicken breasts
- 2 tablespoons butter
- 1/4 bottle buffalo wing sauce
- 1 tablespoon honey
- 1 teaspoon cider vinegar
- 1 tablespoons tabasco sauce

Directions:

1. Place all ingredients in the Ninja Foodi.
2. Install pressure lid. Close Ninja Foodi, press the pressure button, choose high settings, and set time to 20 minutes.
3. Once done cooking, do a quick release.
4. Once cooked, take the chicken out and shred using forks.
5. Serve and enjoy.

Nutrition information:
Calories: 685; carbohydrates: 23.2g; protein: 61g; fat: 38.6g

One-Pot Thai Red Curry

Serving: 2, Cooking time: 20 minutes

Ingredients:

- 1 1/2 tablespoon Thai red curry paste
- 1/2 can coconut milk
- 3/4-pound chicken breasts, sliced into chunks
- ¼ cup chicken broth
- 1 tablespoon fish sauce
- 1 teaspoon sear button sugar
- 1/2 tablespoon lime juice
- 1/2 cup red and green bell pepper
- 1/2 cup carrots, peeled and sliced
- ½ cup cubed onion
- 2 lime leaves
- 6 thai basil leaves

Directions:

1. Place all ingredients in the Ninja Foodi and give a good stir.
2. Install pressure lid. Close Ninja Foodi, press the manual button, choose high settings, and set time to 20 minutes.
3. Once done cooking, do a quick release.
4. Serve and enjoy.

Nutrition information:
Calories: 528; carbohydrates: 15.9g; protein: 53.4g; fat: 27.8g

Jamaican Style Curried Chicken

Serving: 2, Cooking time: 25 minutes

Ingredients:

- 2 tablespoons oil
- 1 tablespoon minced garlic
- 1 cup chopped onion
- 1 ½ tablespoon jamaican curry powder
- 1 scotch bonnet pepper, sliced
- ½ teaspoon ground allspice
- 3 sprigs of thyme
- 1-pound boneless chicken thighs, chunked
- Salt and pepper to taste
- 1 large potato, cut into chunks
- 1 cup water

Directions:

1. Press the sauté button on the Ninja Foodi and sauté the garlic, onion, curry powder, scotch bonnet pepper, allspice, and thyme until fragrant.
2. Stir in the chicken thighs and cook until lightly golden. Season with salt and pepper to taste. Add the potatoes and water.
3. Install pressure lid and place valve to vent position.
4. Close Ninja Foodi, press the pressure button, choose high settings, and set time to 20 minutes.
5. Once done cooking, do a quick release. Serve and enjoy.

Nutrition information:

Calories: 1099;   carbohydrates: 78.5g; protein: 48.6g; fat: 65.6g

Tasty Chicken Tetrazzini

Serving: 2, Cooking time: 15 minutes

Ingredients:

- 1 tablespoon butter
- 1 tablespoon flour
- 2 tbsp heavy cream
- 1/3 cup parmesan cheese
- ¼ cup cheddar cheese
- 2 chicken thighs, boneless, skinless and sliced
- 3/4 cup chicken broth
- Salt and pepper to taste
- ¼-lb spaghetti, cooked according to package instructions

Directions:

1. Press the sauté button on the Ninja Foodi and melt the butter. Whisk in the flour until it dissolves. Stir in the heavy cream, parmesan cheese, and cheddar cheese. Stir until melted. Set aside and clean the Ninja Foodi.
2. Still with the sauté button on, stir in the chicken thighs and allow to sear until lightly golden. Season with salt and pepper to taste. Stir in chicken broth and spaghetti. Pour over the cheese sauce.

3. Install pressure lid. Close Ninja Foodi, press the pressure button, choose high settings, and set time to 10 minutes.
4. Once done cooking, do a quick release. Serve and enjoy.

Nutrition information:
Calories: 726; carbohydrates: 32.7g; protein: 50.5g; fat: 43.6g

Chicken Shawarma Middle-East

Serving: 2, Cooking time: 20 minutes

Ingredients:
- ¼ teaspoon coriander
- ¼ teaspoon cumin
- ½ teaspoon paprika
- 1 teaspoon cardamom
- ½ teaspoon cinnamon powder
- ¼ teaspoon cloves
- ¼ teaspoon nutmeg
- ¼ cup lemon juice
- ¼ cup yogurt
- 2 tablespoons garlic, minced
- 1-pound boneless chicken breasts, cut into strips
- 2 bay leaves
- Salt and pepper to taste
- 2 pita bread
- ¼ cup greek yogurt
- For garnish: tomatoes, lettuce, and cucumber

Directions:

1. Place in the Ninja Foodi the coriander, cumin, paprika, cardamom, cinnamon powder, cloves, nutmeg, lemon juice, yogurt, garlic, and chicken breasts. Add the bay leaves and season with salt and pepper to taste.
2. Install pressure lid. Close Ninja Foodi, press the pressure button, choose high settings, and set time to 20 minutes.
3. Once done cooking, do a quick release. Place the chicken in the pita bread and drizzle with Greek yogurt. Garnish with tomatoes, lettuce, and cucumber.
4. Serve and enjoy.

Nutrition information:
Calories: 372; carbohydrates: 21.8g; protein: 55.1g; fat: 7.1g

Creamy 'n Tasty Chicken Chowder

Serving: 2, Cooking time: 20 minutes

Ingredients:
- 1/2-pound chicken thighs, cut into bite-sized pieces
- 3 strips of bacon, chopped
- ½ cup diced onions
- ½ cup chopped celery
- 1 teaspoon minced garlic
- ½ teaspoon dried thyme
- ½ teaspoon dried oregano
- 2 cups chicken stock
- 1/2 cup heavy cream
- Salt and pepper to taste
- 1 cup spinach

Directions:
1. Press the sauté button on the Ninja Foodi and stir in the chicken and bacon. Add the onions, celery, garlic, thyme, and oregano until fragrant.
2. Add the stock and heavy cream. Season with salt and pepper to taste.
3. Install pressure lid. Close Ninja Foodi, press the manual button, choose high settings, and set time to 15 minutes.
4. Once done cooking, do a quick release.
5. Open the lid and stir in the spinach last.
6. Serve and enjoy.

Nutrition information:
Calories: 485; carbohydrates: 13.9g; protein: 27.2g; fat: 35.6g

Indian Keema Matar Chicken

Serving: 2, Cooking time: 25 minutes

Ingredients:
- 2 tablespoons oil
- 1 tablespoon garlic paste
- 1 tablespoon ginger paste
- 1 onion, chopped
- 1-pound ground chicken
- 2 teaspoon coriander powder
- 1 teaspoon cayenne pepper
- 1 teaspoon garam masala
- ½ teaspoon ground cumin
- Salt and pepper to taste
- 2 tomatoes, diced
- ½ cup green peas
- ¼ cup water
- 1 tablespoon lemon juice
- ½ cup mint leaves

Directions:
1. Press the sauté button on the Ninja Foodi and heat the oil and sauté the garlic and ginger paste. Add the onion and sauté until fragrant.
2. Stir the chicken and season with coriander powder, cayenne pepper, garam masala, and cumin. Season with salt and pepper to taste. Stir for 3 minutes.

3. Add the tomato, green peas, water, and lemon juice.
4. Install pressure lid. Close Ninja Foodi, press the manual button, choose high settings, and set time to 20 minutes.
5. Once done cooking, do a quick release. Garnish with chopped mint leaves.
6. Serve and enjoy.

Nutrition information:
Calories: 560; carbohydrates:20.7g; protein: 44.8g; fat: 33.1g

Chicken Meatballs Buffalo Flavored

Serving: 2, Cooking time: 15 minutes

Ingredients:
- ¾-pound ground chicken
- 1/4 cup almond meal
- 1/2 teaspoon salt
- 2 cloves of garlic, minced
- 2 green onions, sliced thinly
- 1 tablespoon ghee
- 2 tablespoons coconut oil, melted
- ½ cup water
- 2 tablespoons hot sauce
- Salt and pepper to taste
- 1/2 tablespoon cornstarch + 1 tablespoon water

Directions:
1. Place all ingredients in the mixing bowl except for the hot sauce, coconut oil, and cornstarch mix.
2. Mix until well combined and form small balls using your hands. Allow to set in the fridge for at least 3 hours.
3. Press the sauté button on the Ninja Foodi and heat the oil. Slowly add the meatballs and allow to sear on all sides. Add water, hot sauce, salt and pepper.
4. Install pressure lid. Close Ninja Foodi, press the pressure button, choose high settings, and set time to 10 minutes.
5. Once done cooking, do a quick release.
6. Open the lid and press the sauté button. Stir in the cornstarch slurry and allow to simmer until the sauce thickens.
7. Serve and enjoy.

Nutrition information:
Calories: 356; carbohydrates: 3g; protein: 23g; fat: 28g

Crispy Garlic-Parmesan Wings

Serving: 2, Cooking time: 20 minutes

Ingredients:
- 1-lb chicken wings/drumettes
- Seasoned salt, to season the wings
- 1/2 cup of chicken broth

Sauce Ingredients:
- 1 stick of salted butter, melted
- 1/2 tsp of garlic better than bouillon (or 1 tbsp of crushed garlic)
- 1/2 cup of grated parmesan cheese
- 1 tsp of garlic powder
- 1/2 tsp of black pepper
- 1/2 tsp of dried parsley flakes

Directions:
1. Lightly rub the seasoned salt on both sides of the chicken wings
2. Add the wings to the Ninja Foodi followed by the broth.
3. Install pressure lid. Close Ninja Foodi, press pressure button, select high settings, and cook for 8 minutes.
4. While the wings are pressure cooking, make the garlic parmesan sauce by combining the butter, garlic, parmesan, pepper, garlic powder and parsley flakes in a large bowl. Mix together well.
5. Once the wings are done cooking, do a quick release.
6. Transfer to bowl of sauce and discard liquid. Remove pressure lid.
7. Add the trivet to pot, spray with non-stick spray and place wings.
8. Lower the tendercrisp lid and hit "broil" and go for 8-10 minutes (the longer you go, the crispier the wings so be sure to check on them). It is a good idea to flip the wings midway through the crisping process.
9. Enjoy!

Nutrition information:
Calories: 957; carbohydrates: 5.5g; protein: 63.0g; fat: 75.9g

Roasted Crisp Whole Chicken

Serving: 2, Cooking time: 25 minutes

Ingredients:
- 1 whole Cornish Hen
- 1/2 tsp seasoned salt
- Juice of 1/2 lemon
- 1 tbsp honey
- ¼ cup hot water
- 1/4 teaspoon salt
- 1/2 teaspoon whole peppercorns (optional)
- 1 sprigs of fresh thyme
- 2 cloves of garlic
- 1 tsp canola oil

Directions:

1. Combine lemon juice, honey, water, salt, peppercorns, thyme, and garlic in pot.
2. Season the chicken inside, outside and underneath the skin with seasoned salt.
3. Place the chicken in the air crisp basket then place into the pot.
4. Install pressure lid. Close pot, choose high, and cook for 15 minutes.
5. Once done cooking, do a quick release. Remove pressure lid.
6. Brush the chicken with canola oil
7. Close the crisping lid and select roast.
8. Set the time for 15 minutes and halfway through cooking time turn chicken over.
9. The juices in the bottom of the cooking pot make a delicious sauce.

Nutrition information:
Calories: 196; carbohydrates: 10.5g; protein: 24.2g; fat: 6.3g

Ranch Flavored Tender Wings

Serving: 2, Cooking time: 20 minutes

Ingredients:
- 1/2 cup water
- 1/4 cup hot pepper sauce
- 2 tablespoons unsalted butter, melted
- 1/2 tablespoons apple cider vinegar
- 1-pound chicken wings
- 1/4 (1-ounce) envelope ranch salad dressing mix
- 1/2 teaspoon paprika
- Nonstick cooking spray

Directions:
1. Pour the water, hot pepper sauce, butter, and vinegar into the pot. Place the wings in the cook & crisp basket and place the basket in the pot.
2. Install pressure lid. Close pot, press pressure button, select high settings, and cook for 5 minutes.
3. Once done, do a quick release. Remove pressure lid.
4. Sprinkle the chicken wings with the dressing mix and paprika. Coat with cooking spray.
5. Close Ninja Foodi, press air crisp, set the temperature to 375°F, and crisp for 15 minutes. Halfway through cooking time, turnover wings.
6. Serve and enjoy.

Nutrition information:
Calories: 351; carbohydrates: 1.3g; protein: 50.5g; fat: 16.0g

Ginger-Balsamic Glazed Chicken

Serving: 2, Cooking time: 15 minutes

Ingredients:
- 4 chicken thighs, skinless
- 1/4 cup balsamic vinegar
- 1 1/2 tablespoons mustard
- 1 tablespoon ginger garlic paste
- 4 cloves of garlic, minced
- 1-inche fresh ginger root
- 2 tablespoons honey
- Salt and pepper to taste

Directions:
1. Place all ingredients in the Ninja Foodi. Stir to combine everything.
2. Install pressure lid. Close Ninja Foodi, press the manual button, choose high settings, and set time to 15 minutes.
3. Once done cooking, do a quick release. Remove pressure lid.
4. Mix and turnover chicken.
5. Cover, press roast, and roast for 5 minutes.
6. Serve and enjoy.

Nutrition information:
Calories: 476; carbohydrates:12.5g; protein: 32.4g; fat: 32.9g

Tasty Sesame-Honeyed Chicken

Serving: 2, Cooking time: 16 minutes

Ingredients:
- 1 tablespoon olive oil
- 1/2 onion, diced
- 2 cloves of garlic, minced
- 1-pound chicken breasts
- 1/4 cup soy sauce
- 2 tbsp ketchup
- 1 tsp sesame oil
- 1/4 cup honey
- ½ teaspoon red pepper flakes
- 1 tablespoon cornstarch + 1 1/2 tablespoons water
- Green onions for garnish
- 1 tablespoon sesame seeds for garnish

Directions:
1. Press the sauté button on the Ninja Foodi and heat the oil. Stir in the onion and garlic until fragrant.
2. Add the chicken breasts. Allow to sear on all sides for three minutes.
3. Stir in the soy sauce, ketchup, sesame oil, honey, and red pepper flakes.
4. Install pressure lid. Close Ninja Foodi, press the pressure button, choose high settings, and set time to 10 minutes.
5. Once done cooking, do a quick release.
6. Open the lid and press the sauté button. Stir in the cornstarch slurry and allow to simmer until the sauce thickens.

7. Garnish with green onions and sesame seeds last.
8. Serve and enjoy.

Nutrition information:
Calories: 568; carbohydrates: 49.1g; protein: 50.9g; fat: 34.6g

Traditional Chicken   'n Dumplings

Serving: 2, Cooking time: 25 minutes

Ingredients:
- 1-pound chicken breasts, cut into cubes
- 2 cloves of garlic, minced
- 1/2 cup chopped onion
- 1/2 cup chopped celery
- 1/2 teaspoon dried thyme
- 1/2 tablespoon bouillon
- 1 cup frozen vegetables (peas and carrots)
- 1 1/2 cups chicken stock
- 1 can cream of chicken
- Salt and pepper to taste
- 1/2 can southern homestyle biscuits
- 2 tbsp parsley, chopped

Directions:
1. Press the sauté button on the Ninja Foodi and stir in the chicken, garlic, onion, celery, and thyme. Stir constantly and allow the onions to sweat.
2. Stir in bouillon, vegetables, stock, and cream of chicken. Stir in the cream of chicken and season with salt and pepper to taste. Allow to simmer for a few minutes. Add the biscuits on top.
3. Install pressure lid. Close Ninja Foodi, press the pressure button, choose high settings, and set time to 15 minutes.
4. Once done cooking, do a quick release.
5. Remove pressure lid. Cover, press roast, and roast for 5 minutes at 400°F.
6. Garnish with parsley.
7. Serve and enjoy.

Nutrition information:
Calories: 726; carbohydrates: 51.2g; protein: 63.8g; fat: 29.6g

Garlic Chicken In Creamy Tuscan Style

Serving: 2, Cooking time: 15 minutes

Ingredients:

- 1 tablespoon olive oil
- 1-pound skinless chicken breasts, halved and pounded
- 2 cloves of garlic, minced
- ½ tablespoon Italian seasoning
- 1/2 teaspoon salt
- 1/3 cup chicken stock
- 1/3 cup heavy cream
- 1/3 cup parmesan cheese
- 1/4 cup sun-dried tomato

Directions:

1. Press the sauté button on the Ninja Foodi and sear the chicken breasts on all sides.
2. Stir in the garlic, Italian seasoning, and salt.
3. Pour in the chicken stock and the rest of the ingredients.
4. Install pressure lid. Close Ninja Foodi, press the pressure button, choose high settings, and set time to 10 minutes.
5. Once done cooking, do a quick release.
6. Serve and enjoy.

Nutrition information:

Calories: 521; carbohydrates: 10.8g; protein: 59.9g; fat: 26.5g

Green Curry Chicken Thai Style

Serving: 2 , Cooking time: 15 minutes

Ingredients:

- 1 tablespoon Thai green curry paste
- 1/3 cup coconut milk
- 1/2 teaspoon coriander powder
- ½ teaspoon cumin powder
- 1/3-pound chicken breasts, bones removed and cut into chunks
- ¼ cup chicken broth
- 1 tablespoon fish sauce
- 1/4 tablespoon sear button sugar
- 1/2 tablespoon lime juice
- 1 lime leaves, crushed
- 1/4 cup bamboo shoots, sliced
- 1/4 cup onion, cubed
- Salt and pepper to taste
- 1/3 cup green bell pepper
- 1/3 cup zucchini, sliced
- 2 tbsp Thai basil leaves

Directions:

1. Press the sauté button on the Ninja Foodi. Place the Thai green curry paste and the coconut milk. Stir until the mixture bubbles. Stir in the coriander and cumin powder and cook for 30 seconds.
2. Stir in the chicken and coconut broth. Season with fish sauce, sear button sugar, lime juice, bamboo shoots, lime leaves, and onion.

Season with salt and pepper to taste.

3. Install pressure lid. Close Ninja Foodi, press the manual button, choose high settings, and set time to 10 minutes.
4. Once done cooking, do a quick release. Open the lid and press the sauté button. Stir in the green bell pepper, zucchini, and basil leaves. Allow to simmer for at least 5 minutes to cook the vegetables.
5. Serve and enjoy.

Nutrition information:
Calories: 208; carbohydrates:9 g; protein:16 g; fat: 12g

Savory   'n Aromatic Chicken Adobo

Serving: 2, Cooking time: 20 minutes

Ingredients:
- 1-pound boneless chicken thighs
- 1/4 cup white vinegar
- ½ cup water
- 1/4 cup soy sauce
- 1/2 head garlic, peeled and smashed
- 2 bay leaves
- ½ teaspoon pepper
- 1 tsp oil

Directions:
1. Place all ingredients in the Ninja Foodi.
2. Install pressure lid. Close Ninja Foodi, press the pressure button, choose high settings, and set time to 10 minutes.
3. Once done cooking, do a quick release.
4. Open the lid and press the sauté button. Allow the sauce to reduce so that the chicken is fried slightly in its oil, around 10 minutes.
5. Serve and enjoy.

Nutrition information:
Calories: 713; carbohydrates: 3.2g; protein: 43.9g; fat: 58.3g

Mexican Cheesy Chicken Ole

(Cooking Time: 30 minutes | Serves: 6)

Ingredients

- 2 tbsps. sesame oil
- 1½ lbs. chicken breasts
- Salt and ground black pepper
- 10 oz. salsa
- 1 c. shredded Queso Añejo cheese

Directions:

1. Press the SEAR/SAUTÉ button and set to High; add olive oil. Once hot, cook the chicken breasts for a few minutes per side. Add salt, pepper, and salsa.
2. Secure the pressure lid; press the PRESSURE button and cook for 20 minutes at High Pressure. Once cooking is complete, use a quick release; remove the lid carefully.
3. Scatter shredded cheese over the chicken breasts.
4. Secure the crisping lid and choose the BROIL function. Set temperature to 390 degrees F with a time of 10 minutes; press the START/STOP button. Bon appétit!

Nutritional Info: Calories 322; Fat 16.3g; Carbs 3g; Protein 38.9g

Creamy Chicken Breasts

(Cooking Time: 25 minutes | Serves: 4)

Ingredients:

- 1 small onion
- 2 tbsps. butter
- 1 lb. chicken breasts
- ½ c. sour cream
- Salt

Directions:

1. Apply salt to the chicken breasts generously and keep aside.
2. Heat butter in a skillet on medium-low heat and add onions.
3. Sauté for 3 minutes and add chicken breasts.
4. Cover the lid and cook for about 10 minutes.
5. Stir in the sour cream and cook for about 4 minutes.
6. Stir gently and dish out to serve.

Nutritional Info: 447 calories, 26.9g fat, 3.8g carbs, 45.3g protein

Ham Stuffed Turkey Rolls

(Cooking Time: 30 minutes | Serves: 8)

Ingredients:

- 4 tbsps. fresh sage leaves
- 8 ham slices
- 8 turkey cutlets
- Salt and black pepper
- 2 tbsps. melted butter

Directions:

1. Season the turkey cutlets with salt and black pepper.
2. Roll the turkey cutlets and wrap each one with ham slices tightly.
3. Coat each roll with butter and place the sage leaves evenly over each cutlet.
4. Press "Bake/Roast" on Ninja Foodi and add turkey rolls.
5. Bake for about 10 minutes at 360 degrees F and flip the sides.
6. Bake for another 10 minutes and dish out to serve.

Nutritional Info: 467 calories, 24.8g fat, 1.7g carbs, 56g protein

Stuffed Whole Chicken

(Cooking Time: 8 hours 10 minutes | Serves: 6)

Ingredients:

- 1 c. mozzarella cheese
- 4 peeled garlic cloves,
- 2 lbs. whole chicken, clean and dried
- Salt and black pepper
- 2 tbsps. fresh lemon juice

Directions:

1. Stuff the chicken cavity with garlic cloves mozzarella cheese.
2. Season the chicken with salt and black pepper.
3. Transfer the chicken in the Ninja Foodi and drizzle lemon juice.
4. Press "Slow Cooker" and cook on Low for about 8 hours.
5. Dish out and serve hot.

Nutritional Info: 309 calories, 12.1g fat, 1.6g carbs, 45.8g protein

Creamy Turkey Breast

(Cooking Time: 2 hours 10 mins | Serves: 6)

Ingredients:

- 1½ c. Italian dressing
- 2 minced garlic cloves
- 2 lbs. bone-in turkey breast
- 2 tbsps. butter
- Salt and black pepper

Directions:

1. Mix together garlic cloves, salt and black pepper and rub the turkey breast with this mixture.

2. Grease the pot of Ninja Foodi with butter and arrange turkey breasts.

3. Top evenly with Italian dressing and press "Bake/Roast".

4. Bake for about 2 hours at 330 degrees F and dish out to serve immediately.

Nutritional Info: 369 calories, 23.2g fat, 6.5g carbs, 35.4g protein

Caprese Hasselback Chicken

(Cooking Time: 1 hour 10 minutes | Serves: 8)

Ingredients:

- 4 tbsps. butter
- Salt and black pepper
- 2 c. freshly sliced mozzarella cheese
- 8 large chicken breasts
- 4 roma tomatoes, sliced

Directions:

1. Make a few deep slits in the chicken breasts and season with salt and black pepper.

2. Stuff the mozzarella cheese slices and tomatoes in the chicken slits.

3. Grease the pot of Ninja Foodi with butter and arrange stuffed chicken breasts.

4. Press "Bake/Roast" and bake for about 1 hour at 365 degrees F.

5. Dish out and serve hot.

Nutritional Info: 287 calories, 15g fat, 3.8g carbs, 33.2g protein

Mediterranean Turkey Cutlets

(Cooking Time: 25 minutes | Serves: 4)

Ingredients:

- 1 tsp. Greek seasoning
- 1 lb. turkey cutlets
- 2 tbsps. olive oil
- 1 tsp. turmeric powder
- ½ c. almond flour

Directions:

1. Combine Greek seasoning, turmeric powder and almond flour in a bowl.
2. Dredge turkey cutlets in it and set aside for about 30 minutes.
3. Press "Sauté" on Ninja Foodi and add oil and turkey cutlets.
4. Sauté for about 2 minutes and add turkey cutlets.

5. Press "Pressure" and set to "Lo:Md" for about 20 minutes.
6. Dish out in a serving platter.

Nutritional Info: 340 calories, 19.4g fat, 3.7g carbs, 36.3g protein

Chicken Congee

(Cooking Time: 65 minutes | Serves: 7)
Ingredients:
- 6 chicken drumsticks
- 7 c. water
- 1 c. Jasmine rice
- 1 tbsp. ginger, fresh
- Salt

Directions:
1. Rinse rice under cool water for a few minutes.
2. Pour rice, water, ginger, and drumsticks into Ninja Foodi. Seal the lid.
3. Select "PRESSURE" and cook at HIGH pressure for 30 minutes.

4. When time is up, press CANCEL and wait for a natural pressure release.
5. When safe, open the lid and press "SAUTÉ".
6. Keep stirring while the congee thickens.
7. Season with salt.
8. Pull off the chicken with tongs, and throw away the bones.
9. Serve right away!

Nutritional Info: 181 calories, 6g fat, 21g carbs, 12g protein

Chicken Alfredo Pasta

(Cooking Time: 5 minutes | Serves: 3)

Ingredients:
- 8 oz. fettuccine
- 15 oz. Alfredo sauce
- 2 c. water
- 1 c. cooked chicken, diced
- 2 tsps. chicken seasoning

Directions:
1. Break your pasta in half so it fits in the cooker.
2. Add pasta, water, and chicken seasoning to Ninja Foodi.
3. Seal the lid. Select STEAM and cook at HIGH pressure for 3 minutes.
4. When the timer beeps, press CANCEL and use a quick release.
5. Drain the pasta and add to serving bowl.
6. Mix in Alfredo sauce and chicken. Serve!

Nutritional Info: 225 calories, 6.3g fat, 21.8g carbs, 20.1g protein

The Shiny Chicken Stock

(Cooking Time: 2 hours 10 mins | Serves: 4)

Ingredients
- 2 lbs. meaty chicken bones
- ¼ tsp. salt
- 3½ c. water

Directions:
1. Place chicken parts in Foodi and season with salt
2. Add water, place the pressure cooker lid and seal the valve, cook on HIGH pressure for 90 minutes
3. Release the pressure naturally over 10 minutes
4. Line a cheesecloth on a colander and place it over a large bowl, pour chicken parts and stock into the colander and strain out the chicken and bones
5. Let the stock cool and let it peel off any layer of fat that might accumulate on the surface
6. Use as needed!

Nutritional Info: 51 calories, 3g fat, 2g carbs. 6g protein

Succulent Roasted Chicken

Serves: 6, Prep Time: 15 minutes, Cooking Time: 35 minutes

Ingredients:
- 1 (5-lb.) whole chicken, necks and giblets removed
- Salt and freshly ground black pepper, to taste
- ¼ C. honey
- ¼ C. fresh lemon juice
- ¼ C. hot water

Directions:
1) Season the chicken inside, outside and underneath the skin with the salt and black pepper generously.
2) In the pot of Ninja Foodi, place the honey, lemon juice, water, salt and black pepper and mix until well combined.
3) Place the chicken into the "Cook & Crisp Basket". Arrange the "Cook & Crisp Basket" in the pot.
4) Cover the Ninja Foodi with the pressure lid and place the pressure valve to "Seal" position. Select "Pressure" and set to "High" for about 15 minutes.
5) Press "Start/Stop" to begin. Switch the valve to "Vent" and do a "Quick" release.
6) Once all the pressure is released, open the lid, Spray the chicken with the cooking spray evenly.
7) Now, close the Ninja Foodi with the crisping lid and select "Air Crisp".
8) Set the temperature to 400 degrees F for 15-20 minutes.
9) Press "Start/Stop" to begin. Open the lid and transfer the chicken onto a cutting board for about 10 minutes before carving.
10) Cut into desired sized pieces and serve.

Nutrition Information:
Calories: 616; Carbohydrates: 11.9g; Protein: 109.7g; Fat: 11.5g; Sugar: 11.8g; Sodium: 26mg; Fiber: 0.1g

Smoky Roasted Chicken

Serves: 5, Prep Time: 20 minutes, Cooking Time: 40 minutes

Ingredients:
- 1 (4-lb.) whole chicken, necks and giblets removed
- Salt and freshly ground black pepper, to taste
- 1 tsp. liquid smoke
- 2 tbsp. chicken rub

Directions:
1) Season the chicken inside, outside and underneath the skin with the salt and black pepper generously.
2) In the pot of Ninja Foodi, place 1 C. of water and liquid smoke, Place the

chicken into the "Cook & Crisp Basket". Arrange the "Cook & Crisp Basket" in the pot.

3) Cover the Ninja Foodi with the pressure lid and place the pressure valve to "Seal" position. Select "Pressure" and set to "High" for about 15 minutes.

4) Press "Start/Stop" to begin. Switch the valve to "Vent" and do a "Quick" release.

5) Once all the pressure is released, open the lid . Spray the chicken with the cooking spray and then, coat with half of the chicken rub.

6) Now, close the Ninja Foodi with the crisping lid and select "Air Crisp".

7) Set the temperature to 400 degrees F for 10 minutes.

8) Press "Start/Stop" to begin. Again, spray the chicken with the cooking spray and then, coat with half of the chicken rub.

9) Close the Ninja Foodi with the crisping lid and cook for 10 minutes more.

10) Open the lid and transfer the chicken onto a cutting board for about 10 minutes before carving. Cut into desired sized pieces and serve.

Nutrition Information:
Calories: 557; Carbohydrates: 1.2g; Protein: 3.2105.2g; Fat: 11g; Sugar: 0g; Sodium: 446mg; Fiber: 0g

Aromatic Roasted Chicken

Serves: 7, Prep Time: 20 minutes, Cooking Time: 1 hour 29 minutes

Ingredients:
- 1 (6-lb.) whole chicken, necks and giblets removed
- Salt and freshly ground black pepper, to taste
- 3 fresh rosemary sprigs, divided
- 1 lemon, zested and cut into quarters
- 2 large onions, sliced,
- 4 C. chicken broth

Directions:
1) Stuff the cavity of chicken with 2 rosemary sprigs and lemon quarters.

2) Season the chicken with salt and black pepper evenly. Chop the remaining rosemary sprig and set aside.

3) Select "Sauté/Sear" setting of Ninja Foodi and place the chicken into the pot.

4) Press "Start/Stop" to begin and cook, uncovered for about 5-7 minutes per side.

5) Remove chicken from the pot and arrange onto a roasting rack.

6) In the pot, place the onions and broth. Arrange the roasting rack into the pot and sprinkle the chicken with reserved chopped rosemary and lemon zest.

7) Close the Ninja Foodi with the crisping lid and select "Bake/Roast".

8) Set the temperature to 375 degrees F for 1¼ hours and press "Start/Stop" to begin. Open the lid and transfer

the chicken onto a cutting board for about 10 minutes before carving.

9) Cut into desired sized pieces and serve.

Nutrition Information:
Calories: 628; Carbohydrates: 5.1g; Protein: 116g; Fat: 12.7g; Sugar: 2.3g; Sodium: 706mg; Fiber: 1.2g

Crispy Fried Chicken

Serves: 4, Prep Time: 15 minutes, Cooking Time: 40 minutes

Ingredients:
- 3 C. seasoned flour
- 1 C. milk
- 2 eggs
- 1 (2-2½-lb.) chicken, cut into 8 pieces
- ½ C. canola oil

Directions:
1) In a shallow bowl, place the flour.
2) In another shallow bowl, add the milk and eggs and beat well.
3) Coat the chicken with the flour, then dip into milk mixture and finally, coat with flour again.
4) Select "Sauté/Sear" setting of Ninja Foodi and place the oil into the pot.
5) Press "Start/Stop" to begin and heat for about 5 minutes.
6) Add the chicken into the pot and cook, uncovered for about 4-5 minutes per side.
7) Now, set on "High" setting and cook, uncovered for about 20 minutes, flipping occasionally.
8) With a slotted spoon, transfer the chicken pieces onto a paper towel-lined plate to drain.
9) Serve warm.

Nutrition Information:
Calories: 920; Carbohydrates: 93.2g; Protein: 3.2g; Fat: 3g; Sugar: 11.9g; Sodium: 1000mg; Fiber: 6.7g

Simple Homestyle Chicken Thighs

Serves: 4, Prep Time: 10 minutes, Cooking Time: 14 minutes

Ingredients:
- 4 (6-oz.) boneless skin-on chicken thighs
- 1 tbsp. extra-virgin olive oil
- 2 tsp. poultry seasoning
- 1 tsp. salt

Directions:
1) In the pot of Ninja Foodi, place 1 C. of water. arrange the reversible rack in higher position.
2) Arrange the chicken thighs over the rack, skin side up.
3) Cover the Ninja Foodi with the pressure lid and place the pressure valve to "Seal" position.
4) Select "Pressure" and set to "High" for about 4 minutes.
5) Press "Start/Stop" to begin.
6) Switch the valve to "Vent" and do a "Quick" release.
7) Once all the pressure is released, open the lid
8) Coat the chicken thighs with oil evenly and season with poultry seasoning and salt.
9) Now, close the Ninja Foodi with the crisping lid and select "Broil".
10) Set time to 10 minutes and select "Start/Stop" to begin.
11) Open the lid and serve hot.

Nutrition Information:
Calories: 394; Carbohydrates: 0.5g; Protein: 30.2g; Fat: 29.2g; Sugar: 0g; Sodium: 710mg; Fiber: 0.1g

Tender Chicken Thighs

Serves: 6, Prep Time: 10 minutes, Cooking Time: 28 minutes

Ingredients:
- 2 tbsp. butter
- 1 onion, chopped
- 2 lb. chicken thighs
- ¾ C. chicken broth
- Salt and freshly ground black pepper, to taste

Directions:
1) Select "Sauté/Sear" setting of Ninja Foodi and place the butter into the pot.
2) Press "Start/Stop" to begin and heat for about 2-3 minutes.
3) Add the onion and cook for about 5 minutes.
4) Press "Start/Stop" to stop cooking and stir in remaining ingredients.
5) Cover the Ninja Foodi with the pressure lid and place the pressure valve to "Seal" position.
6) Select "Pressure" and set to "High" for about 20 minutes.
7) Press "Start/Stop" to begin.
8) Switch the valve to "Vent" and do a "Quick" release.
9) Once all the pressure is released, open the lid

10) Serve hot.

Nutrition Information:

Calories: 333; Carbohydrates: 1.8g; Protein: 44.6g; Fat: 15.2g; Sugar: 0.9g; Sodium: 281mg; Fiber: 0.4g__

Creamy Tomato Chicken

Serves: 6, Prep Time: 10 minutes, Cooking Time: 6 hours

Ingredients:
- ¾ C. chicken broth
- 1 C. sour cream
- 1½ C. fresh tomatoes, chopped finely
- Salt and freshly ground black pepper, to taste
- 6 (6-oz.) boneless, skinless chicken breasts

Directions:
1) In the pot of Ninja Foodi, add all the ingredients and stir to combine.
2) Close the crisping lid and select "Slow Cooker".
3) Set on "Low" for about 6 hours.
4) Press "Start/Stop" to begin.
5) Open the lid and serve hot.

Nutrition Information:
Calories: 418; Carbohydrates: 3.5g; Protein: 51.4g; Fat: 20.9g; Sugar: 1.3g; Sodium: 291mg; Fiber: 0.5g__

Chicken Taco Filling

Serves: 8, Prep Time: 15 minutes, Cooking Time: 4 hours

Ingredients:
- ¼ C. low-sodium soy sauce
- ¼ C. blackberry jam
- ¼ C. honey
- ½ tsp. red pepper flakes, crushed
- 5 (8-oz.) boneless, skinless chicken breasts

Directions:
6) Grease the pot of Ninja Foodi generously.
7) In a bowl, add all the ingredients except the chicken breasts and mix well.
8) In the prepared pot, place the chicken breasts and top with the honey mixture.
9) Close the crisping lid and select "Slow Cooker".
10) Set on "High" for about 4 hours.
11) Press "Start/Stop" to begin.
12) Open the lid and with 2 forks, shred the meat and stir with sauce well.
13) Serve hot.

Nutrition Information:
Calories: 329; Carbohydrates: 15.8g; Protein: 41.6g; Fat: 10.5g; Sugar: 15.2g; Sodium: 562mg; Fiber: 0.1g__

Italian Chicken Dinner

Serves: 6, Prep Time: 15 minutes, Cooking Time: 8 hours 15 minutes

Ingredients:
- 1 tbsp. olive oil
- 6 skinless, boneless chicken breasts
- 4 C. fresh button mushrooms, sliced
- 1 C. chicken broth
- Salt and freshly ground black pepper, to taste

Directions:
1) Select "Sauté/Sear" setting of Ninja Foodi and place the oil into the pot.
2) Press "Start/Stop" to begin and heat for about 2-3 minutes.
3) Add the chicken and cook, uncovered for about 5 minutes per side.
4) Press "Start/Stop" to stop cooking and stir in the remaining ingredients.
5) Close the crisping lid and select "Slow Cooker".
6) Set on "Low" for about 7-8 hours.
7) Press "Start/Stop" to begin.
8) Open the lid and serve hot.

Nutrition Information:
Calories: 249; Carbohydrates: 1.7g; Protein: 40.3g; Fat: 8.8g; Sugar: 0.9g; Sodium: 218mg; Fiber: 0.5g__

Teriyaki Chicken & Broccoli

Serves: 3, Prep Time: 15 minutes, Cooking Time: 14 minutes

Ingredients:
- 2 (8-oz.) boneless, skinless chicken breasts
- 1 head broccoli, cut in 2-inch florets
- 1 tbsp. olive oil
- Salt and freshly ground black pepper, to taste
- ¼ C. teriyaki sauce

Directions:
1) In the pot of Ninja Foodi, place 1 C. of water.
2) In the pot, arrange the reversible rack in higher position.
3) Arrange the chicken breasts over the rack.
4) Cover the Ninja Foodi with the pressure lid and place the pressure valve to "Seal" position.
5) Select "Pressure" and set to "High" for about 2 minutes.
6) Press "Start/Stop" to begin.
7) Meanwhile, in a bowl, add the broccoli, oil salt and black pepper and toss to coat well.
8) Switch the valve to "Vent" and do a "Natural" release for about 10 minutes. Then do a "Quick" release.
9) Once all the pressure is released, open the lid
10) Coat the chicken breasts with teriyaki sauce generously.
11) Arrange the broccoli florets around the chicken breasts.

12) Now, close the Ninja Foodi with the crisping lid and select "Broil".
13) Set time to 12 minutes and select "Start/Stop" to begin.
14) Open the lid and serve the chicken breasts with alongside the broccoli.

Nutrition Information:
Calories: 387; Carbohydrates: 11.3g; Protein: 48.3g; Fat: 16.2g; Sugar: 5.3g; Sodium: 1000mg; Fiber: 3g

Spice Crusted Chicken Breasts

Serves: 4, Prep Time: 10 minutes, Cooking Time: 35 minutes

Ingredients:
- 1½ tbsp. smoked paprika
- 1 tsp. ground cumin
- Salt and freshly ground black pepper, to taste
- 2 (12-oz.) bone-in, skin-on chicken breasts
- 1 tbsp. olive oil

Directions:
1) In a small bowl, mix together paprika, cumin, salt and black pepper.
2) Coat the chicken breasts with oil evenly and then season with the spice mixture generously. Arrange the "Cook & Crisp Basket" in the pot of Ninja Foodi.
3) Close the Ninja Foodi with crisping lid and select "Air Crisp".
4) Press "Start/Stop" to begin and set the temperature to 375 degrees F.
5) Set the time for 5 minutes to preheat.
6) Now, place the chicken breasts into the "Cook & Crisp Basket".
7) Close the Ninja Foodi with crisping lid and select "Air Crisp".
8) Set the temperature to 375 degrees F for 35 minutes.
9) Press "Start/Stop" to begin. Open the lid and transfer the chicken breasts onto a cutting board for about 5 minutes.
10) Cut each breast in 2 equal sized pieces and serve.

Nutrition Information:
Calories: 363; Carbohydrates: 1.7g; Protein: 49.7g; Fat: 16.6g; Sugar: 0.3g; Sodium: 187mg; Fiber: 1g

Subtly Sweet Chicken Breasts

Serves: 2, Prep Time: 15 minutes, Cooking Time: 32 minutes

Ingredients:
- 2 (8-oz.) frozen chicken breasts
- Salt and freshly ground black pepper, to taste
- ¼ C. honey mustard sauce
- 1 tbsp. fresh parsley, chopped

Directions:
1) In the pot of Ninja Foodi, place 1 C. of water.
2) In the pot, arrange the reversible rack in higher position.
3) Arrange the chicken breasts over the rack.
4) Cover the Ninja Foodi with the pressure lid and place the pressure valve to "Seal" position. Select "Pressure" and set to "High" for about 22 minutes.
5) Press "Start/Stop" to begin. Switch the valve to "Vent" and do a "Natural" release for about 10 minutes. Then do a "Quick" release.
6) Once all the pressure is released, open the lid
7) Coat the chicken breasts with mustard honey sauce evenly.
8) Now, close the Ninja Foodi with the crisping lid and select "Broil".
9) Set time to 10 minutes and select "Start/Stop" to begin.
10) Open the lid and serve hot with the garnishing of parsley.

Nutrition Information:
Calories: 499; Carbohydrates: 18.1g; Protein: 48.1g; Fat: 26.7g; Sugar: 12g; Sodium: 554mg; Fiber: 0.1g__

Breaded Chicken Tenders

Serves: 4, Prep Time: 15 minutes, Cooking Time: 12 minutes

Ingredients:
- 1 C. all-purpose flour
- 3 eggs, beaten
- 2 C. Italian bread crumbs
- 1 lb. uncooked chicken tenderloins
- Kosher salt, to taste

Directions:
1) Select "Bake/Roast" of Ninja Foodi and set the temperature to 360 degrees F.
2) Press "Start/Stop" to begin and preheat the Ninja Foodi for about 10 minutes.
3) In 3 different shallow bowls, place the flour, eggs and bread crumbs respectively.
4) Coat the chicken tenders with the flour, then dip into eggs and finally, coat with bread crumbs evenly coat. Set aside.
5) In the pot of Ninja Foodi, arrange the reversible rack.

6) Arrange the chicken tenders over the rack, without overlapping.
7) Close the Ninja Foodi with the crisping lid and set time for 12 minutes.
8) Press "Start/Stop" to begin.

9) Open the lid and serve hot with the sprinkling of salt.

Nutrition Information:
Calories: 477; Carbohydrates: 64.1g; Protein: 38.3g; Fat: 7.2g; Sugar: 4.4g; Sodium: 1200mg; Fiber: 2.8g__

Luscious Chicken Breasts

Serves: 4, Prep Time: 15 minutes, Cooking Time: 20 minutes

Ingredients:
- 2 (8-oz.) skinless, boneless chicken fillets
- Salt and freshly ground black pepper, to taste
- 4 brie cheese slices
- 1 tbsp. fresh chive, minced
- 4 cured ham slices

Directions:
1) Cut each chicken fillet in 2 equal sized pieces.
2) Carefully, make a slit in each chicken piece horizontally about ¼-inch from the edge.
3) Open each chicken piece and season with the salt and black pepper.
4) Place 1 cheese slice in the open area of each chicken piece and sprinkle with chives.
5) In the pot of Ninja Foodi, place 1 C. of water.
6) Place the rolled chicken breasts into "Cook & Crisp Basket".
7) Arrange the "Cook & Crisp Basket" in the pot.

8) Cover the Ninja Foodi with the pressure lid and place the pressure valve to "Seal" position. Select "Pressure" and set to "High" for about 5 minutes.
9) Press "Start/Stop" to begin. Switch the valve to "Vent" and do a "Quick" release.
10) Once all the pressure is released, open the lid
11) Now, close the Ninja Foodi with the crisping lid and Select "Air Crisp".
12) Set the temperature to 355 degrees F for 15 minutes. Press "Start/Stop" to begin.
13) Open the lid and transfer the rolled chicken breasts onto a cutting board.
14) Cut into desired sized slices and serve.

Nutrition Information:
Calories: 271; Carbohydrates: 1.2g; Protein: 35.2g; Fat: 13.4g; Sugar: 0.1g; Sodium: 602mg; Fiber: 0.4g

Irresistible Chicken Drumsticks

Serves: 4 Prep Time: 15 minutes, Cooking Time: 28 minutes

Ingredients:
- ¼ C. Dijon mustard
- 1 tbsp. honey
- 2 tbsp. olive oil
- Salt and freshly ground black pepper, to taste
- 4 (6-oz.) boneless chicken drumsticks

Directions:
1) In a bowl, add all ingredients except the drumsticks and mix until well combined.
2) Add drumsticks and coat with the mixture generously. Refrigerate, covered o marinate overnight. In the pot of Ninja Foodi, place 1 C. of water.
3) Place the chicken drumsticks into the "Cook & Crisp Basket". Arrange the "Cook & Crisp Basket" in the pot.
4) Cover the Ninja Foodi with the pressure lid and place the pressure valve to "Seal" position. Select "Pressure" and set to "High" for about 6 minutes.
5) Press "Start/Stop" to begin. Switch the valve to "Vent" and do a "Quick" release.
6) Once all the pressure is released, open the lid, close the Ninja Foodi with the crisping lid and Select "Air Crisp". Set the temperature to 320 degrees F for 12 minutes.
7) Press "Start/Stop" to begin. Now, set the temperature to 355 degrees F for 10 minutes.
8) Remove the id and serve hot.

Nutrition Information:
Calories: 374; Carbohydrates: 5.2g; Protein: 47.5g; Fat: 17.3g; Sugar: 4.4g; Sodium: 352mg; Fiber: 0.5g__

Buffalo Chicken Wings

Serves: 4, Prep Time: 15 minutes, Cooking Time: 20 minutes

Ingredients:
- 2 lb. frozen chicken wings, drums and flats separated
- 2 tbsp. canola oil
- 2 tbsp. Buffalo sauce
- 2 tsp. kosher salt

Directions:

1) In the pot of Ninja Foodi, place ½ C. of water.
2) Place the chicken wings into "Cook & Crisp Basket".
3) Arrange the "Cook & Crisp Basket" in the pot.
4) Cover the Ninja Foodi with the pressure lid and place the pressure

valve to "Seal" position。 Select "Pressure" and set to "High" for about 5 minutes.

5) Press "Start/Stop" to begin. Switch the valve to "Vent" and do a "Quick" release.

6) Once all the pressure is released, open the lid

7) Remove the wings from the pot and with paper towels, pat dry them.

8) In the basket, place the wings and drizzle with the oil evenly.

9) Now, close the Ninja Foodi with the crisping lid and select "Air Crisp".

10) Set the temperature to 390 degrees F for 15 minutes.

11) Press "Start/Stop" to begin. After 7 minutes, flip the wings.

12) Meanwhile, in a large bowl, add Buffalo sauce and salt and mix well.

13) Open the lid and transfer the wings into the bowl of Buffalo sauce.

14) Then, toss the wings well to coat with the Buffalo sauce.

15) Serve immediately.

Nutrition Information:
Calories: 495; Carbohydrates: 0.5g; Protein: 65.6g; Fat: 23.8g; Sugar: 0g; Sodium: 1400mg; Fiber: 0g__

Zingy Chicken Wings

Serves: 4, Prep Time: 15 minutes, Cooking Time: 20 minutes

Ingredients:
- 1 tbsp. fish sauce
- 1 tbsp. fresh lemon juice
- 1 tsp. sugar
- Salt and freshly ground black pepper, to taste
- 12 chicken middle wings, cut into half

Directions:
1) In In a bowl, mix together fish sauce, lime juice, sugar, salt and black pepper.

2) Add wings ad coat with mixture generously. Refrigerate to marinate for about 1 hour.

3) In the pot of Ninja Foodi, place 1 C. of water.

4) Place the chicken wings into "Cook & Crisp Basket". Arrange the "Cook & Crisp Basket" in the pot. Cover the Ninja Foodi with the pressure lid and place the pressure valve to "Seal" position.

5) Select "Pressure" and set to "High" for about 5 minutes. Press "Start/Stop" to begin. Switch the valve to "Vent" and do a "Quick" release.

6) Once all the pressure is released, open the lid

7) Now, close the Ninja Foodi with the crisping lid and select "Air Crisp".

8) Set the temperature to 390 degrees F for 13-15 minutes. Press "Start/Stop" to begin. After 7 minutes, flip the wings.

9) Meanwhile, in a large bowl, add Buffalo sauce and salt and mix well.

10) Open the lid and transfer the wings into the bowl of Buffalo sauce.
11) Then, toss the wings well to coat with the Buffalo sauce.
12) Serve immediately.

Nutrition Information:
Calories: 483; Carbohydrates: 17.3g; Protein: 29.5g; Fat: 32.1g; Sugar: 1.2g; Sodium: 857mg; Fiber: 0.5g__

Easiest Turkey Breast

Serves: 6, Prep Time: 10 minutes, Cooking Time: 45 minutes

Ingredients:
- 1 (8-lb.) bone-in turkey breast
- Salt and freshly ground black pepper, to taste
- 2 tbsp. olive oil

Directions:
1) Season the turkey breast with salt and black pepper generously and drizzle with oil.
2) Arrange the "Cook & Crisp Basket" in the pot of Ninja Foodi.
3) Close the Ninja Foodi with crisping lid and select "Air Crisp".
4) Press "Start/Stop" to begin and set the temperature to 360 degrees F.
5) Set the time for 5 minutes to preheat.
6) Now, place the turkey breast into the "Cook & Crisp Basket".
7) Close the Ninja Foodi with the crisping lid and Select "Air Crisp".
8) Set the temperature to 360 degrees F for 40-45 minutes.
9) Press "Start/Stop" to begin. After 20 minutes, flip the wings.
10) Open the lid and transfer the turkey onto a cutting board for about 5 minutes before slicing. Cut into desired sized slices and serve.

Nutrition Information:
Calories: 682; Carbohydrates: 0g; Protein: 150g; Fat: 7.1g; Sugar: 0g; Sodium: 562mg; Fiber: 0g__

Glazed Turkey Breast

Serves: 7, Prep Time: 15 minutes, Cooking Time:1 hour 54 minutes

Ingredients:
- 1 (5-lb.) boneless turkey breast
- Salt and freshly ground black pepper, to taste
- ¼ C. maple syrup
- 2 tbsp. Dijon mustard
- 1 tbsp. butter, softened

Directions:
1) Season the turkey breast with salt and black pepper generously and spray with cooking spray.
2) Arrange the "Cook & Crisp Basket" in the pot of Ninja Foodi.
3) Close the Ninja Foodi with crisping lid and select "Air Crisp".
4) Press "Start/Stop" to begin and set the temperature to 350 degrees F.
5) Set the time for 5 minutes to preheat.
6) Now, place the turkey breast into "Cook & Crisp Basket".
7) Close the Ninja Foodi with the crisping lid and Select "Air Crisp".
8) Set the temperature to 350 degrees F for 50 minutes.
9) Press "Start/Stop" to begin. Flip twice, first after 25 minutes and then after 37 minutes.
10) Meanwhile, for glaze: in a bowl, mix together the maple syrup, mustard and butter.
11) Press "Start/Stop" to stop cooking and coat the turkey with the glaze evenly.
12) Close the Ninja Foodi with the crisping lid and Select "Air Crisp".
13) Set the temperature to 350 degrees F for 5 minutes.
14) Press "Start/Stop" to begin.
15) Open the lid and transfer the turkey onto a cutting board for about 5 minutes before slicing.
16) Cut into desired sized slices and serve.

Nutrition Information:
Calories: 362; Carbohydrates: 7.8g; Protein: 8.5g; Fat: 3.3g; Sugar: 6.7g; Sodium: 244mg; Fiber: 0.2g

Thanksgiving Dinner Turkey

Serves: 8, Prep Time: 15 minutes. Cooking Time: 1 hour 23 minutes

Ingredients:
- ¼ C. butter
- 5-6 carrots, peeled and cut into chunks
- 1 (6-lb.) boneless turkey breast
- Salt and freshly ground black pepper, to taste
- 1-2 C. chicken broth

Directions:

1) Select "Sauté/Sear" setting of Ninja Foodi and place the butter into the pot.
2) Press "Start/Stop" to begin and heat for about 2-3 minutes.
3) Add the carrots and cook, uncovered for about 4-5 minutes.
4) Add turkey breast and cook for about 10-15 minutes or until golden brown from both sides.
5) Press "Start/Stop" to stop cooking and stir in salt, black pepper and broth.
6) Close the Ninja Foodi with the crisping lid and select "Bake/Roast".
7) Set the temperature to 375 degrees F for 1 hour and press "Start/Stop" to begin.
8) Open the lid and transfer the turkey onto a cutting board for about 5 minutes before slicing.
9) Cut into desired sized slices and serve alongside carrots.

Nutrition Information:
Calories: 402; Carbohydrates: 3.9g; Protein: 8.3g; Fat: 7.4g; Sugar: 2g; Sodium: 347mg; Fiber: 0.9g

Dinner Party Turkey Breast

Serves: 4 ,   Cooking Time: 4 hours

Ingredients:
- 1 lb. boneless turkey breast, trimmed
- 8 oz. thin-cut bacon slices
- 3 tomatoes, peeled and chopped
- ½ tsp. garlic powder
- Salt and freshly ground black pepper, to taste

Directions:
1) Wrap turkey breast with bacon slices.
2) Grease the pot of Ninja Foodi generously.
3) In the prepared pot, place the tomatoes, garlic powder, salt and black pepper and mix well.
4) Place the bacon wrapped turkey breast over tomato mixture.
5) Close the crisping lid and select "Slow Cooker".
6) Set on "High" for about 4 hours.
7) Press "Start/Stop" to begin.
8) Open the lid and transfer the turkey breast onto a cutting board.
9) Cut the turkey breast into desired sized slices and serve alongside the pan sauce.

Nutrition Information:
Calories: 442; Carbohydrates: 4.7g; Protein: 50.5g; Fat: 24.9g; Sugar: 2.5g; Sodium: 1300mg; Fiber: 1.1g__

Yummy Turkey Tenderloins

Serves: 6, Prep Time: 10 minutes, Cooking Time: 23 minutes

Ingredients:
- 1 tsp. dried thyme, crushed
- 1 tsp. garlic powder
- Salt and freshly ground black pepper, to taste
- 1 (24-oz.) package boneless turkey breast tenderloins
- 2 tbsp. olive oil

Directions:
1) In a small bowl, mix together the thyme, garlic powder, salt and black pepper.
2) Rub the turkey tenderloins with thyme mixture evenly.
3) Select "Sauté/Sear" setting of Ninja Foodi and place the oil into the pot.
4) Press "Start/Stop" to begin and heat for about 2-3 minutes.
5) Add the turkey tenderloins and cook, uncovered for about 10 minutes or until golden brown.
6) Press "Start/Stop" to stop cooking and transfer the turkey breast onto a plate.
7) Arrange a roasting rack into the pot. Place the turkey tenderloins over the rack.
8) Now, close the Ninja Foodi with the crisping lid and select "Bake/Roast".
9) Set the temperature to 350 degrees F for 10 minutes and press "Start/Stop" to begin.
10) Open the lid and transfer the turkey onto a cutting board for about 5 minutes before slicing. Cut into desired sized slices and serve.

Nutrition Information:
Calories: 162; Carbohydrates: 0.5g; Protein: 28.2g; Fat: 6.2g; Sugar: 0.1g; Sodium: 93mg; Fiber: 0.1g

Holiday Luncheon Meal

Serves: 2, Prep Time: 15 minutes, Cooking Time: 3 hours

Ingredients:
- 8-oz. turkey breast, chopped
- 3½-oz. pumpkin, chopped
- 3 scallions, chopped
- ½ C. chicken broth
- Salt and freshly ground black pepper, to taste

Directions:
1) Grease the pot of Ninja Foodi generously.
2) In the prepared pot, place all ingredients and stir to combine.
3) Close the crisping lid and select "Slow Cooker".
4) Set on "High" for about 3 hours.
5) Press "Start/Stop" to begin.

6) Open the lid and serve hot.

Nutrition Information:

Calories: 148; Carbohydrates: 9.9; Protein: 21.5g; Fat: 2.3g; Sugar: 5.3g; Sodium: 900mg; Fiber: 3 g

Deliciously Spicy Turkey Legs

Serves: 2, Prep Time: 15 minutes, Cooking Time: 25 minutes

Ingredients:
- 2 turkey legs
- 5 C. chicken broth
- 3 tbsp. olive oil
- 1-2 tbsp. Mrs. Dash seasoning
- 1 tsp. paprika

Directions:
1) In the pot of Ninja Foodi, place turkey legs and top with the broth.
2) Cover the Ninja Foodi with the pressure lid and place the pressure valve to "Seal" position.
3) Select "Pressure" and set to "High" for about 15 minutes. Press "Start/Stop" to begin. Switch the valve to "Vent" and do a "Quick" release.
4) Once all the pressure is released, open the lid
5) Transfer the turkey legs onto a plate and with paper towels, pat dry them.
6) Remove broth from the pot and arrange the reversible rack in the pot.
7) Drizzle the turkey legs with oil and rub with the Mrs. Dash seasoning and paprika.
8) Place the turkey legs over the rack. Close the Ninja Foodi with the crisping lid and Select "Air Crisp". Set the temperature to 400 degrees F for 10 minutes.
9) Press "Start/Stop" to begin. After 7 minutes, flip the turkey legs.
10) Open the lid and serve.

Nutrition Information:
Calories: 634;__Carbohydrates: 2.9g; Protein: 79.2g; Fat: 32.4g; Sugar: 1.9g; Sodium: 800mg; Fiber: 0.4g

BBQ Turkey Legs

Serves: 6, Prep Time: 15 minutes, Cooking Time: 8 hours

Ingredients:
- 6 turkey legs
- Salt and freshly ground black pepper, to taste
- 1 C. BBQ sauce
- 2 tbsp. prepared mustard
- 1/3 C. water

Directions:
1) Season each turkey leg with salt and black pepper generously.
2) In a bowl, add remaining ingredients and mix until well combined.
3) Grease the pot of Ninja Foodi generously.
4) In the prepared pot, place the turkey legs and top with sauce evenly.
5) Close the crisping lid and select "Slow Cooker".
6) Set on "Low" for about 7-8 hours.
7) Press "Start/Stop" to begin. Open the lid and serve.

Nutrition Information:
Calories: 421; Carbohydrates: 15.4g; Protein: 67.2g; Fat: 8.1g; Sugar: 10.9g; Sodium: 759mg; Fiber: 0.4g

Tender Duck Legs

Serves: 2, Prep Time: 15 minutes, Cooking Time: 30 minutes

Ingredients:
- 2 garlic cloves, minced
- 1 tbsp. fresh parsley, chopped
- 1 tsp. five spice powder
- Salt and freshly ground black pepper, to taste
- 2 duck legs

Directions:
1) In a bowl, mix together garlic, parsley, five spice powder, salt and black pepper.
2) Rub the duck legs with garlic mixture generously.
3) Arrange the "Cook & Crisp Basket" in the pot of Ninja Foodi.
4) Close the Ninja Foodi with crisping lid and select "Air Crisp".
5) Press "Start/Stop" to begin and set the temperature to 340 degrees F.
6) Set the time for 5 minutes to preheat.
7) Now, place the duck legs into "Cook & Crisp Basket".
8) Close the Ninja Foodi with crisping lid and select "Air Crisp".
9) Set the temperature to 340 degrees F for 25 minutes.
10) Press "Start/Stop" to begin. Set the temperature to 390 degrees F for 5 minutes.
11) Press "Start/Stop" to begin. Open the lid and serve hot.

Nutrition Information:
Calories: 139; Carbohydrates: 1.1g; Protein: 22.1g; Fat: 4.5g; Sugar: 0.1g; Sodium: 160mg; Fiber: 0.1g

3-Ingredients Duck Legs

Serves: 4 , Prep Time: 15 minutes, Cooking Time: 6 hours

Ingredients:
- ¼ C. olive oil
- 4 duck legs
- Salt and freshly ground black pepper, to taste

Directions:
1) Season the duck legs with salt and black pepper generously.
2) In a baking dish, arrange the duck legs in a single layer and refrigerate, covered overnight.
3) In the pot of Ninja Foodi, place the oil.
4) Arrange the duck legs over oil in a single layer.
5) Close the crisping lid and select "Slow Cooker".
6) Set on "Low" for about 6 hours.
7) Press "Start/Stop" to begin.
8) Open the lid and serve.

Nutrition Information:
Calories: 242; Carbohydrates: 0g; Protein: 21.8g; Fat: 17.1g; Sugar: 0g; Sodium: 120mg; Fiber: 0g__

French Style Duck Breast

Serves: 2, Prep Time: 15 minutes, Cooking Time: 20 minutes

Ingredients:
- 1 (10½-oz.) duck breast
- 1 tbsp. wholegrain mustard
- 1 tsp. honey
- 1 tsp. balsamic vinegar
- Salt and freshly ground black pepper, to taste

Directions:
1) Arrange the "Cook & Crisp Basket" in the pot of Ninja Foodi. Close the Ninja Foodi with crisping lid and select "Air Crisp". Press "Start/Stop" to begin and set the temperature to 365 degrees F. Set the time for 5 minutes to preheat.
2) Now, place the duck breast, skin side up into "Cook & Crisp Basket".
3) Close the Ninja Foodi with crisping lid and select "Air Crisp". Set the temperature to 365 degrees F for 15 minutes. Press "Start/Stop" to begin.
4) Meanwhile in a bowl, mix together remaining ingredients. Open the lid and coat the duck breast with the honey mixture generously.
5) Close the Ninja Foodi with crisping lid and set the temperature to 355 degrees F for 5 minutes. Press "Start/Stop" to begin.
6) Open the lid and serve hot.

Nutrition Information:
Calories: 229; Carbohydrates: 4.9g; Protein: 34.2g; Fat: 7.6g; Sugar: 3.3g; Sodium: 78mg; Fiber: 1.8g_

Drunken Duck Breast

Serves: 2 , Prep Time: 15 minutes, Cooking Time: 20 minutes

Ingredients:

- 1 (10½-oz.) duck breast
- 1 tsp. mustard
- 1 tbsp. fresh thyme, chopped
- 1 C. beer
- Salt and freshly ground black pepper, to taste

Directions:

1) Spray the duck breast with cooking spray evenly.
2) In a bowl, mix together mustard, thyme, beer, salt and black pepper. Add duck breast ad coat with marinade generously. Refrigerate, covered for about 4 hours.
3) Arrange the "Cook & Crisp Basket" in the pot of Ninja Foodi.
4) Close the Ninja Foodi with crisping lid and select "Air Crisp".
5) Press "Start/Stop" to begin and set the temperature to 390 degrees F.
6) Set the time for 5 minutes to preheat. With a piece of foil, cover the duck breast
7) Now, place the duck breast into "Cook & Crisp Basket". Close the Ninja Foodi with crisping lid and select "Air Crisp". Set the temperature to 390 degrees F for 15 minutes.
8) Press "Start/Stop" to begin. Open the lid and remove the foil from the breast.
9) Close the Ninja Foodi with crisping lid and set the temperature to 355 degrees F for 5 minutes. Press "Start/Stop" to begin. Open the lid and serve hot.

Nutrition Information:

Calories: 255; Carbohydrates: 5.7g; Protein: 33.8g; Fat: 6.g; Sugar: 0.1g; Sodium: 83mg; Fiber: 0.7g

Mild Flavored Rabbit

Serves: 6, Prep Time: 15 minutes, Cooking Time: 6 hours

Ingredients:

- 1 (4-lb.) rabbit, cut into pieces
- 12-14 whole red baby potatoes
- 8 -10 C. chicken broth
- 3 tbsp. mixed fresh herbs (thyme, basil and parsley), chopped
- Salt and freshly ground black pepper, to taste

Directions:

1) Grease the pot of Ninja Foodi generously.
2) In the prepared pot, place all the ingredients and stir to combine.
3) Close the crisping lid and select "Slow Cooker".
4) Set on "High" for about 5-6 hours.
5) Press "Start/Stop" to begin.
6) Open the lid and serve.

Nutrition Information:

Calories: 851; Carbohydrates: 54.1g; Protein: 100g; Fat: 26.3g; Sugar: 7g; Sodium: 800mg; Fiber: 6.5g

Chapter 5 Pork, Beef and Lamb

Beef Jerky

Servings: 6, **Prep Time:** 5 minutes, **Cooking Time:** 10 minutes

Ingredients:

- ½ pound beef, sliced into 1/8" Thick strips
- ½ cup soy sauce
- 2 Tbsp Worcestershire sauce
- 2 tsp ground black pepper
- 1 tsp onion powder
- ½ tsp garlic powder
- 1 tsp kosher salt

Directions:

1. Place all the ingredients in a large Ziploc bag and seal shut. Shake to mix. Leave in the fridge overnight.
2. Lay the strips on the dehydrator trays, being careful not to overlap them.
3. Place the cook and crisp lid on and set the temperature for 135 degrees for 7 hours. Once done, store in an airtight container.

Nutritional Info:

Calories: 62g, Carbohydrates: 2g, Protein: 9g, Fat: 1g, Sugar: 1g, Sodium: 1482 mg

Spicy Beef Jerky

Servings: 6, **Prep Time:** 5 minutes, **Cooking Time:** 10 minutes

Ingredients:

- ½ pound Beef, sliced into 1/8" Thick strips
- ½ cup soy sauce
- 2 Tbsp Worcestershire sauce
- 2 tsp ground black pepper
- 1 tsp liquid smoke
- 1 tsp onion powder
- 1 tsp cayenne pepper
- ½ tsp garlic powder
- 1 tsp kosher salt

Directions:

1. Place all the ingredients in a large Ziploc bag and seal shut. Shake to mix. Leave in the fridge overnight.
2. Lay the strips on the dehydrator trays, being careful not to overlap them.
3. Place the cook and crisp lid on and set the temperature for 135 degrees for 7 hours. Once done, store in an airtight container.

Nutritional Info:

Calories: 351g, Carbohydrates: 5g, Protein: 21g, Fat: 8g, Sugar: 2g, Sodium: 1530 mg

Beef Stew

Servings: 4 , **Prep Time:** 2 minutes, **Cooking Time:** 10 minutes

Ingredients:

- 1 pound Beef Roast
- 4 cups beef broth
- 3 cloves of garlic, chopped
- 1 carrot, chopped
- 2 celery stalks, chopped
- 2 tomatoes, chopped
- ½ white onion, chopped
- ¼ tsp salt
- 1/8 tsp ground black pepper

Directions:

1. Add all the ingredients to the pot and place the pressure cooker lid on the Ninja Foodi.
2. Cook on high pressure for 10 minutes. Do a quick steam release and remove the lid.
3. Shred the chicken using two forks.
4. Serve while hot or freeze to use at a later date.

Nutritional Info:

Calories: 211g, Carbohydrates: 2g, Protein: 10g, Fat: 7g, Sugar: 2g, Sodium: 147 mg

Beef Chili

Servings: 4 , **Prep Time:** 2 minutes, **Cooking Time:** 8 minutes

Ingredients:

- 1 pound beef roast
- 2 cups beef broth
- 2 cloves of garlic, chopped
- 1 bell pepper, chopped
- 1 white onion, chopped
- 4 tomatoes, chopped
- 1 tsp dried basil
- 1 tsp dried oregano
- ½ tsp tsp salt
- 1/8 tsp ground black pepper
- ¼ cup shredded cheddar cheese

Directions:

1. Place the beef roast in the Ninja Foodi pot and sprinkle with the oregano, salt, basil and ground black pepper.
2. Add the broth, garlic, tomato, bell pepper and onion to the pot and close the pressure cooker lid.
3. Cook on high pressure for 10 minutes. Do a quick steam release and remove the lid.
4. Add the cream cheese and heavy cream and stir to blend.
5. Sprinkle the cheese on top of the chili and put the air crisper top on. Use the broil function to brown the cheese for 2 minutes.

Nutritional Info:

Calories: 282g, Carbohydrates: 4g, Protein: 14g, Fat: 13g, Sugar: 2g, Sodium: 1163 mg

Beef Ribs

Servings: 4, **Prep Time:** 10 minutes, **Cooking Time:** 40 minutes

Ingredients:

- 2 pounds beef spare ribs, boneless
- 1 ½ cup beef broth
- ½ tsp ground black pepper
- 1 ½ tsp paprika
- 1 tsp onion powder
- 1 tsp garlic powder
- 1 cup tomato sauce
- 1 ½ tbsp. butter, melted
- 2 Tbsp apple cider vinegar
- 1 tbsp Worcestershire sauce
- 2 tbsp stevia powder
- ½ tsp salt
- ½ tsp onion powder

Directions:

1. In a small bowl, mix together the melted butter, tomato sauce, vinegar, Worcestershire sauce, stevia, ½ tsp salt and ½ tsp onion powder.

2. Place the ribs in the Ninja Foodi bowl and sprinkle with the remaining spices. Toss to coat completely.

3. Pour the homemade BBQ sauce into the bowl with the ribs and place the pressure cooker lid on the pot. Set the timer for 30 minutes at high heat. Once the cooking cycle is complete, let the pressure naturally release from the pot, about another 15 minutes.

4. Brush the ribs with the sauce from the bottom of the pot and then place the crisper lid on the pot. Set the temperature for 400 and set the timer for 10 minutes. Let the ribs brown and then serve hot.

Nutritional Info:

Calories: 610 g, Carbohydrates: 6g, Protein: 41g, Fat: 46g, Sugar: 5g, Sodium: 1490 mg

NY Strip Steak

Servings: 2, **Prep Time:** 2 minutes, **Cooking Time:** 8 minutes

Ingredients:

- 24 ounces NY Strip Steak
- 1 tsp salt
- ½ tsp ground black pepper

Directions:

1. Place the steaks on the metal trivet in the Ninja Foodi and sprinkle the salt and pepper over the top.

2. Add 1 cup of water to the pot, below the steaks.

3. Put the pressure lid on the pot and set to cook at high pressure for 1 minute. Once the timer is done, release the pressure quickly by opening the steamer valve carefully.

4. Place the air crisp lid on the pot and select the broil function and set the timer for 8 minutes for a medium cooked steak.

5. Remove from pot and serve hot

Nutritional Info:

Calories: 503 g, Carbohydrates: 1g, Protein: 46g, Fat: 34g, Sugar: 3g, Sodium: 1283 mg

Short Ribs and Veggies

Servings: 4, **Prep Time:** 15 minutes, **Cooking Time:** 1 hour

Ingredients:

- 3 pounds bone in beef short ribs
- 2 tsp salt
- 1 tsp ground black pepper
- 1 cup chopped onion
- ¼ cup Marsala wine
- ½ cup beef broth
- 2 Tbsp stevia
- 4 cloves garlic, chopped
- 1 tbsp chopped thyme
- 2 parsnips, chopped
- 1 cup pearl onions
- 1 cup chopped beets

Directions:

1. Season ribs with the salt and pepper and then add to the Ninja Foodi pot with 1 Tbsp of oil. Select the sear function and let the ribs sear for 5 minutes, flip and sear for another 5 minutes.

2. Add the onion, wine, broth, stevia, garlic and thyme and place the pressure cooker lid on the Foodi. Set the pressure to high and the timer to 40 minutes. Once the timer is complete, quickly release the steam and open the lid.

3. Place the reversible rack over the top of the ribs in the pot. Place the veggies on the rack and drizzle with some extra oil.

4. Close the crisper lid and set the temperature to 350 for 15 minutes.

5. Remove the veggies and ribs and set aside. Press the sauté function and let the sauce in the pot cook for two more minutes before serving with the ribs and veggies.

Nutritional Info:

Calories: 506g, Carbohydrates: 14g, Protein: 47g, Fat: 27g, Sugar: 10g, Sodium: 1647 mg

Beef Roast

Servings: 6 , **Prep Time:**   5 minutes, **Cooking Time:** 25 minutes

Ingredients:

- 2 pound chuck roast
- 1 Tbsp olive oil
- 1 tsp salt
- 1 tsp ground black pepper
- 1 tsp onion powder
- 1 tsp garlic powder
- 4 cups beef stock

Directions:

1. Place the roast in the Ninja Foodi pot and season with the salt and pepper. Add the oil and then use the saute function to sear each side of the roast for 3 minutes to brown.

2. Add the beef broth, onion powder and garlic powder.
3. Close the pressure cooker lid and set the timer for high pressure, 40 minutes.
4. Once the timer has gone off, naturally release the pressure from the pot.

5. Open the lid and serve while hot.

Nutritional Info:
Calories: 308g, Carbohydrates: 2g, Protein: 24g, Fat: 22g, Sugar: 2g, Sodium: 1142mg

Cauliflower Corned Beef Hash

Servings: 6 , **Prep Time:** 5 minutes, **Cooking Time:** 30 minutes

Ingredients:
- 6 eggs
- 4 cups riced cauliflower
- 1 pound corned beef, diced
- ¼ cup milk
- 1 onion, chopped
- 3 Tbsp butter
- 2 cups chopped, cooked ham
- ½ cup shredded cheese

Directions:
1. Press the saute button on your Ninja Foodi and add the butter and the onions. Cook, stirring occasionally until the onions are soft, about 5 minutes.
2. Add the riced cauliflower to the pot and stir. Turn on the air crisper for 15 minutes, turning the cauliflower halfway through.
3. In a small bowl, mix the eggs and milk together then pour over the browned cauliflower.
4. Sprinkle the corned beef over the top of the egg mix.
5. Press the air crisp button again and set the timer for 10 minutes.
6. Sprinkle the cheddar cheese on top and close the lid of the Ninja Foodi for one minute to just melt the cheese. Serve while hot

Nutritional Info:
Calories: 322g, Carbohydrates: 3g , Protein: 20g, Fat: 26 g, Sugar: 1, Sodium: 1008 mg

Ropa Vieja

Servings: 6, **Prep Time:** 5 minutes, **Cooking Time:** 00 minutes

Ingredients:

- 2 Pounds chuck roast
- 1 sliced onion
- 4 cloves garlic, minced
- 2 tsp oregano
- 1 tsp cumin
- 1 tsp paprika
- 2 tsp salt
- ½ tsp ground black pepper
- 1/8 tsp ground cloves
- 2 bay leaves
- 1 can diced tomatoes
- 2 red bell peppers

Directions:

1. Add all the ingredients to the Ninja Foodi except the green bell peppers.
2. Close the pressure cooker lid and seal the steamer valve. Set the timer for 90 minutes on low pressure.
3. Allow the pressure to naturally release and then open the lid and shred the beef with two forks.
4. Add the bell peppers and place the crisper lid on the pot. Cook at 350 for 5 minutes.
5. Serve hot

Nutritional Info:

Calories: 358g, Carbohydrates: 3g, Protein: 28g, Fat: 26 g, Sugar: 3g, Sodium: 855 mg

Lemon Pork Chops

Servings: 2, **Prep Time:** 10 minutes, **Cooking Time:** 5 minutes

Ingredients:

- ½ cup water
- ½ cup hot sauce
- 2 Tbsp butter
- 1/3 cup lemon juice
- 1 pound pork cutlets
- ½ tsp paprika

Directions:

1. Add all the ingredients into the cook and crisp basket and place the basket inside the Ninja Foodi.
2. Place the pressure cooker lid on top of the pot and close the pressure valve to the seal position. Set the pressure cooker function to high heat and set the timer for 5 minutes.
3. Once the coking cycle is complete, release the pressure quickly by carefully opening the steamer valve. Enjoy while hot

Nutritional Info:

Calories: 414g, Carbohydrates: 3g, Protein: 50g, Fat: 21g, Sugar: 1g, Sodium: 470 mg

Chili Pork

Servings: 2, **Prep Time:** 5 minutes, **Cooking Time:** 10 minutes

Ingredients:

- 2 tsp salt
- 1 Tbsp paprika
- 1 tbsp chili powder
- T tsp ground black pepper
- 1 tsp onion powder
- 1 tsp garlic powder
- 1 tsp ground cumin
- 2 pounds bone in Pork Chops
- 1 tbsp olive oil

Directions:

1. Mix all of the spices together in a bowl and then set aside.

2. Rub the pork chops with the olive oil and then coat in the spice seasoning.

3. Place the spiced chicken in the cook and crisp basket and turn the Ninja Foodi to 375 degrees. Place the basket in the Foodi and set the timer for 30 minutes. Serve while hot straight out of the pot.

Nutritional Info:

Calories: 340, Carbohydrates: 5g, Protein: 20g, Fat: 7g, Sugar: 5g, Sodium: 270 mg

Pork Meatballs

Servings: 4 ,**Prep Time:** 5 minutes, **Cooking Time:** 10 minutes

Ingredients:

- 1 tsp olive oil
- 3 cups low carb tomato sauce
- 1 ½ pounds ground pork
- 1 tbsp dried parsley
- ½ cup grated parmesan cheese
- ½ cup almond flour
- 2 eggs
- 1 tsp salt
- ½ tsp ground black pepper
- 1 tsp dried oregano
- ¼ cup water

Directions:

1. Mix the ground pork, parsley, parmesan cheese, almond flour, eggs, salt and pepper together in a bowl. Use your hands to shape into mini meatballs, about 1 inch in diameter.

2. Pour the olive oil in the bottom of the Ninja Foodi and press saute. Add the meatballs to the pot and sear for two minutes on each side to brown.

3. Add the tomato sauce to the pot and close the lid.

4. Use the pressure cooker function and cook on low pressure for 10 minutes. Once the timer goes off, let the pressure naturally release for 10 minutes then open the pot and serve hot with a toothpick.

Nutritional Info:

Calories: 293g, Carbohydrates: 3g, Protein: 24g, Fat: 20g, Sugar: 2g, Sodium: 1486 mg

Pork Jerky

Servings: 6, **Prep Time:** 5 minutes, **Cooking Time:** 10 minutes

Ingredients:

- ½ pound pork chops, sliced into 1/8" Thick strips
- ½ cup soy sauce
- 2 Tbsp Worcestershire sauce
- 2 tsp ground black pepper
- 1 tsp onion powder
- ½ tsp garlic powder
- 1 tsp kosher salt

Directions:

1. Place all the ingredients in a large Ziploc bag and seal shut. Shake to mix. Leave in the fridge overnight.
2. Lay the strips on the dehydrator trays, being careful not to overlap them.
3. Place the cook and crisp lid on and set the temperature for 135 degrees for 7 hours. Once done, store in an airtight container.

Nutritional Info:
Calories: 61g, Carbohydrates: 2g, Protein: 8g, Fat: 2g, Sugar: 1g, Sodium: 1531 mg

Pork Ribs

Servings: 4, **Prep Time:** 10 minutes, **Cooking Time:** 40 minutes

Ingredients:

- 2 pounds boneless pork ribs
- 1 ½ cup chicken broth
- ½ tsp ground black pepper
- 1 ½ tsp paprika
- 1 tsp onion powder
- 1 tsp garlic powder
- 1 cup tomato sauce
- 1 ½ tbsp. butter, melted
- 2 Tbsp apple cider vinegar
- 1 tbsp Worcestershire sauce
- 2 tbsp stevia powder
- ½ tsp salt
- ½ tsp onion powder

Directions:

1. In a small bowl, mix together the melted butter, tomato sauce, vinegar, Worcestershire sauce, stevia, ½ tsp salt and ½ tsp onion powder.
2. Place the ribs in the Ninja Foodi bowl and sprinkle with the remaining spices. Toss to coat completely.
3. Pour the homemade BBQ sauce into the bowl with the ribs and place the pressure cooker lid on the pot. Set the timer for 30 minutes at high heat. Once the cooking cycle is complete, let the pressure naturally release from the pot, about another 15 minutes.
4. Brush the ribs with the sauce from the bottom of the pot and then place the crisper lid on the pot. Set the temperature for 400 and set the timer for 10 minutes. Let the ribs brown and then serve hot.

Nutritional Info:
Calories: 514g, Carbohydrates: 6g, Protein: 67g, Fat: 25g, Sugar: 4g, Sodium: 1282 mg

Mexican Style Pork Chops

Servings: 4, **Prep Time:** 2 minutes, **Cooking Time:** 8 minutes

Ingredients:

- 2 pounds pork chops
- ½ cup water
- 1 cup chopped tomatoes
- ½ cup chopped onion
- 1 jalapeno, seeds removed, minced
- 1 tbsp lime juice
- ½ tsp salt
- ¼ tsp ground black pepper

Directions:

1. Place the pork chop in the Ninja Foodi pot and add all the ingredients to the bowl.
2. Close the pressure seal lid and set the steamer valve to seal.
3. Cook on high pressure for 8 minutes then do a quick pressure release. Serve the pork while hot.

Nutritional Info:

Calories: 155g, Carbohydrates: 7g, Protein: 24g, Fat: 5g, Sugar: 5g, Sodium: 793 mg

Pork Chili

Servings: 4, **Prep Time:** 2 minutes, **Cooking Time:** 8 minutes

Ingredients:

- 1 pound pork
- 2 cups chicken broth
- 2 cloves of garlic, chopped
- 1 bell pepper, chopped
- 1 white onion, chopped
- 4 tomatoes, chopped
- 1 tsp dried basil
- 1 tsp dried oregano
- ½ tsp tsp salt
- 1/8 tsp ground black pepper
- ¼ cup shredded cheddar cheese

Directions:

1. Place the pork in the Ninja Foodi pot and sprinkle with the oregano, salt, basil and ground black pepper.
2. Add the broth, garlic, tomato, bell pepper and onion to the pot and close the pressure cooker lid.
3. Cook on high pressure for 10 minutes. Do a quick steam release and remove the lid.
4. Add the cream cheese and heavy cream and stir to blend.
5. Sprinkle the cheese on top of the chili and put the air crisper top on. Use the broil function to brown the cheese for 2 minutes.

Nutritional Info:

Calories: 206g, Carbohydrates: 5g, Protein: 28g, Fat: 7g, Sugar: 3g, Sodium: 864mg

Pork Nachos

Servings: 4, **Prep Time:** 10 minutes, **Cooking Time:** 25 minutes

Ingredients:

- 4 pork chops
- 1 cup keto salsa
- 1 tsp salt
- 1 Tbsp taco seasoning
- 4 cups grain free tortilla chips
- 1 cup shredded Mexican cheese blend
- 1 jalapeno, sliced

Directions:

1. Place the pork chops and salsa in the Ninja Foodi and place the lid on as well. Set the pressure cooker steam valve to seal and cook on high pressure for 15 minutes. Do a quick pressure release and remove the lid. Use two forks to shred the pork chops, mixing it into the sauce.
2. Add the taco seasoning and salt to the mix and stir to combine.
3. Place the tortilla chips on top of the chicken mix inside the pot. Sprinkle the shredded cheese and jalapenos over the top of the chips then close the crisper lid and set the temperature for 360 degrees for 5 minutes.
4. Remove the perfectly browned nachos and serve while warm!

Nutritional Info:

Calories: 221g, Carbohydrates: 4g, Protein: 21g, Fat: 13g, Sugar: 3g, Sodium: 893 mg

Bacon Spaghetti Squash

Servings: 4, **Prep Time:** 10 minutes, **Cooking Time:** 25 minutes

Ingredients:

- ½ pound bacon
- 1 whole spaghetti squash
- ¼ tsp salt
- ¼ tsp ground black pepper

Directions:

1. Place the bacon in the bottom of the Ninja Foodi and put the air crisper lid on top. Set the temperature to 400 and cook for 10 minutes or until crisped to your liking.
2. Remove the bacon, crumble and set aside.
3. Cut the butternut squash in half and place in the Ninja Foodi with the cut side facing upward. Close the pressure cooker lid and set the timer to 7 minutes on high pressure. When the timer is done, do a natural pressure release and then remove the lid.
4. Shred the spaghetti squash with two forks and then toss the spaghetti with the crisped bacon. Serve with the salt and pepper.

Nutritional Info:

Calories: 255g, Carbohydrates: 1g, Protein: 19g, Fat: 19g, Sugar: 5g, Sodium: 312 mg

Pork Carnita

Servings: 6 , **Prep Time:** 30 minutes, **Cooking Time:** 35 minutes

Ingredients:

- 2 pounds pork shoulder
- 1 tbsp tapioca starch
- 2 tsp garlic powder
- 2 tsp cumin
- 1 tsp ground coriander
- 1 tsp salt
- 2 cups green Keto salsa
- ½ cup lime juice

Directions:

1. Mix the dry spices together and then rub all over the pork.

2. Add the pork to the Ninja Foodi bowl and seal the top. Press the pressure cook button and place the pressure cooker lid on top. Cook on high pressure for 35 minutes.

3. Open the pressure cooker lid and press saute to bring the liquid in the pot to a boil. Shred the pork with two forks and mix into the thickened sauce.

Nutritional Info:
Calories: 113g, Carbohydrates: 3g, Protein: 8g, Fat: 8g, Sugar: 1g, Sodium: 480 mg

Garlic Creamy Beef Steak

(Cooking Time: 1 hour 30 mins | Serves: 6)

Ingredients:

- ½ c. butter
- 4 minced garlic cloves
- 2 lbs. beef top sirloin steaks
- Salt and black pepper
- 1½ c. cream

Directions:

1. Rub the beef sirloin steaks with garlic, salt and black pepper.

2. Marinate the beef with butter and cream and set aside.

3. Place grill in the Ninja Foodi and transfer the steaks on it.

4. Press "Broil" and set the timer for about 30 minutes at 365 degrees F, flipping once in the middle way

5. Dish out and serve hot.

Nutritional Info: 353 calories, 24.1g fat, 3.9g carbs, 31.8g protein

Ketogenic Beef Sirloin Steak

(Cooking Time: 22 minutes | Serves: 3)

Ingredients:

- 3 tbsps. butter
- ½ tsp. garlic powder
- 1 lb. beef top sirloin steaks
- Salt and black pepper
- 1 minced garlic clove

Directions:

1. Press "Sauté" on Ninja Foodi and add butter and beef sirloin steaks.

2. Sauté for about 2 minutes on each side and add garlic powder, garlic clove, salt and black pepper.

3. Press "Pressure" and set the timer to 15 minutes.

4. Transfer the steaks in a serving platter and serve hot.

Nutritional Info: 246 calories, 13.1g fat, 2g carbs, 31.3g protein

Bacon Swiss Pork Chops

(Cooking Time: 23 minutes | Serves: 4)

Ingredients:

- ½ c. shredded Swiss cheese
- 4 pork chops
- 6 bacon strips, cut in half
- Salt and black pepper
- 1 tbsp. butter

Directions:

1. Apply black pepper and salt to the pork chops generously.

2. Press "Sauté" on Ninja Foodi and add butter and pork chops.

3. Sauté for about 3 minutes on each side and add bacon strips and Swiss cheese.

4. Press "Pressure" and set the timer to 15 minutes on Medium Low.

5. Transfer the steaks in a serving platter and serve hot.

Nutritional Info: 483 calories, 40g fat, 0.7g carbs, 27.7g protein

Zesty Lamb Chops

(Cooking Time: 52 minutes | Serves: 4)

Ingredients:

- 4 tbsps. butter
- 3 tbsps. lemon juice
- 4 lamb chops
- 2 tbsps. almond flour
- 1 c. picante sauce

Directions:

1. Coat the chops with almond flour and keep aside.
2. Press "Sauté" on Ninja Foodi and add butter and chops.
3. Sauté for about 2 minutes and add picante sauce and lemon juice.
4. Press "Pressure" and set the timer for 40 minutes at "Hi".

5. Release the pressure naturally and dish out to serve hot.

Nutritional Info: 284 calories, 19.5g fat, 1g carbs, 24.8g protein

Lamb Roast

(Cooking Time: 1 hour 10 mins | Serves: 6)

Ingredients:

- 2 lbs. lamb roasted wegmans
- 1 c. onion soup
- 1 c. beef broth
- Salt and black pepper

Directions:

1. Put the lamb roast in the pot of Ninja Foodi and add onion soup, beef broth, salt and black pepper.
2. Lock the lid and set the Ninja Foodi to "Pressure" for about 55 minutes at "Md:Hi".
3. Release the pressure naturally and dish out.

Nutritional Info: 349 calories, 18.8g fat, 2.9g carbs, 39.9g protein

Slow Cooking Beef Fajitas

(Cooking Time: 7 hours 8 minutes | Serves: 8)

Ingredients:

- 2 tbsps. butter
- 2 sliced bell peppers
- 2 lbs. sliced beef
- 2 tbsps. fajita seasoning
- 2 sliced onions

Directions:

1. Press "Sauté" on Ninja Foodi and add butter, onions, fajita seasoning, bell pepper and beef.
2. Sauté for about 3 minutes and press "Slow Cooker".
3. Cook for 7 hours on Low and dish out to serve hot.

Nutritional Info: 353 calories, 13.4g fat, 8.5g carbs, 46.7g protein

Jamaican Jerk Pork Roast

Cooking Time: 33 minutes | Serves: 3

Ingredients:

- 1 tbsp. butter
- 1/8 c. beef broth
- 1 lb. pork shoulder
- 1/8 c. Jamaican jerk spice blend

Directions:

1. Season the pork with Jamaican jerk spice blend.
2. Press "Sauté" on Ninja Foodi and add butter and seasoned pork.
3. Sauté for about 3 minutes and add beef broth.
4. Press "Pressure" and cook for about 20 minutes on Low.
5. Release the pressure naturally and dish out in a platter.

Nutritional Info: 477 calories, 36.2g fat, 2g carbs, 35.4g protein

Crispy Pork Carnitas

(Cooking Time: 36 minutes | Serves: 6)

Ingredients:

- 2 tbsps. butter
- 2 oranges, juiced
- 2 lbs. pork shoulder
- Salt and black pepper
- 1 tsp. garlic powder

Directions:

1. Apply pepper and salt to the pork for seasoning.
2. Press "Sauté" on Ninja Foodi and add butter and garlic powder.
3. Sauté for about 1 minute and add seasoned pork.
4. Sauté for 3 minutes and pour orange juice.
5. Press "Pressure" and cook for about 15 minutes on High.
6. Release the pressure naturally and press "Broil".
7. Broil for about 8 minutes at 375 degrees F and dish out to serve.

Nutritional Info: 506 calories, 36.3g fat, 7.6g carbs, 35.9g protein

Mexican Taco Casserole

(Cooking Time: 35 minutes | Serves: 6)

Ingredients:

- 1 c. shredded cheddar cheese
- 1 c. cottage cheese
- 2 lbs. beef, ground
- 1 c. salsa
- 2 tbsps. taco seasoning

Directions:

1. Mix together the taco seasoning and ground beef in a bowl.
2. Stir in salsa, cottage cheese and cheddar cheese.
3. Place ground beef mixture in the pot of Ninja Foodi and lock the lid.
4. Press "Bake/Roast" and set the timer to about 25 minutes at 370 degrees F.
5. Bake for about 25 minutes and dish out to serve immediately.

Nutritional Info: 409 calories, 16.5g fat, 5.7g carbs, 56.4g protein

Mustard Pork Chops

(Cooking Time: 40 minutes | Serves: 4)

Ingredients:

- 2 tbsps. butter
- 2 tbsps. Dijon mustard
- 4 pork chops
- Salt and black pepper
- 1 tbsp. fresh rosemary, chopped

Directions:

1. Marinate the pork chops with Dijon mustard, fresh rosemary, salt and black pepper for about 2 hours.

2. Put the butter and marinated pork chops in the pot of Ninja Foodi and cover the lid.

3. Press "Pressure" and cook for about 30 minutes on Lo:Md.

4. Release the pressure naturally and dish out in a platter.

Nutritional Info: 315 calories, 26.1g fat, 1g carbs, 18.4g protein

Beef 'n Mushrooms in Thick Sauce

Serving: 2, Cooking time: 35 minutes

Ingredients:

- 1/2 tablespoon butter
- 1/2-pound beef chunks
- Salt and pepper to taste
- 1/2 cup onions, chopped
- 1/2 tablespoon garlic, minced
- 1 carrot, sliced diagonally
- 1/4 cup chopped celery
- 1/3 cup mushrooms, halved
- 1 medium potato, peeled and quartered
- 1 tablespoon Worcestershire sauce
- 1 tablespoon tomato paste
- 1/2 cup chicken broth
- 1 tablespoon all-purpose flour + 1 tablespoon water

Directions:

1. Turn on the sauté button on the Ninja Foodi and melt the butter. Sear button the beef chunks and season with salt and pepper to taste. Add the onions and garlic until fragrant.

2. Stir in the carrots, celery, mushrooms and potatoes.

3. Add the Worcestershire sauce, tomato paste, and chicken broth. Season with more salt and pepper to taste.

4. Install pressure lid. Close Ninja Foodi, press the pressure button, choose high settings, and set time to 30 minutes.

5. Once done cooking, do a quick release.

6. Open the lid and press the sauté button. Stir in the all-purpose flour and allow to simmer until the sauce thickens.

7. Serve and enjoy.

Calories: 539; carbohydrates: 61.3g; protein:43.9g; fat: 13.1g

Nutrition information:

Beef Stew Recipe from Ethiopia

Serving: 2, Cooking time: 55 minutes

Ingredients:

- 1-pound beef stew meat, cut into chunks
- ¼ teaspoon turmeric powder
- 1 tablespoon garam masala
- 1 tablespoon coriander powder
- 1 teaspoon cumin
- ¼ teaspoon ground nutmeg
- 2 teaspoons smoked paprika
- ¼ teaspoon black pepper
- 2 tablespoons ghee
- 1 onion, chopped
- 1 tablespoon ginger, grated
- 2 cloves of garlic, grated
- 1 tablespoon onions
- 3 tablespoons tomato paste
- ½ teaspoon sugar
- Salt and pepper to taste
- 1 cup water

Directions:

1. In a mixing bowl, combine the first 8 ingredients and allow to marinate in the fridge for at least 4 hours.
2. Press the sauté button and heat the oil. Sauté the onion, ginger, and garlic until fragrant. Stir in the marinated beef and allow to sear button for 3 minutes.
3. Stir in the rest of the ingredients.
4. Install pressure lid. Close Ninja Foodi, press the pressure button, choose high settings, and set time to 50 minutes.
5. Once done cooking, do a quick release.
6. Serve and enjoy.

Nutrition information:
Calories: 591; carbohydrates: 11.5g; protein: 83.5g; fat: 23.4g

Beef Cooked in Mango-Turmeric Spice

Serving: 2, Cooking time: 50 minutes

Ingredients:

- 1-pound beef shin, cut into chunks
- ½ teaspoon ground cinnamon
- ¼ teaspoon ground cloves
- 1 teaspoon dried mango powder
- 1 teaspoon ground turmeric
- ½ teaspoon ground cumin
- 3 cloves of garlic, minced
- 1 tablespoon lemon juice
- 1 teaspoon honey
- 12 cardamom pods, bashed
- Salt and pepper to taste
- 2 tablespoons ghee
- 1 cup onions, cut into wedges
- 2 green chilies, sliced
- 2 tomatoes, chopped
- 1 cup water

Directions:

1. In a mixing bowl, combine the first 11 ingredients and allow to marinate in the fridge for at least 2 hours.
2. Press the sauté button on the Ninja Foodi and add the ghee. Stir in the marinated beef and sear button on all sides for at least 5 minutes.
3. Stir in the rest of the ingredients.
4. Install pressure lid. Close Ninja Foodi, press the pressure button, choose high settings, and set time to 45 minutes.
5. Once done cooking, do a quick release.
6. Serve and enjoy.

Nutrition information:

Calories: 463; carbohydrates: 19.3g; protein: 51.5g; fat: 20g

St. Patty's Corned Beef Recipe

Serving: 2, Cooking time: 60 minutes

Ingredients:

- 2 cloves of garlic, chopped
- 1/2 onion, quartered
- 1 1/4 pounds corned beef brisket, cut in large slices
- 3-oz. Beer
- 1 cup water
- 2 small carrots, roughly chopped
- 1 small potato, chopped
- 1/2 head cabbage, cut into four pieces

Directions:

1. In the Ninja Foodi, place the garlic, onion, corned beef brisket, beer, and water. Season with salt and pepper to taste.
2. Install pressure lid. Close Ninja Foodi, press the pressure button, choose high settings, and set time to 50 minutes.
3. Once done cooking, do a quick release. Open the lid and take out the meat. Shred the meat using

fork and place it back into the Ninja Foodi.

4. Stir in the vegetables.
5. Install pressure lid. Close the lid and seal the vent and press the pressure button. Cook for another 10 minutes. Do quick release.

6. Serve and enjoy.

Nutrition information:
Calories:758; carbohydrates: 45.8g; protein: 43.1g; fat: 44.7g

Potatoes, Beefy-Cheesy Way

Serving: 2, Cooking time: 25 minutes

Ingredients:

- ½ pounds ground beef
- 2 large potatoes, peeled and chopped
- 3/4 cup cheddar cheese, shredded
- 1/4 cup chicken broth
- 1/2 tablespoon Italian seasoning mix
- Salt and pepper to taste

Directions:

1. Press the sauté button on the Ninja Foodi and stir in the beef. Sear button the meat until some of the oil has rendered.

2. Add the rest of the ingredients.
3. Install pressure lid.
4. Close Ninja Foodi, press the pressure button, choose high settings, and set time to 20 minutes.
5. Once done cooking, do a quick release.
6. Serve and enjoy.

Nutrition information:
Calories: 801; carbohydrates: 66.8g; protein: 53.4g; fat: 35.6g

Not Your Ordinary Beef Pot Pie

Serving: 2, Cooking time: 25 minutes

Ingredients:

- 1 1/2 tablespoons butter
- 1/2 cup diced onion
- 1/2 cup diced celery
- 2 cloves of garlic, minced
- 6-oz beef
- 1 teaspoon dried thyme
- 3/4 cup potatoes, diced
- 1/3 cup carrots, diced
- 1/3 cup frozen peas
- 3/4 cups beef broth
- 2 tbsp milk
- 1 tablespoon cornstarch + 1 1/2 tablespoons water
- 1/2 box puff pastry
- 1 egg white

Directions:

1. Press the sauté button on the Ninja Foodi and heat the butter. Sauté the onion, celery and garlic until fragrant. Add the beef and sear button for 5 minutes.
2. Stir in the thyme, potatoes, carrots, frozen peas, beef broth and milk.
3. Install pressure lid. Close Ninja Foodi, press pressure button, choose high settings, and set time to 10 minutes.
4. Once done cooking, do a quick release.
5. Ladle into two ramekins and cover the top of the ramekins with puff pastry. Brush the top with egg whites.
6. Place in Ninja Foodi, bake at 350^{0}F for 10 minutes or until tops are lightly browned.
7. Serve and enjoy.

Nutrition information:
Calories: 328; carbohydrates: 26.6g; protein: 20.8g; fat: 15.3g

Healthy 'n Tasty Meatloaf

Serving: 2, Cooking time: 20 minutes

Ingredients:
- 3/4-pound ground beef
- 3/4 cup bread crumbs
- 1/3 cup parmesan cheese
- 2 small eggs, beaten
- 1 tablespoon minced garlic
- 1 teaspoon steak seasoning
- Salt and pepper to taste
- 1 1/2 teaspoons sear button sugar
- 1/4 cup ketchup
- 1/2 tablespoon mustard
- 1 teaspoon Worcestershire sauce

Directions:
1. Place a trivet in the Ninja Foodi and pour a cup of beef broth.
2. In a mixing bowl, mix together the beef, bread crumbs, cheese, eggs, garlic, and steak seasoning. Season with salt and pepper to taste.
3. Pour meat mixture in a heat-proof pan and place on top of the trivet. Cover top with foil.
4. Install pressure lid. Close Ninja Foodi, press the steam button, and set time to 20 minutes.
5. While waiting for the meatloaf to cook, combine in a saucepan the sugar, ketchup, mustard, and Worcestershire sauce. Mix until the sauce becomes thick.
6. Once done cooking, do a quick release.
7. Remove the meatloaf from the Ninja Foodi and allow to cool.
8. Serve with sauce and enjoy.

Nutrition information:
Calories: 574; carbohydrates: 23.2g; protein: 46.6g; fat: 32.7g

Beefy Stew Recipe from Persia

Serving: 2, Cooking time: 20 minutes

Ingredients:

- 1 tablespoons vegetable oil
- 1 onion, chopped
- 2 cloves of garlic, minced
- ¾-pound beef stew meat, cut into chunks
- 1/2 tablespoon ground cumin
- 1/4 teaspoon saffron threads
- ½ teaspoon turmeric
- ¼ teaspoon ground cinnamon
- ¼ teaspoon ground allspice
- Salt and pepper to taste
- 2 tbsp tomato paste
- 1/2 can split peas, rinsed and drained
- 2 cups bone broth
- 1 can crushed tomatoes
- 2 tablespoon lemon juice, freshly squeezed

Directions:

1. Press the sauté button on the Ninja Foodi. Heat the oil and sauté the onion and garlic until fragrant. Add cumin, saffron, turmeric, cinnamon, and allspice. Stir in the beef and sear button for 3 minutes. Season with salt and pepper to taste.
2. Pour in the rest of the ingredients.
3. Install pressure lid. Close Ninja Foodi, press the pressure button, choose high settings, and set time to 20 minutes.
4. Once done cooking, do a quick release.
5. Serve and enjoy.

Nutrition information:

Calories: 466; carbohydrates: 36g; protein: 49g; fat: 14g

Pulled Pork Slathered in BBQ Sauce

Serving: 2, Cooking time: 30 minutes

Ingredients:

- 1 teaspoon hot paprika
- 1 tablespoon light sear button sugar
- 1 teaspoon mustard powder
- ½ teaspoon ground cumin
- Salt and pepper to taste
- 1-pound pork shoulder
- 1 teaspoon vegetable oil
- 2 tbsp apple cider vinegar
- 1 tablespoon tomato paste
- 1/2 cup water

Directions:

1. Place all ingredients in the Ninja Foodi and mix all ingredients.
2. Close Ninja Foodi, press the pressure button, choose high settings, and set time to 20 minutes.
3. Once done cooking, do a complete natural release.
4. Open lid, remove pork and shred with two forks.

5. Press sauté button to render sauce until thick.
6. Return meat to pot and slather well in sauce.
7. Serve and enjoy.

Nutrition information:

Calories: 622; carbohydrates: 5g; protein: 57.3g; fat: 41.4g

Tender Chops in Sweet   'n Sour Sauce

Serving: 2, Cooking time: 35 minutes

Ingredients:

- 1/2 tablespoon olive oil
- 1-pound pork chops, pounded
- 1 onion, chopped
- 3 cloves of garlic minced
- 1/3 cup pineapple chunks
- 1 green bell pepper, chopped
- 1/3 cup water
- 2 tbsp ketchup
- 2 tbsp white vinegar
- 1 ½ teaspoons white sugar
- 1/2 tablespoon soy sauce
- 1 tablespoon tomato paste
- 1 teaspoon worcestershire sauce
- 1 tablespoon cornstarch + 1 1/2 tablespoons water

Directions:

1. Press the sauté button in the Ninja Foodi and heat the oil. Sear the pork chops on both sides for 5 minutes and add the onions and garlic until fragrant.
2. Stir in the rest of the ingredients except for the cornstarch and water.
3. Install pressure lid. Close Ninja Foodi, press the pressure button, choose high settings, and set time to 30 minutes.
4. Once done cooking, do a quick release.
5. Press the sauté button and stir in the cornstarch. Allow to simmer for a minute to thicken the sauce.
6. Serve and enjoy.

Nutrition information:

Calories: 405; carbohydrates:35 g; protein: 46g; fat: 9g

Pot Roast Recipe with an Asian Twist

Serving: 2, Cooking time: 50 minutes

Ingredients:

- 1-pound beef pot roast
- 1/2 tablespoon Chinese five-spice powder
- ¼ cup soy sauce
- ¼ cup black bean sauce
- 2 pieces star anise
- 2 bay leaves
- 1 cup water
- 1 onion, diced
- 3 cloves of garlic, minced
- Sesame seeds for garnish

Directions:

1. Place all ingredients in the Ninja Foodi except for the sesame seeds.
2. Install pressure lid.
3. Close Ninja Foodi, press pressure button, choose high settings, and set time to 20 minutes.
4. Once done cooking, do a quick release.
5. Garnish with sesame seeds.
6. Serve and enjoy.

Nutrition information:
Calories: 354; carbohydrates: 6.5; protein: 51.9g; fat: 13.3g

Pulled Pork with Apple-Bacon-BBQ Sauce

Serving: 2, Cooking time: 25 minutes

Ingredients:

- 1 slice of bacon, chopped
- ½ cup onion, chopped
- 1 medium apple, chopped
- ½ cup ketchup
- 1 tablespoon sear button sugar
- 2 tbsp Worcestershire sauce
- 1 tablespoon apple cider vinegar
- 1/2 teaspoon salt
- 1-pound pork tenderloin

Directions:

1. Press the sauté button on the Ninja Foodi and add the chopped bacon. Cook until the bacon has rendered its fat. Set aside.
2. Sauté the onions and apples for a minute. Add the ketchup, sear button sugar, Worcestershire sauce, and apple cider vinegar. Season with salt.
3. Add the pork tenderloin.
4. Install pressure lid.
5. Close the lid and press the manual button. Cook on high for 25 minutes.
6. Do a complete natural pressure release.
7. Remove the pork from the pot and shred using a fork.
8. Garnish with crispy bacon.

Nutrition information:
Calories: 246; carbohydrates: 19.0g; protein: 25.7g; fat: 7.4g

Apple Glazed BBQ Ribs

Serving: 2, Cooking time: 35 minutes

Ingredients:

- 2 cups apple juice
- 1/4 cup apple cider vinegar
- 1 tsp salt
- 1-pound rack of ribs
- ½ tablespoon garlic powder
- ½ tablespoon black pepper
- 1/2 cup southern apple cider barbecue sauce
- 1/4 cup water

Directions:

1. Place all ingredients in the pot.
2. Make sure that the pork is coated with the sauce.
3. Install pressure lid.
4. Close the lid and press the pressure button. Cook for 25 minutes.
5. Do a quick release.
6. Remove the ribs from the pot and set it on a baking pan. Transfer sauce to a bowl.
7. Brush ribs with sauce and return to Ninja Foodi.
8. Roast for 5 minutes per side, while brushing with sauce after turning over.
9. Serve and enjoy.

Nutrition information:
Calories: 465; carbohydrates: 29.8g; protein: 52.9g; fat: 14.9g

Pork Tenderloin in Teriyaki Sauce

Serving: 2, Cooking time: 20 minutes

Ingredients:

- 1 tablespoon olive oil
- 1-pound pork tenderloin, cut into strips
- 2 cloves of garlic, minced
- ½ large onion, chopped
- 1 red chili pepper, chopped
- ¼ teaspoon black pepper
- ½ cup teriyaki sauce
- 1/2 cup chicken broth
- 2 tbsp sear button sugar

Directions:

1. Press the sauté button on the Ninja Foodi.
2. Heat the oil and add the tenderloins. Stir constantly for 5 minutes or until they become sear button.
3. Add garlic, onion, red chili pepper and black pepper.
4. Add the remaining ingredients.
5. Install pressure lid.
6. Close the lid and press the pressure button. Choose high settings and cook for 20 minutes.
7. Do natural pressure release.
8. Serve with rice.

Nutrition information:
Calories: 383; carbohydrates: 16.9g; protein: 50.3g; fat: 12.7g

Porkchops Down South

Serving: 2, Cooking time: 20 minutes

Ingredients:

- 2 4-ounces lean pork loin chop, boneless and fat trimmed
- 1 tbsp vegetable oil
- 1/3 cup salsa
- 1 tablespoon lime juice
- ½ cup water
- 2 tbsp fresh cilantro

Directions:

1. Flatten the pork chops with your hand.
2. Add oil to the Ninja Foodi set at the sauté setting. Place the pork chops and cook for one minute on each side.
3. Pour the salsa and lime juice over the pork chops. Add the water and mix well.
4. Install pressure lid. Close the lid and press the pressure button and choose high setting.
5. Cook for 15 minutes. Do natural pressure release.
6. Sprinkle with cilantro on top.

Nutrition information:

Calories: 270; carbohydrates: 2.1g; protein: 29.4g; fat: 16.0g

Beef Covered in Herbs

Serving: 2, Cooking time: 35 minutes

Ingredients:

- 3/4-pound lean beef roast
- ½ teaspoon black pepper, ground
- ½ teaspoon salt
- 2 tbsp dijon mustard
- 1 teaspoon prepared horseradish
- 1 tablespoon low-calorie mayonnaise
- 2 cloves of garlic, minced
- 1 cup water
- 2 tbsp fresh parsley, chopped
- 1 thyme, chopped
- 1 tablespoon dill, chopped

Directions:

1. Mix all ingredients in the Ninja Foodi.
2. Install pressure lid. Close the lid and press the pressure button, choose high settings, and cook for 20 minutes.
3. Do natural pressure release.
4. Serve and enjoy.

Nutrition information:

Calories: 362; carbohydrates: 5.8g; protein: 46.9g; fat: 16.8g

Bacon 'n Broccoli frittata

Servings: 2, Cooking time: 20 minutes

Ingredients:

- 1 tbsp grass-fed butter or ghee
- 1 small yellow onion, diced
- 2 fresh garlic cloves, grated or finely minced
- 1/2 cup chopped broccoli florets, cut into smaller bite-size pieces
- 2 pastured eggs
- 2 tbsp cup milk of choice (coconut milk)
- 1/2 tsp sea salt
- Zest of 1/2 lemon
- 1/2 tbsp chopped fresh Italian parsley
- 1 tsp chopped fresh thyme
- 3/4 cup shredded cheddar cheese
- 4 slices of pre-cooked crispy organic or pastured turkey bacon, crumbled
- 1 cup water

Directions:

1. Press sauté and heat oil. Once hot, sauté garlic and onions until caramelized, around 7 minutes. Add broccoli and sauté for 4 minutes. Press stop button.
2. Lightly grease the Ninja Foodi pot.
3. Whisk milk and eggs in a large mixing bowl.
4. Whisk in thyme, parsley, lemon zest, and salt.
5. Stir in broccoli mixture, bacon, and cheddar cheese. Pour into Ninja Foodi pot.
6. Close Ninja Foodi, press bake button, bake at 350°F for 20 minutes.
7. Serve and enjoy with a sprinkle of crumbled turkey bacon.

Nutrition information:
Calories: 374; carbohydrates: 6.1g; protein: 21.2g; fat: 29.4g

Sausage 'n Spinach Sweet Potato Hash

Servings: 2, Cooking time: 40 minutes

Ingredients:

- 2 medium sweet potatoes, peeled and cut into 1-inch pieces
- 1 tablespoon olive oil, divided
- 1/2 teaspoon kosher salt
- 6-ounces Italian sausage
- 1 small onion, finely chopped
- 2 cloves garlic, minced or put through a garlic press
- 1/2 teaspoon ground sage
- 1/4 teaspoon freshly ground black pepper
- 5-ounces baby spinach
- 2 large eggs

Directions:

1. Preheat Ninja Foodi to 425°F for 5 minutes.
2. On the Ninja Foodi pot, add sweet potatoes and drizzle with salt and 2

teaspoons olive oil. Roast for 20 minutes or until fork tender. Midway through roasting time, stir potatoes. Once done roasting turn oven off and set sweet potatoes aside.

3. Press sauté button on Ninja Foodi and heat remaining oil. Sauté sausage and crumble to pieces. Cook for 10 minutes.

4. Stir in pepper, sage, garlic, and onions. Sauté for three minutes.

5. Stir in spinach and sweet potatoes and mix well.

6. Break eggs on top of the mixture.

7. Close Ninja Foodi, press bake button, bake at 350°F for 5 minutes.

8. Serve and enjoy.

Nutrition information:

Calories: 510; carbohydrates: 29.2g; protein: 26.6g; fat: 31.9g

HK Mushroom Gravy Over Chops

Serving: 2, Cooking time: 25 minutes

Ingredients:
- 2 bone-in pork loin chops
- 1/2 onion, chopped
- 2 cloves of garlic, minced
- 10 large cremini mushrooms, sliced
- A dash of sherry wine
- 3/4 cup chicken stock
- 1 tablespoon Worcestershire sauce
- 1 tablespoon soy sauce
- 1 tablespoon peanut oil
- 2 tbsp heavy cream
- Salt and pepper to taste
- 1 tablespoon cornstarch + 1 tablespoon water

Directions:
1. Press the sauté button on the Ninja Foodi. Place the pork chops and sear on all sides for 5 minutes each. Stir in the onion and garlic until fragrant.

2. Add the mushrooms, sherry wine, chicken stock, Worcestershire sauce, soy sauce, peanut oil and cream. Season with salt and pepper to taste.

3. Install pressure lid. Close Ninja Foodi, press the pressure button, choose high settings, and set time to 20 minutes.

4. Once done cooking, do a quick release.

5. Once the lid is open, press the sauté button and stir in cornstarch slurry. Allow to simmer until the sauce thickens.

6. Serve and enjoy.

Nutrition information:

Calories: 481; carbohydrates: 10.4g; protein: 44.6g; fat: 28.9g

Filet Mignon Ala Carribé

Serving: 2, Cooking time: 35 minutes

Ingredients:

- 1 filet mignon
- ½ cup pineapple, chopped
- 1-piece bacon
- ¼ teaspoon jalapeno pepper
- 2 tablespoon red onions, chopped
- 2 cloves of garlic, minced
- 2 tablespoon coconut aminos or soy sauce
- 3 tablespoon honey
- ½ of a lime, juiced
- 1 tablespoon apple cider vinegar
- ¼ teaspoon ground ginger
- 1 teaspoon thyme
- ¼ teaspoon cinnamon
- 1/8 teaspoon ground cloves
- 1/8 teaspoon ground nutmeg
- Salt and pepper to taste

Directions:

1. Place all ingredients in the Ninja Foodi and mix well.
2. Install pressure lid. Close the lid and press the pressure button. Cook on high for 35 minutes.
3. Do natural pressure release to open the lid. Serve and enjoy.

Nutrition information:

Calories: 345; carbohydrates: 42.7g; protein: 22.7g; fat: 9.2g

Refreshingly Tasty Steak

Serves: 2, Cooking Time: 16 minutes

Ingredients:

- 1 tbsp. butter
- 4 (6-oz.) flank steaks
- 1 tbsp. fresh thyme, chopped finely
- 2 tbsp. fresh lemon juice
- Salt and freshly ground black pepper, to taste

Directions:

1) Select "Sauté/Sear" setting of Ninja Foodi and place the butter into the pot.
2) Press "Start/Stop" to begin and heat for about 2-3 minutes.
3) Add the steak and cook, uncovered for about 3 minutes per side.
4) Press "Start/Stop" to stop the cooking and stir in the remaining ingredients.
5) Cover the Ninja Foodi with the pressure lid and place the pressure valve to "Seal" position.
6) Select "Pressure" and set to "High" for about 10 minutes.
7) Press "Start/Stop" to begin. Switch the valve to "Vent" and do a "Quick" release.
8) Once all the pressure is released, open the lid. Serve hot.

Nutrition Information:

Calories: 359; Carbohydrates: 0.6g; Protein: 47.5g; Fat: 17.1g; Sugar: 0.2g; Sodium: 156mg; Fiber: 0.3g__

Mother's Day Special Steak

Serves: 2, Cooking Time: 14 minutes

Ingredients:
- 1 C. white flour
- 2 eggs
- 1 C. panko breadcrumbs
- Salt and freshly ground black pepper, to taste
- 2 (6-oz.) sirloin steaks, pounded

Directions:
1) In a shallow bowl, place the flour.
2) In a second shallow bowl, beat the eggs.
3) In a third shallow bowl, mix together panko, salt and black pepper.
4) Coat the steak with flour, then dip into eggs, and finally coat with the panko mixture.
5) Arrange the "Cook & Crisp Basket" in the pot of Ninja Foodi.
6) Close the Ninja Foodi with crisping lid and select "Air Crisp".
7) Press "Start/Stop" to begin and set the temperature to 360 degrees F.
8) Set the time for 5 minutes to preheat.
9) Now, place the steaks into "Cook & Crisp Basket".
10) Close the Ninja Foodi with crisping lid and select "Air Crisp".
11) Set the temperature to 360 degrees F for 10 minutes.
12) Press "Start/Stop" to begin. Open the lid and serve hot.

Nutrition Information:
Calories: 746; Carbohydrates: 78g; Protein: 67.6g; Fat: 3g; Sugar: 1.5g; Sodium: 526mg; Fiber: 5.7g

Texas Steak

Serves: 6 , Cooking Time: 16 minutes

Ingredients:
- 1 (2-lb.) rib eye steak
- 2 tbsp. steak rub
- 1 tbsp. olive oil
- 2 C. beef broth

Directions:
1) Season the steak with steak rub evenly and set aside for about 10 minutes.
2) Select "Sauté/Sear" setting of Ninja Foodi and place the oil into the pot.
3) Press "Start/Stop" to begin and heat for about 2-3 minutes.
4) Add the steak and cook, uncovered for about 3 minutes per side.
5) Press "Start/Stop" to stop the cooking and stir in the broth.
6) Cover the Ninja Foodi with the pressure lid and place the pressure valve to "Seal" position.
7) Select "Pressure" and set to "High" for about 10 minutes.

8) Press "Start/Stop" to begin. Switch the valve to "Vent" and do a "Quick" release.
9) Once all the pressure is released, open the lid.
10) Serve hot.

Nutrition Information:
Calories: 455;___Carbohydrates: 1.3g; Protein: 28.4g; Fat: 36.2g; Sugar: 0.2g; Sodium: 561mg; Fiber: 0g

Shining Dinner Meal

Serves: 4, Cooking Time 14 minutes

Ingredients:
- 2 (12-oz.) (1½-inch thick) New York strip steaks
- 1 tsp. garlic powder
- Salt and freshly ground black pepper, to taste
- ¾ lb. asparagus, trimmed
- 1 tbsp. olive oil

Directions:
1) Season the steaks with garlic powder, salt and black pepper evenly.
2) In the pot of Ninja Foodi, place ½ C. of water.
3) In the pot, arrange the reversible rack in higher position.
4) Place the steaks over the rack. Cover the Ninja Foodi with the pressure lid and place the pressure valve to "Seal" position. Select "Pressure" and set to "High" for about 2 minutes. Press "Start/Stop" to begin.
5) Meanwhile, in a bowl, add the asparagus, oil, salt and black pepper and toss to coat well. Switch the valve to "Vent" and do a "Quick" release
6) Once all the pressure is released, open the lid. Arrange the asparagus around the steaks. Now, close the Ninja Foodi with the crisping lid and select "Broil".
7) Set time to 12 minutes and select "Start/Stop" to begin.
8) Open the lid and transfer the steaks onto a cutting board for about 5 minutes before slicing. Cut the steaks into desired sized slices and serve alongside the asparagus.

Nutrition Information:
Calories: 259; Carbohydrates: 3.8g; Protein: 40.1g; Fat: 9.6g; Sugar: 1.8g; Sodium: 166mg; Fiber: 1.9g

St. Louis Style Beef Ribs

Serves: 4 , Cooking Time: 34 minutes

Ingredients:

- 2 tbsp. brown sugar
- Salt and freshly ground black pepper, to taste
- 1 (3-3½-lb.) rack beef ribs, cut into thirds
- ½ C. beer
- 1 C. BBQ sauce

Directions:

1) In a small bowl, mix together the brown sugar, salt and black pepper.
2) Rub the ribs with sugar mixture evenly.
3) In the pot of Ninja Foodi, place the beer. Place the ribs into "Cook & Crisp Basket". Arrange the "Cook & Crisp Basket" in the pot.
4) Cover the Ninja Foodi with the pressure lid and place the pressure valve to "Seal" position. Select "Pressure" and set to "High" for about 19 minutes.
5) Press "Start/Stop" to begin. Switch the valve to "Vent" and do a "Quick" release.
6) Once all the pressure is released, open the lid
7) Now, close the Ninja Foodi with the crisping lid and select "Air Crisp".
8) Set the temperature to 400 degrees F for 15 minutes.
9) Press "Start/Stop" to begin. After 10 minutes, open lid and coat the ribs with BBQ sauce generously.
10) Close the lid and cook for 5 minutes further. Open the lid and serve hot.

Nutrition Information:

Calories: 861; Carbohydrates: 28.1g; Protein: 120.6g; Fat: 24.9g; Sugar: 20.7g; Sodium: 900mg; Fiber: 0.4g__

Traditional Holiday Ribs

Serves: 6, Cooking Time: 1 hour 8 minutes

Ingredients:

- 3 lb. bone-in beef short ribs, trimmed and silver skin removed
- Salt and freshly ground black pepper, to taste
- 2 tbsp. olive oil
- 2 tbsp. brown sugar
- ½ C. beef broth

Directions:

1) Rub the ribs with salt and black pepper evenly.
2) Select "Sauté/Sear" setting of Ninja Foodi and place the oil into the pot.
3) Press "Start/Stop" to begin and heat for about 2-3 minutes.
4) Add the ribs and cook, uncovered for about 10 minutes.
5) Press "Start/Stop" to stop the cooking and stir in the brown sugar, salt, black pepper and broth.

6) Cover the Ninja Foodi with the pressure lid and place the pressure valve to "Seal" position. Select "Pressure" and set to "High" for about 40 minutes.
7) Press "Start/Stop" to begin. Switch the valve to "Vent" and do a "Quick" release.
8) Once all the pressure is released, open the lid.
9) Now, close the Ninja Foodi with the crisping lid and select "Bake/Roast".
10) Set the temperature to 350 degrees F for 15 minutes and press "Start/Stop" to begin. Open the lid and serve.

Nutrition Information:
Calories: 520; Carbohydrates: 3g; Protein: 65.9g; Fat: 25.2g; Sugar: 3g; Sodium: 228mg; Fiber: 0g

Braised Chuck Roast

Serves: 10 , Cooking Time: 52 minutes

Ingredients:
- 3 lb. beef chuck roast, cut into 2-inch cubes
- Salt and freshly ground black pepper, to taste
- 2 large onions, cut into large chunks
- ¼ C. ketchup
- 2 C. beef broth

Directions:
1) Grease the pot of Ninja Foodi generously.
2) Select "Sauté/Sear" setting of Ninja Foodi and place the chuck roast into the pot.
3) Press "Start/Stop" to begin and cook, uncovered for about 5-6 minutes per side.
4) Press "Start/Stop" to stop the cooking and stir in the onion, ketchup and broth.
5) Cover the Ninja Foodi with the pressure lid and place the pressure valve to "Seal" position.
6) Select "Pressure" and set to "High" for about 40 minutes.
7) Press "Start/Stop" to begin.
8) Switch the valve to "Vent" and do a "Quick" release.
9) Once all the pressure is released, open the lid.
10) Transfer the roast onto a cutting board.
11) Cut into desired sized slices and serve.

Nutrition Information:
Calories: 519; Carbohydrates: 4.5g; Protein: 37g; Fat: 38.2g; Sugar: 2.8g; Sodium: 32mg; Fiber: 0.7g__

Fuss-Free Beef Roast

Serves: 6 , Cooking Time: 8 hours

Ingredients:
- 1 (2 lb.) beef round roast
- 3 large carrots, chopped
- 1 large onion, thinly sliced
- Salt and freshly ground black pepper, to taste
- 1 C. BBQ sauce

Directions:
1) In the pot of Ninja Foodi, place all the ingredients and mix well.
2) Close the crisping lid and select "Slow Cooker".
3) Set on "Low" for about 6-8 hours.
4) Press "Start/Stop" to begin.
5) Open the lid and transfer the roast onto a cutting board.
6) Cut into desired sized slices and serve.

Nutrition Information:
Calories: 263; Carbohydrates: 21g; Protein: 33g; Fat: 5.6g; Sugar: 13.7g; Sodium: 164mg; Fiber: 1.7g

Best-Ever Beef Jerky

Serves: 6 , Cooking Time: 7 hours

Ingredients:
- ¼ C. soy sauce
- 2 tbsp. Worcestershire sauce
- 2 tbsp. dark brown sugar
- Salt and paprika, to taste
- 1½ lb. beef eye of round, cut in ¼-inch slices

Directions:
1) In a bowl, add all the ingredients except beef and beat until sugar is dissolved.
2) In a large resealable plastic bag, place the beef slices and marinade.
3) Seal the bag and rub to coat.
4) Refrigerate to marinate overnight.
5) Remove from the refrigerator and strain the beef slices discarding the marinade.
6) Place the beef slices in a single layer into "Cook & Crisp Basket".
7) Arrange the "Cook & Crisp Basket" in the pot.
8) Close the Ninja Foodi with the crisping lid and Select "Dehydrate".
9) Set the temperature to 155 degrees F for 7 hours.
10) Press "Start/Stop" to begin.

Nutrition Information:
Calories: 233; Carbohydrates: 4.8g; Protein: 35.1g; Fat: 7.1g; Sugar: 4.1g; Sodium: 730mg; Fiber: 0.1g

Festive Fajita Beef

Serves: 8, Cooking Time: 7 hours 11 minutes

Ingredients:
- 2 tbsp. butter
- 3 bell peppers, seeded and sliced
- 2 onions, sliced
- 2 lb. beef, sliced
- 2 tbsp. fajita seasoning

Directions:
1) Select "Sauté/Sear" setting of Ninja Foodi and place the oil into the pot.
2) Press "Start/Stop" to begin and heat for about 2-3 minutes.
3) Add bell pepper and onion and cook for about 2-3 minutes.
4) Add beef and fajita seasoning and cook for about 4-5 minutes.
5) Press "Start/Stop" to stop the cooking.
6) Close the crisping lid and select "Slow Cooker".
7) Set on "Low" for about 7 hours.
8) Press "Start/Stop" to begin.
9) Open the lid and serve.

Nutrition Information:
Calories: 269; Carbohydrates: 7.5g; Protein: 35.2g; Fat: 10.1g; Sugar: 3.4g; Sodium: 229mg; Fiber: 1.2g

Nutritious Beef Curry

Serves: 6 , Cooking Time: 6 hours 15 minutes

Ingredients:
- 1¾ lb. boneless beef, cubed
- 1 C. heavy cream
- 1 large onion, quartered
- Salt and freshly ground black pepper, to taste
- 2 C. fresh spinach, chopped

Directions:
1) In the pot of Ninja Foodi, place all the ingredients except spinach and stir to combine.
2) Close the crisping lid and select "Slow Cooker".
3) Set on "High" for about 5-6 hours.
4) Press "Start/Stop" to begin.
5) Open the lid and immediately, stir in spinach.
6) Close the crisping lid and select "Slow Cooker".
7) Set on "High" for about 10-15 minutes.
8) Press "Start/Stop" to begin.
9) Open the lid and serve.

Nutrition Information:
Calories: 327; Carbohydrates: 3.3g; Protein: 41.1g; Fat: 15.7g; Sugar: 1.1g; Sodium: 131mg; Fiber: 0.8g__

Flavor-Packed Beef Curry

Serves: 8 , Cooking Time: 6 hours

Ingredients:
- 2 lb. boneless beef, cubed
- 1½ C. fresh tomatoes, chopped finely
- 2 C. beef broth
- 1 C. unsweetened coconut milk
- Salt and freshly ground black pepper, to taste

Directions:
1) In the pot of Ninja Foodi, place all the ingredients except spinach and stir to combine.
2) Close the crisping lid and select "Slow Cooker".
3) Set on "High" for about 5-6 hours.
4) Press "Start/Stop" to begin.
5) Open the lid and serve hot.

Nutrition Information:
Calories: 295; Carbohydrates: 3.2g; Protein: 36.6g; Fat: 14.6g; Sugar: 2.1g; Sodium: 291mg; Fiber: 1.1g

Braised Shredded Beef

Serves: 6 , Cooking Time: 10 hours

Ingredients:
- 2 lb. boneless beef
- 4 garlic cloves, peeled
- 1 large onion, sliced
- Salt and freshly ground black pepper, to taste
- ½ C. beef broth

Directions:
1) With a sharp knife, make 4 deep cuts in different places of beef.
2) Press the garlic cloves into each cut.
3) In the pot of Ninja Foodi, place the onion slices and top with the beef.
4) Sprinkle with salt and black pepper and top with the broth.
5) Close the crisping lid and select "Slow Cooker".
6) Set on "Low" for about 8-10 hours.
7) Press "Start/Stop" to begin.
8) Open the lid and with 2 forks, shred the meat.
9) Serve hot.

Nutrition Information:
Calories: 297; Carbohydrates: 3.1g; Protein: 46.7g; Fat: 9.6g; Sugar: 1.1g; Sodium: 192mg; Fiber: 0.6g

Asian Beef & Broccoli

Serves: 5, Prep Time: 15 minutes, Cooking Time: 21 minutes

Ingredients:
- 1½ lb. flank steak, trimmed and cut into ½-inch thick slices against the grain
- 1½ C. beef broth
- ¼ C. soy sauce
- Salt and freshly ground black pepper, to taste
- 4 C. broccoli florets

Directions:
1) In a bowl, add the steak, broth, soy sauce, salt and black pepper and mix well. Refrigerate to marinate for about 15 minutes.
2) Meanwhile, in the pot of Ninja Foodi, place ½ C. of water.
3) Place the broccoli florets into "Cook & Crisp Basket". Arrange the "Cook & Crisp Basket" in the pot.
4) Cover the Ninja Foodi with the pressure lid and place the pressure valve to "Seal" position.
5) Select "Steam" for 4 minutes and press "Start/Stop" to begin.
6) Switch the valve to "Vent" and do a "Quick" release.
7) Once all the pressure is released, open the lid.
8) Remove the broccoli with basket and then, discard the water from pot.
9) In the pot of Ninja Foodi, add the steak with marinade.
10) Cover the Ninja Foodi with the pressure lid and place the pressure valve to "Seal" position.
11) Select "Pressure" and set to "High" for about 12 minutes.
12) Press "Start/Stop" to begin.
13) Switch the valve to "Vent" and do a "Quick" release.
13) Once all the pressure is released, open the lid.
14) Select "Sauté/Sear" setting of Ninja Foodi and stir in the broccoli.
15) Press "Start/Stop" to begin and cook for about 5 minutes.
16) Press "Start/Stop" to stop the cooking and serve hot.

Nutrition Information:
Calories: 307; Carbohydrates: 6.1g; Protein: 42.2g; Fat: 12g; Sugar: 1.7g; Sodium: 1000mg; Fiber: 2g

Thai Egg Rolls

Serves: 4, Prep Time: 15 minutes, Cooking Time: 8 minutes

Ingredients:
- 2 C. cooked beef, shredded
- ¼ C. Thai peanut sauce
- 1 medium carrot, peeled and julienned
- 1 red bell pepper, seeded and julienned
- 4 egg roll wrappers

Directions:
1) In a bowl, add the beef and peanut sauce and toss to coat well.
2) In another bowl, mix together the carrot and bell pepper.
3) With a damp cloth, cover the wrappers to avoid the drying.
4) Arrange 1 wrapper onto a clean, smooth surface.
5) Place about ¼ of the carrot mixture onto the bottom third of 1 wrapper, followed by ½ C. of the beef mixture. With wet fingers, moisten the outside edges of wrapper. Fold the sides of the wrapper over the filling, then roll up from the bottom.
6) Pinch the center to create a round, sausage-like roll. Repeat with the remaining wrappers and filling. Spray each egg roll with cooking spray evenly.
7) Arrange the "Cook & Crisp Basket" in the pot of Ninja Foodi. Close the Ninja Foodi with crisping lid and select "Air Crisp".
8) Press "Start/Stop" to begin and set the temperature to 390 degrees F.
9) Set the time for 5 minutes to preheat. place the rolls into "Cook & Crisp Basket".
10) Close the Ninja Foodi with crisping lid and select "Air Crisp".
11) Set the temperature to 390 degrees F for 8 minutes.
12) Press "Start/Stop" to begin. Open the lid and cut each roll in 2 equal sized portions before serving.

Nutrition Information:
Calories: 461; Carbohydrates: 42.3g; Protein: 42.8g; Fat: 12.9g; Sugar: 10.8g; Sodium: 741mg; Fiber: 2.9g

Favorite Beef Taquitos

Serves: 12, Prep Time: 15 minutes, Cooking Time: 15 minutes

Ingredients:
- 8-oz. cream cheese, softened
- 2 tbsp. buffalo sauce
- 2 C. cooked beef, shredded
- 12 small corn tortillas

Directions:
1) In a bowl, add cream cheese and buffalo sauce and mix until smooth.
2) Add the shredded beef and mix well. Arrange the corn tortillas onto a clean, smooth surface. Spread about 2-3 tbsp. of the chicken mixture onto center of each tortillas in a thin layer. Roll each tortilla up tightly around the chicken mixture.
3) Arrange the greased "Cook & Crisp Basket" in the pot of Ninja Foodi.
4) Close the Ninja Foodi with crisping lid and select "Air Crisp".
5) Press "Start/Stop" to begin and set the temperature to 360 degrees F.
6) Set the time for 5 minutes to preheat.
7) Now, place the rolls into the greased "Cook & Crisp Basket". Close the Ninja Foodi with crisping lid and select "Air Crisp". Set the temperature to 400 degrees F for 15 minutes.
8) Press "Start/Stop" to begin. Open the lid and cut each roll in 2 equal sized portions. Serve warm.

Nutrition Information:
Calories: 202; Carbohydrates: 11.9g; Protein: 14.3g; Fat: 10.8g; Sugar: 0.4g; Sodium: 92mg; Fiber: 1.5g

Awesome Beef Enchilada

Serves: 2, Prep Time: 15 minutes, Cooking Time: 10 minutes

Ingredients:
- 1 (12-inch) flour tortilla
- 1 C. cooked beef, shredded and divided
- 5-oz. Mexican cheese blend, shredded and divided
- 1 large Roma tomato, chopped and divided
- 2 corn tostadas, divided

Directions:
1) Arrange the tortillas onto a clean, smooth surface.
2) Place about ½ C. of shredded beef onto center of tortilla, followed by 2-oz. of the cheese, half of tomatoes and 1 tostada. Repeat the layers once and finally top with the remaining 1-oz. of cheese.
3) Gently fold tortilla over the filling in 4 layers.
4) With a broken piece of tostada, cover the center opening of the enchilada to secure the filling.
5) Arrange the "Cook & Crisp Basket" in the pot of Ninja Foodi.
6) Close the Ninja Foodi with crisping lid and select "Air Crisp".
7) Press "Start/Stop" to begin and set the temperature to 360 degrees F.
8) Set the time for 5 minutes to preheat. Coat the enchilada with cooking spray.
9) Place the enchilada, seam-side down into "Cook & Crisp Basket".
10) Close the Ninja Foodi with crisping lid and select "Air Crisp". Set the temperature to 360 degrees F for 8 minutes.
11) Press "Start/Stop" to begin. Open the lid and cut the enchilada in 2 equal sized portions. Serve warm.

Nutrition Information:
Calories: 441; Carbohydrates: 36.4g; Protein: 53g; Fat: 37.1g; Sugar: 2.6g; Sodium: 852mg; Fiber: 3.8g___

Beef Taco Casserole

Serves: 6, Prep Time: 15 minutes, Cooking Time: 25 minutes

Ingredients:
- 2 lb. ground beef
- 2 tbsp. taco seasoning
- 1 C. cheddar cheese, shredded
- 1 C. cottage cheese
- 1 C. salsa

Directions:
1) Select "Bake/Roast" of Ninja Foodi and set the temperature to 370 degrees F.
2) Press "Start/Stop" to begin and preheat the Ninja Foodi for about 10 minutes.
3) In a bowl, add the beef and taco seasoning and mix well.
4) Add cheeses and salsa and stir to combine.
5) Grease the pot of Ninja Foodi generously.
6) In the prepared pot, place the beef mixture and slightly, press to smooth the top surface.
7) Close the Ninja Foodi with crisping lid and set the time for 25 minutes.
8) Press "Start/Stop" to begin.
9) Open the lid and serve.

Nutrition Information:
Calories: 407; Carbohydrates: 5.3g; Protein: 56.4g; Fat: 16.5g; Sugar: 1.8g; Sodium: 734mg; Fiber: 0.7g

Herbed Lamb Chops

Serves: 4, Prep Time: 15 minutes, Cooking Time: 10 hours

Ingredients:
- 1 lb. lamb chops
- 1½ C. tomatoes, chopped finely
- 1 C. chicken broth
- Salt and freshly ground black pepper, to taste
- 3 tbsp. mixed fresh herbs (oregano, thyme, sage), chopped

Directions:
1) In the pot of Ninja Foodi, place all the ingredients and mix well.

2) Close the crisping lid and select "Slow Cooker".
3) Set on "Low" for about 8 hours.
4) Press "Start/Stop" to begin.
5) Open the lid and serve hot.

Nutrition Information:
Calories: 237; Carbohydrates: 3.8g; Protein: 33.8g; Fat: 9g; Sugar: 2g; Sodium: 319mg; Fiber: 1.4g__

Zesty Lamb Chops

Serves: 4, Prep Time: 15 minutes, Cooking Time: 40 minutes

Ingredients:
- 4 (6-oz.) bone-in lamb chops
- 2 tbsp. all-purpose flour
- 4 tbsp. butter
- 1 C. picante sauce
- 3 tbsp. fresh lemon juice

Directions:
1) Coat the lamb chops with almond flour evenly and set aside.
2) Select "Sauté/Sear" setting of Ninja Foodi and place the butter into the pot.
3) Press "Start/Stop" to begin and heat for about 2-3 minutes.
4) Add the chops and cook, uncovered for about 4-5 minutes or until browned from both sides. Press "Start/Stop" to stop the cooking and stir in the picante sauce and lemon juice.
5) Cover the Ninja Foodi with the pressure lid and place the pressure valve to "Seal" position. Select "Pressure" and set to "High" for about 40 minutes.
6) Press "Start/Stop" to begin. Switch the valve to "Vent" and do a "Quick" release.
7) Once all the pressure is released, open the lid. Serve hot.

Nutrition Information:
Calories: 452; Carbohydrates: 6.2g; Protein: 49.1g; Fat: 24.3g; Sugar: 2.1g; Sodium: 513mg; Fiber: 0.5g

Hawaiian Lamb Chops

Serves: 3, Prep Time: 15 minutes, Cooking Time: 40 minutes

Ingredients:
- 3 (8-oz.) lamb shoulder chops
- Salt and freshly ground black pepper, to taste
- ¼ C. brown sugar
- 4-5 pineapple slices
- ¼-½ C. pineapple juice

Directions:
1) Select "Bake/Roast" of Ninja Foodi and set the temperature to 375 degrees F.
2) Press "Start/Stop" to begin and preheat the Ninja Foodi for about 10 minutes.
3) Season the pork chops with salt and black pepper generously.
4) In the pot of Ninja Foodi, place the chops and top with the brown sugar, pineapple slices and pineapple juice.
5) Close the Ninja Foodi with crisping lid and set the time for 40 minutes.
6) Press "Start/Stop" to begin.
7) After 20 minutes of cooking, baste the chops with juices.
8) Open the lid and serve.

Nutrition Information:
Calories: 408; Carbohydrates: 17g; Protein: 44.3g; Fat: 18.1g; Sugar: 15.7g; Sodium: 215mg; Fiber: 0.3g__

Almonds Coated Lamb

Serves: 6, Prep Time: 15 minutes, Cooking Time: 35 minutes

Ingredients:
- 1¾ lb. rack of lamb
- Salt and freshly ground black pepper, to taste
- 1 egg
- 1 tbsp. breadcrumbs
- 3-oz. almonds, chopped finely

Directions:
1) Season the rack of lamb with salt and black pepper evenly and then, drizzle with cooking spray. In a shallow dish, beat the egg.

2) In another shallow dish mix together breadcrumbs and almonds.
3) Dip the rack of lamb in egg and then coat with the almond mixture.
4) Arrange the "Cook & Crisp Basket" in the pot of Ninja Foodi. Close the Ninja Foodi with crisping lid and select "Air Crisp". Press "Start/Stop" to begin and set the temperature to 220 degrees F. Set the time for 5 minutes to preheat.
5) Now, place the rack of lamb into "Cook & Crisp Basket". Close the Ninja Foodi with crisping lid and select "Air Crisp". Set the temperature to 220 degrees F for 30 minutes.
6) Press "Start/Stop" to begin. Now, set the temperature to 390 degrees F for 5 minutes. Open the lid and serve.

Nutrition Information:
Calories: 319; Carbohydrates: 3.9g; Protein: 31g; Fat: 19.6g; Sugar: 0.7g; Sodium: 139mg; Fiber: 1.8g__

Garlicky Leg of Lamb

Serves: 10 , Prep Time: 15 minutes, Cooking Time: 8 hours

Ingredients:
- 3 lb. boneless leg of lamb, rolled
- 6 garlic cloves, minced
- Salt and freshly ground black pepper, to taste
- ½ C. beef broth
- 2-3 tbsp. fresh lemon juice

Directions:
6) In the pot of Ninja Foodi, place all the ingredients and mix well.
7) Close the crisping lid and select "Slow Cooker".
8) Set on "Low" for about 8 hours.
9) Press "Start/Stop" to begin.
10) Open the lid and transfer the leg of lamb onto a cutting board.
11) Cut the leg of lamb into desired sized pieces and serve.

Nutrition Information:
Calories: 258; Carbohydrates: 0.7g; Protein: 38.6g; Fat: 10.1g; Sugar: 0.1g; Sodium: 158mg; Fiber: 0.1g__

Herb Infused Leg of Lamb

Serves: 6, Prep Time: 15 minutes, Cooking Time: 1¼ hours

Ingredients:
- 2¼ lb. boneless leg of lamb
- 2 tbsp. olive oil
- Salt and freshly ground black pepper, to taste
- 2 fresh rosemary sprigs
- 2 fresh thyme sprigs

Directions:
1) Coat the leg of lamb with oil and sprinkle with salt and black pepper.
2) Wrap the leg of lamb with herb sprigs.
3) Arrange the "Cook & Crisp Basket" in the pot of Ninja Foodi.
4) Close the Ninja Foodi with crisping lid and select "Air Crisp".
5) Press "Start/Stop" to begin and set the temperature to 300 degrees F.
6) Set the time for 5 minutes to preheat. place the leg of lamb into "Cook & Crisp Basket".
7) Close the Ninja Foodi with crisping lid and select "Air Crisp".
8) Set the temperature to 300 degrees F for 75 minutes.
9) Press "Start/Stop" to begin. Open the lid and transfer the leg of lamb onto a cutting board. Cut into desired sized pieces and serve.

Nutrition Information:
Calories: 360; Carbohydrates: 0.7g; Protein: 47.8g; Fat: 17.3g; Sugar: 0g; Sodium: 157mg; Fiber: 0.5g__

Christmas Dinner Platter

Serves: 6, Prep Time: 15 minutes, Cooking Time: 8 hours

Ingredients:
- 1 (3¼ lb.) bone-in leg of lamb
- 4-5 medium Desiree potatoes, chopped into chunks
- 1 head garlic, peeled
- Salt and freshly ground black pepper, to taste
- 1 C. wine

Directions:

1) Grease the pot of Ninja Foodi generously. Press "Start/Stop" to begin and heat for about 2-3 minutes. Add the lamb and cook, uncovered for about 10 minutes or until browned completely.
2) Press "Start/Stop" to stop the cooking and transfer the lamb onto a plate.
3) In the bottom of pot, place the potatoes and about half of the garlic cloves.
4) Place the lamb on top of the potatoes and rub with remaining garlic cloves.
5) Sprinkle with salt and black pepper and pour wine on top.
6) Close the crisping lid and select "Slow Cooker". Set on "Low" for about 6-8 hours.
7) Press "Start/Stop" to begin. Open the lid and transfer the leg of lamb onto a cutting board. Cut into desired sized pieces and serve alongside the potatoes.

Nutrition Information:
Calories: 946; Carbohydrates: 24.7g; Protein: 74.9g; Fat: 55.1g; Sugar: 2g; Sodium: 270mg; Fiber: 3.5g__

Out of World Deer

Serves: 10 Prep Time: 15 minutes, Cooking Time: 2½ hours

Ingredients:
- 3-4 lb. deer, thawed
- Salt and freshly ground black pepper, to taste
- 1 (12-oz.) can beer
- ¼ C. Worcestershire sauce
- 1 tbsp. honey

Directions:
1) Grease the pot of Ninja Foodi generously.
2) Select "Sauté/Sear" setting of Ninja Foodi and place the deer meat.
3) Press "Start/Stop" to begin and cook, uncovered for about 15 minutes per side.
4) Press "Start/Stop" to stop the cooking and stir in the remaining ingredients.
5) Close the crisping lid and select "Slow Cooker".
6) Set on "High" for about 2 hours.
7) Press "Start/Stop" to begin.
8) Open the lid and with 2 forks, shred the meat.
9) Serve hot.

Nutrition Information:
Calories: 242; Carbohydrates: 4.1g; Protein: 41.3g; Fat: 4.3g; Sugar: 2.9g; Sodium: 156mg; Fiber: 0g__

Creamy Shredded Venison

Serves: 12 Prep Time: 15 minutes, Cooking Time: 6 hours 10 minutes

Ingredients:
- 1 (4-lb.) venison roast
- ½ C. Italian salad dressing
- ½ can Dr. pepper soda
- 1 small onion, chopped
- 1 packet dry Italian dressing

Directions:
1) In the pot of Ninja Foodi, place all the ingredients, except dressing packets and stir to combine.
2) Close the crisping lid and select "Slow Cooker".
3) Set on "High" for about 4 hours.
4) Press "Start/Stop" to begin.
5) Now, set on "Low" for about 2-3 hours.
6) Press "Start/Stop" to begin.
7) Open the lid and with 2 forks, shred the meat.
8) Select "Sauté/Sear" setting of Ninja Foodi and stir in the dressing packets.
9) Press "Start/Stop" to begin and cook, uncovered for about 10 minutes.
10) Press "Start/Stop" to stop the cooking and serve.

Nutrition Information:
Calories: 290; Carbohydrates: 3.4g; Protein: 53g; Fat: 6.2g; Sugar: 2.9g; Sodium: 6mg; Fiber: 0.1g__

Italian Venison

Serves: 12 Prep Time: 15 minutes, Cooking Time: 12 hours

Ingredients:
- 1 C. beef broth
- ½ C. water
- 1 (12-oz.) jar pepperoncini
- 2 packets Italian seasoning
- 1 (4-lb.) venison roast

Directions:

1) In a large bowl, add broth, water, pepperoncini and Italian seasoning and mix well.
2) Add the venison roast and coat with the marinade generously.
3) Cover the bowl tightly and refrigerate to marinate for about 8 hours.
4) In the pot of Ninja Foodi, place the venison roast with marinade.
5) Close the crisping lid and select "Slow Cooker".
6) Set on "Low" for about 12 hours.
7) Press "Start/Stop" to begin.
8) Open the lid and serve.

Nutrition Information:
Calories: 248; Carbohydrates: 3.2g; Protein: 45.6g; Fat: 5.1g; Sugar: 0.5g; Sodium: 590mg; Fiber: 0g___

Special Thanksgiving Roast

Serves: 12 Prep Time: 15 minutes, Cooking Time: 8 hours

Ingredients:
- 12-oz. beef broth
- 1 (14-oz.) can whole berry cranberries
- 5 tsp. horseradish
- Salt and freshly ground black pepper, to taste
- 1 (4-lb.) venison roast

Directions:
1) For sauce: in a pan, add all the ingredients except the roast over medium heat and bring to a boil, stirring frequently.
2) In the pot of Ninja Foodi, place the roast and top with the hot sauce.
3) Close the crisping lid and select "Slow Cooker".
4) Set on "Low" for about 6-8 hours.
5) Press "Start/Stop" to begin.
6) Open the lid and transfer the roast onto a cutting board.
7) Cut into desired sized slices and serve.

Nutrition Information:
Calories: 346; Carbohydrates: 12.2g; Protein: 55.5g; Fat: 6.1g; Sugar: 10.6g; Sodium: 192mg; Fiber: 0.5g___

Family Dinner Pork Shoulder

Serves: 10, Prep Time: 15 minutes, Cooking Time: 10 minutes

Ingredients:
- 3 lb. boneless pork shoulder, trimmed and cut in 2-inch cubes
- 4 tbsp. barbecue seasoning
- 1 C. apple cider vinegar
- 1 can (6 oz.) tomato paste
- 1 (16.3-oz.) tube refrigerated biscuit dough

Directions:
1) In the pot of Ninja Foodi, place pork, barbecue seasoning and vinegar.
2) Cover the Ninja Foodi with the pressure lid and place the pressure valve to "Seal" position. Select "Pressure" and set to "High" for about 35 minutes.
3) Press "Start/Stop" to begin. Switch the valve to "Vent" and do a "Quick" release.
4) Once all the pressure is released, open the lid. Now, select "Sauté/Sear" setting of Ninja Foodi and stir in the tomato paste. Select "Md:Hi" and press "Start/Stop" to begin. Cook for about 10 minutes, stirring occasionally to shred the meat.
5) Meanwhile, tear each uncooked biscuit in 2 halves. Press "Start/Stop" to stop the cooking. Arrange the biscuit halves across the surface of the pork evenly.
6) Now, close the Ninja Foodi with crisping lid and select "Bake/Roast".
7) Set the temperature to 350 degrees F for 10 minutes.
8) Press "Start/Stop" to begin, Open the lid and serve immediately.

Nutrition Information:
Calories: 363; Carbohydrates: 21.9g; Protein: 39.9g; Fat: 12g; Sugar: 4.3g; Sodium: 567mg; Fiber: 1.4g__

Jamaican Jerk Pork

Serves: 3 , Prep Time: 15 minutes, Cooking Time: 30 minutes

Ingredients:
- 1 lb. pork shoulder
- 2 tbsp. Jamaican jerk spice blend
- 1 tbsp. butter
- ¼ C. beef broth

Directions:
1) Select "Sauté/Sear" setting of Ninja Foodi and place the butter into the pot.

2) Press "Start/Stop" to begin and heat for about 2-3 minutes.
3) Add the pork shoulder and cook, uncovered for about 10 minutes or until browned completely. Press "Start/Stop" to stop the cooking and stir in the broth.
4) Cover the Ninja Foodi with the pressure lid and place the pressure valve to "Seal" position. Select "Pressure" and set to "Low" for about 20 minutes.
5) Press "Start/Stop" to begin. Switch the valve to "Vent" and do a "Quick" release.
6) Once all the pressure is released, open the lid. Serve hot.

Nutrition Information:
Calories: 479; Carbohydrates: 0.1g; Protein: 35.6g; Fat: 36.3g; Sugar: 0.1g; Sodium: 194mg; Fiber: 0g__

Citrus Pork Carnitas

Serves: 4 , Cooking Time: 43 minutes
Ingredients:
- 2 lb. pork butt, cut into 2-inch pieces
- Salt and freshly ground black pepper, to taste
- 1 orange, cut in half
- 1 yellow onion, peeled and cut in half
- ½ C. chicken broth

Directions:
1) Season the pork butt with salt and black pepper generously.
2) In the pot of Ninja Foodi, place the pork butt.
3) Squeeze the juice of orange halves over pork butt.
4) Place the squeezed orange halves, onion and broth over the pork.
5) Cover the Ninja Foodi with the pressure lid and place the pressure valve to "Seal" position. Select "Pressure" and set to "High" for about 20 minutes.
6) Press "Start/Stop" to begin. Switch the valve to "Vent" and do a "Quick" release.
7) Once all the pressure is released, open the lid. Remove the orange halves and onion from the pot. Select "Sauté/Sear" setting of Ninja Foodi and set "Md:Hi".
8) Press "Start/Stop" to begin and cook, uncovered for about 10-15 minutes.
9) Press "Start/Stop" to stop the cooking. Now, close the Ninja Foodi with crisping lid and select "Broil". Set time to 8 minutes and select "Start/Stop" to begin.
10) Open the lid and serve hot.

Nutrition Information:
Calories: 475; Carbohydrates: 8.1g; Protein: 71.9g; Fat: 15.4g; Sugar: 5.6g; Sodium: 262mg; Fiber: 1.7g__

Soy Glazed Pork Tenderloin

Serves: 8, Prep Time: 15 minutes, Cooking Time: 8 hours

Ingredients:
- 3 lb. pork tenderloin
- 1 envelope dry onion soup mix
- Salt and freshly ground black pepper, to taste
- 3 tbsp. soy sauce
- 1¾ C. chicken broth

Directions:
1) In the pot of Ninja Foodi, place all ingredients and stir to combine.
2) Close the crisping lid and select "Slow Cooker".
3) Set on "Low" for about 8 hours. Press "Start/Stop" to begin.
4) Open the lid and transfer the pork tenderloin onto a cutting board.
5) Cut into desired sized slices and serve.

Nutrition Information:
Calories: 276; Carbohydrates: 5.3g; Protein: 46.5g; Fat: 6.3g; Sugar: 0.6g; Sodium: 1100mg; Fiber: 0.5g_

Perfect Fall Dinner Pork

Serves: 6 , Prep Time: 15 minutes, Cooking Time: 4 hours

Ingredients:
- 1 medium onion, sliced
- 1½ lb. pork tenderloin
- 2 medium apples, cored and sliced
- Salt and freshly ground black pepper, to taste
- 2 C. chicken broth

Directions:
1) Grease the pot of Ninja Foodi generously.
2) In the bottom of pot, arrange the onion slices and top with the pork tenderloin, followed by apple slices.
3) Sprinkle with salt and black pepper and pour broth on top.
4) Close the crisping lid and select "Slow Cooker".
5) Set on "High" for about 4 hours.
6) Press "Start/Stop" to begin. Open the lid and serve hot.

Nutrition Information:

Calories: 221; Carbohydrates: 12.3g; Protein: 31.7g; Fat: 4.6g; Sugar: 8.7g; Sodium: 348mg; Fiber: 2.2g__

Chinese Pork Chops

Serves: 4, Prep Time: 15 minutes, Cooking Time: 19 minutes

Ingredients:

- 4 (8-oz.) frozen boneless pork chops
- ¼ C. hoisin sauce
- 1/3 C. honey
- 1½ tbsp. soy sauce
- 1 tsp. Chinese five spice powder

Directions:

1) In the pot of Ninja Foodi, place ½ C. of water.
2) In the pot, arrange the reversible rack in higher position.
3) Place the chops over the rack.
4) Cover the Ninja Foodi with the pressure lid and place the pressure valve to "Seal" position. Select "Pressure" and set to "High" for about 4 minutes.
5) Press "Start/Stop" to begin. Switch the valve to "Vent" and do a "Quick" release.
6) Meanwhile, in a bowl add the hoisin sauce, honey, soy sauce and Chinese five spice powder and beat until well combined.
7) Once all the pressure is released, open the lid. Coat the top of pork chops with ½ of sauce generously. Now, close the Ninja Foodi with crisping lid and select "Broil". Set time to 5 minutes and select "Start/Stop" to begin.
8) Open the lid and coat the chops with the remaining sauce.
9) Close the Ninja Foodi with the crisping lid and cook for 10 minutes more.
10) Open the lid and serve.

Nutrition Information:

Calories: 449; Carbohydrates: 30.8g; Protein: 60.3g; Fat: 8.5g; Sugar: 27.7g; Sodium: 727mg; Fiber: 0.6g

Sweet & Sour Pork Chops

Serves: 4, Prep Time: 10 minutes, Cooking Time: 16 minutes

Ingredients:
- 6 pork loin chops
- Salt and freshly ground black pepper, to taste
- 2 tbsp. honey
- 2 tbsp. soy sauce
- 1 tbsp. balsamic vinegar

Directions:
1) With a meat tenderizer, tenderize the chops completely.
2) Sprinkle the chops with a little salt and black pepper.
3) In a large bowl, mix together remaining ingredients. Add the chops and coat with marinade generously. Refrigerate, covered for about 6-8 hours.
4) Arrange the "Cook & Crisp Basket" in the pot of Ninja Foodi. Close the Ninja Foodi with crisping lid and select "Air Crisp".
5) Press "Start/Stop" to begin and set the temperature to 355 degrees F.
6) Set the time for 5 minutes to preheat.
7) Now, place the pork chops into "Cook & Crisp Basket". Close the Ninja Foodi with crisping lid and select "Air Crisp". Set the temperature to 355 degrees F for 16 minutes, flipping once half way through.
8) Press "Start/Stop" to begin. Open the lid and serve hot.

Nutrition Information:
Calories: 281; Carbohydrates: 6.2g; Protein: 18.3g; Fat: 19.9g; Sugar: 5.9g; Sodium: 384mg; Fiber: 0.1g

Inspiring Pork Platter

Serves: 6, Prep Time: 15 minutes, Cooking Time: 12 minutes

Ingredients:
- 2 lb. boneless pork chops
- Salt and freshly ground black pepper, to taste
- 1 small head cabbage, cut into thick chunks
- 2 C. chicken broth
- ¼ C. butter

Directions:
1) Season the pork chops with salt and black pepper evenly.
2) In the pot of Ninja Foodi, place the chops and top with the cabbage, followed by broth and butter.
3) Cover the Ninja Foodi with the pressure lid and place the pressure valve to "Seal" position. Select "Pressure" and set to "High" for about 12 minutes.
4) Press "Start/Stop" to begin. Switch the valve to "Vent" and do a "Natural" release. Once all the pressure is released, open the lid.
5) Serve hot.

Nutrition Information:
Calories: 330; Carbohydrates: 8g; Protein: 43g; Fat: 13.6g; Sugar: 4.5g; Sodium: 446mg; Fiber: 3.3g

Easter Dinner Ham

Serves: 8, Prep Time: 15 minutes, Cooking Time: 1½ hours

Ingredients:
- 1 (4-lb.) bone-in, fully cooked ham
- 2 C. apple cider
- 1 (3-inch) piece fresh ginger, grated finely
- ¼ C. packed brown sugar
- ¼ C. bourbon

Directions:
1) Select "Bake/Roast" of Ninja Foodi and set the temperature to 375 degrees F.
2) Press "Start/Stop" to begin and preheat the Ninja Foodi for about 10 minutes.
3) With a knife, score the ham on all sides in a diamond pattern.
4) In the pot of Ninja Foodi, place the ham and top with the apple cider.

5) Close the Ninja Foodi with crisping lid and set the time for 1½ hours.
6) Press "Start/Stop" to begin. Open the lid and transfer the ham onto a platter.
7) With a piece of foil, cover the ham to and keep warm.
8) Discard the cooking liquid from the pot, reserving 1 C. inside.
9) Now, select "Sauté/Sear" setting of Ninja Foodi and stir in the remaining ingredients.
10) Cook, uncovered for about 10 minutes or until desired thickness of glaze.
11) Coat the ham with glaze and serve.

Nutrition Information:
Calories: 590; Carbohydrates: 11.8g; Protein: 32.5g; Fat: 36.5g; Sugar: 11.2g; Sodium: 3000mg; Fiber: 0.1g__

Richly Cheesy Sausage

Serves: 6, Prep Time: 15 minutes, Cooking Time: 14 minutes

Ingredients:
- 2 lb. pork sausages, casing removed and crumbled
- 16-oz. marinara sauce
- 10-oz. Parmesan cheese, shredded
- 16-oz. mozzarella cheese, shredded

Directions:
1) Select "Bake/Roast" of Ninja Foodi and set the temperature to 360 degrees F.
2) Press "Start/Stop" to begin and preheat the Ninja Foodi for about 10 minutes.
3) Grease the pot of Ninja Foodi generously.
4) In the prepared pot, arrange half of the sausages and top with half of the marinara sauce, followed by half of the mozzarella and Parmesan cheese.
5) Repeat the layer once.
6) Close the Ninja Foodi with crisping lid and set the time for 20 minutes.
7) Press "Start/Stop" to begin.
8) Open the lid and serve.

Nutrition Information:
Calories: 944; Carbohydrates: 14.8g; Protein: 67.3g; Fat: 68.4g; Sugar: 6.7g; Sodium: 2000mg; Fiber: 2g__

Classic Sausage & Bell Peppers

Serves: 6, Prep Time: 20 minutes, Cooking Time: 6 hours

Ingredients:
- 1 lb. sausage, sliced
- 2 medium bell peppers, seeded and sliced
- 2 C. tomatoes, chopped finely
- 1 medium yellow onion, sliced
- Salt and freshly ground black pepper, to taste

Directions:
1) In the pot of Ninja Foodi, place all the ingredients and stir to combine.
2) Close the crisping lid and select "Slow Cooker".
3) Set on "Low" for about 6 hours.
4) Press "Start/Stop" to begin.
5) Open the lid and serve hot.

Nutrition Information:
Calories: 287; Carbohydrates: 7g; Protein: 15.8g; Fat: 21.7g; Sugar: 4.4g; Sodium: 598mg; Fiber: 1.6g__

Chapter 6 Fish & Seafood Recipes

Spicy Flounder

Servings: 2 servings, **Prep Time:** 5 minutes, **Cooking Time:** 15 minutes

Ingredients:

- 2 tsp salt
- 1 Tbsp paprika
- 1 tbsp chili powder
- 1 tsp ground black pepper
- 1 tsp onion powder
- 1 tsp garlic powder
- 1 tsp ground cumin
- 2 filets Flounder, about 1 pound
- 1 tbsp olive oil

Directions:

1. Mix all of the spices together in a bowl and then set aside.
2. Rub the flounder with the olive oil and then coat in the spice seasoning.
3. Place the spiced flounder in the cook and crisp basket and turn the Ninja Foodi to 375 degrees. Place the basket in the Foodi and set the timer for 15 minutes. Serve while hot straight out of the pot.

Nutritional Info:

Calories: 351g, Carbohydrates: 6g, Protein: 51g, Fat: 12g, Sugar: 6g, Sodium: 2658 mg

Lemon Cod

Servings: 2 servings, **Prep Time:** 10 minutes, **Cooking Time:** 5 minutes

Ingredients:

- ½ cup water
- 2 Tbsp butter
- 1/3 cup lemon juice
- 1 pound cod filets
- ½ tsp paprika

Directions:

1. Add all the ingredients into the cook and crisp basket and place the basket inside the Ninja Foodi.
2. Place the pressure cooker lid on top of the pot and close the pressure valve to the seal position. Set the pressure cooker function to high heat and set the timer for 3 minutes.
3. Once the coking cycle is complete, release the pressure quickly by carefully opening the steamer valve. Enjoy while hot

Nutritional Info:

Calories: 492g, Carbohydrates: 3g, Protein: 82g, Fat: 15g, Sugar: 1g, Sodium: 335mg

Lemon Pepper Salmon

Servings: 2 servings, **Prep Time:** 10 minutes, **Cooking Time:** 5 minutes

Ingredients:
- ½ cup water
- 2 Tbsp butter
- 1/3 cup lemon juice
- 1 pound Salmon, de boned
- ½ ground black pepper

Directions:
1. Add all the ingredients into the cook and crisp basket and place the basket inside the Ninja Foodi.
2. Place the pressure cooker lid on top of the pot and close the pressure valve to the seal position. Set the pressure cooker function to high heat and set the timer for 3 minutes.
3. Once the coking cycle is complete, release the pressure quickly by carefully opening the steamer valve. Enjoy while hot

Nutritional Info:
Calories: 314g, Carbohydrates: 8g, Protein: 42g, Fat: 14g, Sugar: 1g, Sodium: 565g

Jambalaya

Servings: 4 servings, **Prep Time:** 2 minutes, **Cooking Time:** 10 minutes

Ingredients:
- 1 pound shrimp, deveined, shells removed
- 2 cups chicken broth
- 2 cloves of garlic, chopped
- 2 bell peppers, chopped
- 1 white onion, chopped
- 4 tomatoes, chopped
- 1 tsp dried basil
- 1 tsp dried oregano
- ½ tsp tsp salt
- 1/8 tsp ground black pepper
- ¼ cup shredded cheddar cheese

Directions:
1. Place the shrimp in the Ninja Foodi pot and sprinkle with the oregano, salt, basil and ground black pepper.
2. Add the broth, garlic, tomato, bell pepper and onion to the pot and close the pressure cooker lid.
3. Cook on high pressure for 10 minutes. Do a quick steam release and remove the lid.
4. Add the cream cheese and heavy cream and stir to blend.
5. Sprinkle the cheese on top of the chili and put the air crisper top on. Use the broil function to brown the cheese for 2 minutes.

Nutritional Info:
Calories: 150g, Carbohydrates: 2g, Protein: 36g, Fat: 0g, Sugar: 2g, Sodium: 438mg

Veggie Fish Soup

Servings: 4 servings, **Prep Time:** 2 minutes, **Cooking Time:** 10 minutes

Ingredients:

- 1 pound cod
- 6 cups chicken broth
- 2 cloves of garlic, chopped
- 1 carrot, chopped
- 1 Bell pepper, chopped
- 1 sweet potato, peeled, diced
- 2 celery stalks, chopped
- ½ white onion, chopped
- ¼ tsp salt
- 1/8 tsp ground black pepper
- ¼ cup shredded cheddar cheese

Directions:

1. Add all the ingredients to the pot and place the pressure cooker lid on the Ninja Foodi.
2. Cook on high pressure for 10 minutes. Do a quick steam release and remove the lid.
3. Remove the chicken from the pot and shred the chicken using two forks.
4. Serve while hot or freeze to use at a later date.

Nutritional Info:

Calories: 250g, Carbohydrates: 4g, Protein: 36g, Fat: 0g, Sugar: 2g, Sodium: 438mg

Spicy Shrimp Soup

Servings: 4 servings, **Prep Time:** 2 minutes, **Cooking Time:** 10 minutes

Ingredients:

- 1 pound shrimp, deveined
- 6 cups chicken broth
- 2 cloves of garlic, chopped
- 1 carrot, chopped
- 2 Bell peppers, chopped
- 2 celery stalks, chopped
- ½ white onion, chopped
- ¼ tsp salt
- ½ tsp cayenne pepper
- 1/8 tsp ground black pepper

Directions:

1. Add all the ingredients to the pot and place the pressure cooker lid on the Ninja Foodi.
2. Cook on high pressure for 10 minutes. Do a quick steam release and remove the lid.
3. Remove the chicken from the pot and shred the chicken using two forks.
4. Serve while hot or freeze to use at a later date.

Nutritional Info:

Calories: 150g, Carbohydrates: 2g, Protein: 36g, Fat: 0g, Sugar: 2g, Sodium: 438mg

Butter Shrimp

Servings: 4 servings, **Prep Time:** 2 minutes, **Cooking Time:** 12 minutes

Ingredients:
- 2 pounds shrimp, deveined and peeled
- 2 Tbsp Butter
- 1 tsp chili powder
- 1 tsp garlic powder
- ½ tsp ground black pepper
- ¼ cup parmesan cheese

Directions:
1. Place the shrimp and butter in the pot and press saute. Sear both sides of the shrimp for 2 minutes.
2. Sprinkle the chili powder, garlic powder and ground black pepper on the shrimp and mix. Sprinkle the cheese over the shrimp and place the air crisp lid on top.
3. Use the roast function set to 375 to cook the shrimp for 10 more minutes. Serve hot.

Nutritional Info:
Calories: 293, Carbohydrates: 2g, Protein: 66g, Fat: 13g, Sugar: 0g, Sodium: 1386 mg

Black Pepper Scallops

Servings: 4 servings, **Prep Time:** 2 minutes, **Cooking Time:** 17 minutes

Ingredients:
- 2 pounds Sea Scallops
- 2 Tbsp Butter
- 1 tsp garlic powder
- 1 tsp ground black pepper
- ¼ cup lemon juice

Directions:
1. Place the scallops and butter in the pot and press saute. Sear both sides of the shrimp for 2 minutes.
2. Sprinkle the chili powder, garlic powder and ground black pepper on the shrimp and mix. Sprinkle the cheese over the shrimp and place the air crisp lid on top.
3. Use the roast function set to 400 to cook the shrimp for 15 more minutes. Serve hot.

Nutritional Info:
Calories: 236 g, Carbohydrates: 11g, Protein: 34g, Fat: 7g, Sugar: 0g, Sodium: 1181 mg

Everyday Flounder

Servings: 4 servings, **Prep Time:** 2 minutes, **Cooking Time:** 12 minutes

Ingredients:
- 2 pounds flounder filets
- 2 Tbsp Butter
- 1 tsp garlic powder
- ½ tsp ground black pepper
- ½ tsp salt
- ¼ cup parmesan cheese

Directions:
1. Place the flounder and butter in the pot and press saute. Sear both sides of the shrimp for 2 minutes.
2. Sprinkle the salt, garlic powder and ground black pepper on the shrimp and mix. Sprinkle the cheese over the flounder and place the air crisp lid on top.
3. Use the roast function set to 375 to cook the shrimp for 10 more minutes. Serve hot.

Nutritional Info:
Calories: 418g, Carbohydrates: 2g, Protein: 60g, Fat: 17g, Sugar: 1g, Sodium: 1267mg

BBQ Shrimp

Servings: 4 servings, **Prep Time:** 10 minutes, **Cooking Time:** 12 minutes

Ingredients:
- 1 ½ pounds Shrimp, deveined and peeled
- 1 Tbsp olive oil
- 1 tsp ground paprika
- ¼ tsp salt
- ¼ tsp ground black pepper
- 1 onion, chopped
- ¼ cup hot sauce
- 1 tsp stevia
- ¼ cup water
- 2 Tbsp vinegar

Directions:
1. Turn the Ninja Foodi on to saute and add the olive oil. Once hot, add the shrimp and sear on each side for 2 minutes.
2. Sprinkle the salt and pepper on the shrimp and then add all the remaining ingredients to the pot.
3. Cover the Foodi and use the pressure cooker function to cook the shrimp for 8 minutes under high heat pressure.
4. Release the pressure using a natural steam and serve warm or chilled

Nutritional Info:
Calories: 207g, Carbohydrates: 1g, Protein: 36g, Fat: 6g, Sugar: 2g, Sodium: 3633mg

Salsa Tuna Steaks

Servings: 4 servings, **Prep Time:**   2 minutes, **Cooking Time:** 10 minutes

Ingredients:
- 4 Tuna Steaks, about 2 pounds
- ½ cup water
- 1 cup chopped tomatoes
- ½ cup chopped onion
- 1 tbsp lemon juice
- ½ tsp salt
- ¼ tsp ground black pepper

Directions:

1. Place the tuna in the Ninja Foodi pot and add all the ingredients to the bowl.
2. Close the pressure seal lid and set the steamer valve to seal.
3. Cook on high pressure for 8 minutes then do a quick pressure release. Serve the tuna while hot.

Nutritional Info:

Calories: 165g, Carbohydrates: 4g, Protein: 24g, Fat: 3g, Sugar: 3g, Sodium: 583 mg

Mexican Swordfish

Servings: 4 servings, **Prep Time:**   2 minutes, **Cooking Time:** 8 minutes

Ingredients:
- 4 Swordfish Steaks
- ½ cup water
- 1 cup chopped tomatoes
- ½ cup chopped onion
- 1 tbsp lime juice
- 1 jalapeno, seeds removed, chopped
- ½ tsp salt
- ¼ tsp ground black pepper

Directions:

1. Place the swordfish in the Ninja Foodi pot and add all the ingredients to the bowl.
2. Close the pressure seal lid and set the steamer valve to seal.
3. Cook on high pressure for 8 minutes then do a quick pressure release. Serve the swordfish while hot.

Nutritional Info:

Calories: 177g, Carbohydrates: 8g, Protein: 23g, Fat: 6g, Sugar: 5g, Sodium: 684

Salmon and Asparagus

Servings: 2 servings, **Prep Time:** 10 minutes, **Cooking Time:** 5 minutes

Ingredients:

- ½ cup water
- 2 Tbsp butter
- 1 lemon, sliced
- 1 pound Salmon, de boned
- ½ ground black pepper
- 1 bunch asparagus, about ½ pound

Directions:

1. Add all the ingredients into the cook and crisp basket, with the asparagus on the bottom, the lemon slices layered on the salmon, and place the basket inside the Ninja Foodi.

2. Place the pressure cooker lid on top of the pot and close the pressure valve to the seal position. Set the pressure cooker function to high heat and set the timer for 3 minutes.

3. Once the cooking cycle is complete, release the pressure quickly by carefully opening the steamer valve. Enjoy while hot

Nutritional Info:

Calories: 342g, Carbohydrates: 13g, Protein: 46g, Fat: 14g, Sugar: 4g, Sodium: 568mg

Chili Lime Salmon

Servings: 2 servings, **Prep Time:** 10 minutes, **Cooking Time:** 5 minutes

Ingredients:

- ½ cup water
- 2 Tbsp butter
- 1/3 cup lime juice
- 1 pound Salmon, de boned
- ½ ground chili powder

Directions:

1. Add the salmon into the cook and crisp basket and place the basket inside the Ninja Foodi.

2. Sprinkle the chili powder over the top of the salmon and then add the water, butter and lime juice around the filets.

3. Place the pressure cooker lid on top of the pot and close the pressure valve to the seal position. Set the pressure cooker function to high heat and set the timer for 3 minutes.

4. Once the cooking cycle is complete, release the pressure quickly by carefully opening the steamer valve. Enjoy while hot

Nutritional Info:

Calories: 349g, Carbohydrates: 8g, Protein: 44g, Fat: 17g, Sugar: 1g, Sodium: 566g

Pepper Crusted Tuna

Servings: 2 servings, **Prep Time:** 10 minutes, **Cooking Time:** 5 minutes

Ingredients:

- ½ cup water
- 2 Tbsp butter
- 1/3 cup lemon juice
- 1 pound Tuna Filets
- T tsp black peppercorns, crushed

Directions:

1. Rub the tuna with the black pepper and then place in the air crisper basket.
2. Place the basket into the Ninja Foodi
3. Sprinkle the chili powder over the top of the salmon and then add the butter and lemon juice around the filets.
4. Place the pressure cooker lid on top of the pot and close the pressure valve to the seal position. Set the pressure cooker function to high heat and set the timer for 3 minutes.
5. Once the cooking cycle is complete, release the pressure quickly by carefully opening the steamer valve. Enjoy while hot

Nutritional Info:

Calories: 564g, Carbohydrates: 3g, Protein: 52g, Fat: 39g, Sugar: 1g, Sodium: 85mg

Tomato Lime Tilapia

Servings: 2 servings, **Prep Time:** 10 minutes, **Cooking Time:** 5 minutes

Ingredients:

- 2 Tbsp butter
- 1/3 cup lime juice
- 1 tomato, diced
- 1 pound Salmon, de boned
- ½ tsp salt
- ¼ tsp ground black pepper

Directions:

1. Add the tilapia into the cook and crisp basket and place the basket inside the Ninja Foodi.
2. Sprinkle the seasoning over the top of the fish and then add the tomatoes, butter and lime juice around the filets.
3. Place the pressure cooker lid on top of the pot and close the pressure valve to the seal position. Set the pressure cooker function to high heat and set the timer for 3 minutes.
4. Once the cooking cycle is complete, release the pressure quickly by carefully opening the steamer valve. Enjoy while hot

Nutritional Info:

Calories: 317g, Carbohydrates: 9g, Protein: 42g, Fat: 14g, Sugar: 4g, Sodium: 1726mg

Cod Topped with Mediterranean-Spiced Tomatoes

Servings: 6, Cooking time: 10 minutes

Ingredients:

- 2 frozen or fresh cod fillet
- 1 tablespoon butter
- 1/2 lemon, juiced
- ½ small onion, sliced thinly
- 1/4 teaspoon salt
- 1/4 teaspoon black pepper
- 1/2 teaspoon oregano
- ¼ tsp cumin
- ¼ tsp rosemary
- 4 roma tomatoes, diced
- ¼ cup water

Directions:

1. Press sauté and melt butter. Stir in lemon juice, onion, salt, black pepper, oregano cumin, rosemary, and diced tomatoes. Cook for 8 minutes.
2. Add fish and spoon sauce over it. Add water and press stop.
3. Install pressure lid and place valve to vent position.
4. Close Ninja Foodi, press steam button, and set time to 2 minutes.
5. Once done cooking, do a quick release. Serve and enjoy.

Nutrition information:

Calories: 184; carbohydrates: 10.0g; protein: 20.7g; fat: 6.8g

Tilapia Filet Topped with Mango-Salsa

Servings: 2, Cooking time: 5 minutes

Ingredients:

- 1 cup coconut milk
- 1/2 to 1 tablespoon Thai green curry paste
- 1 tablespoon fish sauce
- Zest of 1 lime and juice of 1/2 lime
- 2 teaspoons sear button sugar
- 1 teaspoon garlic, minced
- 1 tablespoon fresh ginger, minced
- 2 6-oz Tilapia filet
- 1 lime, cut in thin slices
- A sprinkle of cilantro leaves and chopped scallion

Mango salsa ingredients:

- 1 mango, peeled, seeded, and diced (about 3/4 cup small dice)
- 1 fresno or jalapeno chiles, minced
- 1 scallion, finely chopped
- A handful of cilantro leaves, chopped
- Juice of 1 lime

Directions:

1. In a bowl, mix well coconut milk, Thai green curry paste, fish sauce, lime juice, lime zest, sear button sugar, garlic, and ginger. Add fish and marinate for at least an hour.
2. Meanwhile, make the mango salsa by combining all ingredients in a separate bowl. Keep in the fridge.
3. Cut two 11x11-inch foil. Place one fish fillet in each foil. Top each equally with lime, scallion and cilantro. Seal foil packets.

4. Add a cup of water in Ninja Foodi, place trivet, and add foil packets on trivet.
5. Install pressure lid. Close Ninja Foodi, press pressure button, choose high settings, and set time to 5 minutes.
6. Once done cooking, do a quick release. Serve and enjoy with mango salsa on top.

Nutrition information:
Calories: 372; carbohydrates: 28.5g; protein: 29.3g; fat: 15.6g

Coconut Curry Sea Bass

Servings: 2, Cooking time: 3 minutes

Ingredients:
- 1 (14.5 ounce) can coconut milk
- Juice of 1 lime
- 1 tablespoon red curry paste
- 1 teaspoon fish sauce
- 1 teaspoon coconut aminos
- 1 teaspoon honey
- 2 teaspoons sriracha
- 2 cloves garlic, minced
- 1 teaspoon ground turmeric
- 1 teaspoon ground ginger
- 1/2 teaspoon sea salt
- 1/2 teaspoon white pepper
- 1-pound sea bass, cut into 1" cubes
- 1/4 cup chopped fresh cilantro
- 2 lime wedges

Directions:

1. Whisk well pepper, salt, ginger, turmeric, garlic, sriracha, honey, coconut aminos, fish sauce, red curry paste, lime juice, and coconut milk in a large bowl.
2. Place fish in pot and pour coconut milk mixture over it.
3. Install pressure lid. Close Ninja Foodi, press pressure button, choose high settings, and set time to 3 minutes.
4. Once done cooking, do a quick release.
5. Serve and enjoy with equal amounts of lime wedge and cilantro.

Nutrition information:
Calories: 749; carbohydrates: 16.6g; protein: 58.0g; fat: 50.0g

Tomato-Basil Dressed Tilapia

Servings: 2, Cooking time: 4 minutes

Ingredients:
- 2 (4 oz) tilapia fillets
- Salt and pepper
- 2 roma tomatoes, diced
- 2 minced garlic cloves
- 1/4 cup chopped basil (fresh)
- 1 tbsp olive oil
- 1/4 tsp salt
- 1/8 tsp pepper
- 1 tbsp Balsamic vinegar (optional)

Directions:
1. Add a cup of water in Ninja Foodi, place steamer basket, and add tilapia in basket. Season with pepper and salt.
2. Install pressure lid and place valve to vent position.
3. Close Ninja Foodi, press steam button, and set time to 2 minutes.
4. Meanwhile, in a medium bowl toss well to mix pepper, salt, olive oil, basil, garlic, and tomatoes. If desired, you can add a tablespoon of balsamic vinegar. Mix well.
5. Once done cooking, do a quick release.
6. Serve and enjoy with the basil-tomato dressing.

Nutrition information:
Calories: 196; carbohydrates: 2.0g; protein: 20.0g; fat: 12.0g

Pasta 'n Tuna Bake

Servings: 2, Cooking time: 10 minutes

Ingredients:
- 1 can cream-of-mushroom soup
- 1 1/2 cups water
- 1 1/4 cups macaroni pasta
- 1 can tuna
- 1/2 cup frozen peas
- 1/2 tsp salt
- 1 tsp pepper
- 1/2 cup shredded cheddar cheese

Directions:
1. Mix soup and water in Ninja Foodi.
2. Add remaining ingredients except for cheese. Stir.
3. Install pressure lid.
4. Close Ninja Foodi, press pressure button, choose high settings, and set time to 4 minutes.
5. Once done cooking, do a quick release.
6. Remove pressure lid.
7. Stir in cheese and roast for 5 minutes.
8. Serve and enjoy.

Nutrition information:
Calories: 378; carbohydrates: 34.0g; protein: 28.0g; fat: 14.1g

Salmon-Pesto Over Pasta

Servings: 2, Cooking time: 10 minutes

Ingredients:
- 4 ounces dry pasta
- 1 cup water
- 3-ounces smoked salmon, broken up in bite sized pieces
- 1/4 lemon
- Salt and pepper
- 1/2 teaspoon grated lemon zest
- 1/2 teaspoon lemon juice
- 2 tbsp heavy cream

Pesto-spinach sauce ingredients:
- 1 tbsp walnuts
- 1 clove garlic
- 1 cup packed baby spinach
- 1 ½ tbsp olive oil
- 1/4 cup freshly grated parmesan + more for serving/garnish
- Kosher salt and black pepper to taste
- 1 tsp grated lemon zest
- 1/4 cup heavy cream

Directions:

1. Make the sauce in blender by pulsing garlic and walnuts until chopped. Add ¼ tsp pepper, ¼ tsp salt, ½ cup parmesan, oil, and 2/3s of spinach. Puree until smooth.
2. Add butter, water, and pasta in Ninja Foodi.
3. Install pressure lid. Close Ninja Foodi, press pressure button, choose high settings, and set time to 4 minutes.
4. Once done cooking, do a quick release. Press stop and then press sauté.
5. Stir in remaining parmesan, remaining spinach, sauce, lemon juice, lemon zest, heavy cream, and smoked salmon. Mix well and sauté for 5 minutes.
6. Serve and enjoy.

Nutrition information:
Calories: 465; carbohydrates: 31.0g; protein: 20.1g; fat: 29.0g

Sweet 'n Spicy Mahi-Mahi

Servings: 2, Cooking time: 10 minutes

Ingredients:
- 2 6-oz mahi-mahi fillets
- Salt, to taste
- Black pepper, to taste
- 1-2 cloves garlic, minced or crushed
- 1" piece ginger, finely grated
- ½ lime, juiced
- 2 tablespoons honey
- 1 tablespoon nanami togarashi
- 2 tablespoons sriracha
- 1 tablespoon orange juice

Directions:

1. In a heatproof dish that fits inside the Ninja Foodi, mix well orange juice,

sriracha, nanami togarashi, honey lime juice, ginger, and garlic.

2. Season mahi-mahi with pepper and salt. Place in bowl of sauce and cover well in sauce. Seal dish securely with foil.

3. Install pressure lid and place valve to vent position.

4. Add a cup of water in Ninja Foodi, place trivet, and add dish of mahi-mahi on trivet.

5. Close Ninja Foodi, press steam button and set time to 10 minutes.

6. Once done cooking, do a quick release.

7. Serve and enjoy.

Nutrition information:
Calories: 200; carbohydrates: 20.1g; protein: 28.1g; fat: 0.8g

Easy Veggie-Salmon Bake

Servings: 2, Cooking time: 20 minutes
Ingredients:
- 1 cup chicken broth
- 1 cup milk
- 1 salmon filet
- 2 tbsp olive oil
- Ground pepper to taste
- 1 tsp minced garlic
- 1 cup frozen vegetables
- 1/2 can of cream of celery soup
- ¼ tsp dill
- ¼ tsp cilantro
- 1 tsp Italian spice
- 1 tsp poultry seasoning
- 1 tbsp ground parmesan

Directions:
1. Press sauté button and heat oil.
2. Add the salmon and cook until white on both sides and defrosted enough to split apart, around 2 minutes per side.

3. Add the garlic and just stir into the oil then deglaze the pot with the broth for 3 minutes.

4. Add the spices, milk, vegetables, noodles and stir.

5. Add the cream of celery soup on top and just gently stir so it is mixed in enough on top to not be clumpy.

6. Install pressure lid. Close Ninja Foodi, press pressure cook button, choose high settings, and set time to 8 minutes.

7. Once done cooking, do a quick release.

8. Serve and enjoy with a sprinkle of parmesan.

Nutrition information:
Calories: 616; carbohydrates: 28.7g; protein: 51.8g; fat: 32.6g

Salmon with Orange-Ginger Sauce

Servings: 2, Cooking time: 15 minutes

Ingredients:

- 1-pound salmon
- 1 tablespoon dark soy sauce
- 2 teaspoons minced ginger
- 1 teaspoon minced garlic
- 1 teaspoon salt
- 1 1/2 tsp ground pepper
- 2 tablespoons low sugar marmalade

Directions:

1. In a heatproof pan that fits inside your Ninja Foodi, add salmon.
2. Mix all the sauce ingredients and pour over the salmon. Allow to marinate for 15-30 minutes. Cover pan with foil securely.
3. Put 2 cups of water in Ninja Foodi and add trivet.
4. Place the pan of salmon on trivet.
5. Install pressure lid. Close Ninja Foodi, press pressure button, choose low settings, and set time to 5 minutes.
6. Once done cooking, do a quick release.
7. Serve and enjoy.

Nutrition information:

Calories: 177; carbohydrates: 8.8g; protein: 24.0g; fat: 5.0g

Coconut Curry Fish

Servings: 2, Cooking time: 15 minutes

Ingredients:

- 1-lb fish steaks or fillets, rinsed and cut into bite-size pieces
- 1 tomato, chopped
- 1 green chiles, sliced into strips
- 1 small onions, sliced into strips
- 2 garlic cloves, squeezed
- 1/2 tbsp freshly grated ginger
- 2 bay laurel leaves
- 1 tsp ground coriander
- 1 tsp ground cumin
- ½ tsp ground turmeric
- ½ tsp chili powder
- ½ tsp ground fenugreek
- 1 cup unsweetened coconut milk
- Salt to taste

Directions:

1. Press sauté button and heat oil. Add garlic, sauté for a minute. Stir in ginger and onions. Sauté for 5 minutes. Stir in bay leaves, fenugreek, chili powder, turmeric, cumin, and coriander. Cook for a minute.
2. Add coconut milk and deglaze pot.
3. Stir in tomatoes and green chilies. Mix well.
4. Add fish and mix well. Install pressure lid and place valve to vent position.
5. Close Ninja Foodi, press pressure cook button, choose low settings, and set time to 5 minutes.
6. Once done cooking, do a quick release. Adjust seasoning to taste.
7. Serve and enjoy.

Nutrition information:

Calories: 434; carbohydrates: 11.7g; protein: 29.7g; fat: 29.8g

Seafood Gumbo New Orleans Style

Servings: 2, Cooking time: 20 minutes

Ingredients:

- 1 sea bass filet patted dry and cut into 2" chunks
- 1 tablespoon ghee or avocado oil
- 1 tablespoon Cajun seasoning
- 1 small yellow onion diced
- 1 small bell pepper diced
- 1 celery rib diced
- 2 roma tomatoes diced
- 1 tbsp tomato paste
- 1 bay leaf
- 1/2 cup bone broth
- ¾-pound medium to large raw shrimp deveined
- Sea salt to taste
- Black pepper to taste

Directions:

1. Press sauté button and heat oil.
2. Season fish chunks with pepper, salt, and half of Cajun seasoning. Once oil is hot, sear fish chunks for 3 minutes per side and gently transfer to a plate.
3. Stir in remaining Cajun seasoning, celery, and onions. Sauté for 2 minutes. Press stop.
4. Stir in bone broth, bay leaves, tomato paste, and diced tomatoes. Mix well. Add back fish. Install pressure lid and place valve to vent position.
5. Close Ninja Foodi, press pressure cook button, choose high settings, and set time to 5 minutes.
6. Once done cooking, do a quick release. Stir in shrimps. Cover and let it sit for 5 minutes. Open and mix well.
7. Serve and enjoy.

Nutrition information:

Calories: 357; carbohydrates: 14.8g; protein: 45.9g; fat: 12.6g

Creamy Herb 'n Parm Salmon

Servings: 2, Cooking time: 10 minutes

Ingredients:

- 2 frozen salmon filets
- 1/2 cup water
- 1 1/2 tsp minced garlic
- 1/4 cup heavy cream
- 1 cup parmesan cheese grated
- 1 tbsp chopped fresh chives
- 1 tbsp chopped fresh parsley
- 1 tbsp fresh dill
- 1 tsp fresh lemon juice
- Salt and pepper to taste

Directions:

1. Add water and trivet in pot. Place fillets on top of trivet.
2. Install pressure lid. Close Ninja Foodi, press pressure button, choose high settings, and set time to 4 minutes.
3. Once done cooking, do a quick release.
4. Transfer salmon to a serving plate. And remove trivet.

5. Press stop and then press sauté button on Ninja Foodi. Stir in heavy cream once water begins to boil. Boil for 3 minutes. Press stop and then stir in lemon juice, parmesan cheese, dill, parsley, and chives. Season with pepper and salt to taste. Pour over salmon.

6. Serve and enjoy.

Nutrition information:

Calories: 423; carbohydrates: 6.4g; protein: 43.1g; fat: 25.0g

Stewed Mixed Seafood

Servings: 2, Cooking time: 35 minutes

Ingredients:

- 1 tbsp vegetable oil
- ½ 14.5-oz can fire-roasted tomatoes
- 1/2 cup diced onion
- 1/2 cup chopped carrots, or 1 cup chopped bell pepper
- 1/2 cup water
- 1/2 cup white wine or broth
- 1 bay leaf
- 1/2 tablespoon tomato paste
- 1 tablespoon minced garlic
- 1 teaspoon fennel seeds toasted and ground
- 1/2 teaspoon dried oregano
- 1 teaspoon salt
- 1 teaspoon red pepper flakes
- 2 cups mixed seafood such as fish chunks, shrimp, bay scallops, mussels and calamari rings, defrosted
- 1 tablespoon fresh lemon juice

Directions:

1. Press sauté button on Ninja Foodi and heat oil. Once hot, stir in onion and garlic. Sauté for 5 minutes. Stir in tomatoes, bay leaves, tomato paste, oregano, salt, and pepper flakes. Cook for 5 minutes. Press stop.

2. Stir in bell pepper, water, wine, and fennel seeds. Mix well.

3. Install pressure lid. Close Ninja Foodi, press pressure button, choose high settings, and set time to 15 minutes.

4. Once done cooking, do a quick release.

5. Stir in defrosted mixed seafood. Cover and let it cook for 10 minutes in residual heat.

6. Serve and enjoy with a dash of lemon juice.

Nutrition information:

Calories: 202; carbohydrates: 10.0g; protein: 18.0g; fat: 10.0g

Bok Choy On Ginger-Sesame Salmon

Servings: 2, Cooking time: 6 minutes

Ingredients:

- 1 tablespoon toasted sesame oil
- 1 tablespoons rice vinegar
- 2 tablespoons sear button sugar
- 1/2 cup shoyu (soy sauce)
- 1 garlic clove, pressed
- 1 tablespoon freshly grated ginger
- 1 tablespoon toasted sesame seed
- 2 green onions, sliced reserve some for garnish
- 2 7-oz salmon filet
- 2 baby bok choy washed well
- 1 teaspoon miso paste mixed with a 1/2 cup of water

Directions:

1. On a loaf pan that fits inside your Ninja Foodi, place salmon with skin side down.
2. In a small bowl whisk well sesame oil, rice vinegar, sear button sugar, shoyu, garlic, ginger, and sesame seed. Pour over salmon.
3. Place half of sliced green onions over salmon. Securely cover pan with foil.
4. On a separate loaf pan, place bok choy. In a small bowl, whisk well water and miso paste. Pour over bok choy and seal pan securely with foil.
5. Add water to Ninja Foodi and place trivet. Place pan of salmon side by side the bok choy pan on trivet.
6. Install pressure lid. Close Ninja Foodi, press manual button, choose high settings, and set time to 6 minutes.
7. Once done cooking, do a quick release. Serve and enjoy.

Nutrition information:
Calories: 609; carbohydrates: 30.4g; protein: 56.0g; fat: 29.2g

Eggs 'n Smoked Ramekin

Servings: 2, Cooking time: 4 minutes

Ingredients:

- 2 eggs
- 2 slices of smoked salmon
- 2 slices of cheese
- 2 fresh basil leaves for garnish
- Olive oil

Directions:

1. Add a cup of water in Ninja Foodi and place trivet on bottom.
2. Lightly grease each ramekin with a drop of olive oil each. Spread well.
3. Crack an egg in each ramekin. Place a slice of cheese, a slice of smoked salmon, and basil leaf in each ramekin.
4. Cover each ramekin with foil and place on trivet.
5. Install pressure lid. Close Ninja Foodi, press manual button, choose low settings, and set time to 4 minutes.

6. Once done cooking, do a quick release.
7. Serve and enjoy.

Nutrition information:
Calories: 239; carbohydrates: 0.9g; protein: 17.5g; fat: 18.3g

Salmon Stew

(Cooking Time: 16 minutes | Serves: 3)

Ingredients:
- 1 c. homemade fish broth
- Salt and black pepper
- 1 chopped onion
- 1 lb. salmon fillet, cubed
- 1 tbsp. butter

Directions:
1. Season the salmon fillets with salt and black pepper.
2. Press "Sauté" on Ninja Foodi and add butter and onions.
3. Sauté for about 3 minutes and add salmon and fish broth.
4. Lock the lid and set the Ninja Foodi to "Pressure" for about 8 minutes.
5. Release the pressure naturally and dish out to serve hot.

Nutritional Info: 272 calories, 14.2g fat, 4.4g carbs, 32.1g protein

Paprika Shrimp

(Cooking Time: 20 minutes | Serves: 3)

Ingredients:
- 1 tsp. paprika, smoked
- 3 tbsps. butter
- 1 lb. tiger shrimps
- Salt

Directions:
1. In a bowl, mix all the above ingredients and marinate the shrimps in it.
2. Grease the pot of Ninja Foodi with butter and transfer the seasoned shrimps in it.
3. Press "Bake/Roast" and set the timer to 15 minutes at 355 degrees F.
4. Dish out shrimps from the Ninja Foodi and serve.

Nutritional Info: 173 calories, 8.3g fat, 0.1g carbs, 23.8g protein

Ketogenic Butter Fish

(Cooking Time: 40 minutes | Serves: 3)

Ingredients:

- 1 lb. salmon fillets
- 2 tbsps. ginger-garlic paste
- 3 chopped green chilies
- Salt and black pepper
- ¾ c. butter

Directions:

1. Season the salmon fillets with ginger-garlic paste, salt and black pepper.
2. Place the salmon fillets in the pot of Ninja Foodi and top with green chilies and butter.
3. Press "Bake/Roast" and set the timer to 30 minutes at 360 degrees F.
4. Bake for about 30 minutes and dish out the fillets in a serving platter.

Nutritional Info: 507 calories, 45.9g fat, 2.4g carbs, 22.8g protein

Shrimp Magic

(Cooking Time: 25 minutes | Serves: 3)

Ingredients:

- 2 tbsps. butter
- ½ tsp. paprika, smoked
- 1 lb. deveined shrimps, peeled
- Lemongrass stalks
- 1 chopped red chili pepper, seeded

Directions:

1. In a bowl, combine all the ingredients except lemongrass and marinate for about 1 hour.
2. Press "Bake/Roast" and set the timer to 15 minutes at 345 degrees F.
3. Bake for about 15 minutes and dish out the fillets.

Nutritional Info: 251 calories, 10.3g fat, 3g carbs, 34.6g protein

Sweet and Sour Fish

(Cooking Time: 16 minutes | Serves: 3)

Ingredients:

- 2 drops liquid stevia
- ¼ c. butter
- 1 lb. fish chunks
- 1 tbsp. vinegar
- Salt and black pepper

Directions:

1. Press "Sauté" on Ninja Foodi and add butter and fish chunks.
2. Sauté for about 3 minutes and add stevia, salt and black pepper.
3. Press "Air Crisp" and cook for about 3 minutes at 360 degrees F.
4. Dish out in a serving bowl and serve immediately.

Nutritional Info: 274 calories, 15.4 fat, 2.8g carbs, 33.2g protein

Buttered Scallops

(Cooking Time: 25 minutes | Serves: 6)

Ingredients:

- 4 minced garlic cloves
- 4 tbsps. freshly chopped rosemary,
- 2 lbs. sea scallops
- ½ c. butter
- Salt and black pepper

Directions:

1. Press "Sauté" on Ninja Foodi and add butter, rosemary and garlic.
2. Sauté for about 1 minute and add sea scallops, salt and black pepper.
3. Sauté for about 2 minutes and press "Air Crisp" at 350 degrees F.
4. Set the timer for about 3 minutes and dish out to serve.

Nutritional Info: 279 calories, 16.8g fat, 5.7g carbs, 25.8g protein

Buffalo Fish

(Cooking Time: 21 minutes | Serves: 6)

Ingredients:

- 6 tbsps. butter
- ¾ c. Franks red hot sauce
- 6 fish fillets
- Salt and black pepper
- 2 tsps. garlic powder

Directions:

1. Press "Sauté" on Ninja Foodi and add butter and fish fillets.
2. Sauté for about 3 minutes and add salt, black pepper and garlic powder.
3. Press "Bake/Roast" and bake for about 8 minutes at 340 degrees F.
4. Dish out in a serving platter and serve hot.

Nutritional Info: 317 calories, 22.7g fat, 16.4g carbs, 13.6g protein

Green Chili Mahi-Mahi Fillets

(Cooking Time: 10 minutes | Serves: 2)

Ingredients:

- ¼ c. homemade green chili enchilada sauce
- 2 thawed Mahi-Mahi fillets
- 2 tbsps. butter
- Salt and pepper
- 1 c. water

Directions:

1. Pour 1 cup of water into the Ninja Foodi and set a steamer rack.
2. Grease the bottom of each mahi-mahi fillet with 1 tablespoon of butter, spreading the butter from end to end – this will prevent the fish from sticking to the rack.
3. Put the fillets on the rack. Spread 1/4 cup of enchilada sauce between each fillet using a pastry brush – cover them well.
4. Top with more enchilada sauce, if desired. Season fillets with salt and pepper. Lock the lid and close the steam valve. Press "PRESSURE", set the pressure to HIGH, and set the timer for 5 minutes.
5. When the timer beeps, quickly release the pressure and transfer the fillets into serving plates. Serve.

Fancy "Rich" Guy Smoked Lobster

(Cooking Time: 35 minutes | Serves: 4)

Ingredients
- 6 Lobster Tails
- 4 garlic cloves
- ¼ c. butter

Directions:
1. Preheat the Ninja Foodi to 400 degrees F at first
2. Open the lobster tails gently by using kitchen scissors
3. Remove the lobster meat gently from the shells but keep it inside the shells
4. Take a plate and place it
5. Add some butter in a pan and allow it melt
6. Put some garlic cloves in it and heat it over medium-low heat
7. Pour the garlic butter mixture all over the lobster tail meat
8. Let the fryer to broil the lobster at 130 degrees F
9. Remove the lobster meat from Ninja Foodi and set aside
10. Use a fork to pull out the lobster meat from the shells entirely
11. Pour some garlic butter over it if needed

Nutritional Info: 160 calories, 1g fat, 3g carbs, 20g protein

Mesmerizing Salmon Loaf

(Cooking Time: 6 hours 10 mins | Serves: 6)

Ingredients
- 2 slightly beaten eggs
- 1 c. chicken broth
- ¼ c. shredded cheddar cheese
- 2 c. stuffing croutons, seasoned
- 7 oz. drained salmon, skinless and boneless

Directions:
1. Mix all the ingredients except salmon in a bowl then add salmon and combine it well
2. Spray the inside of the Ninja Foodi with cooking spray
3. Make it into a loaf shape
4. Cook for 4-6 hours on low heat
5. Serve and enjoy!

Nutritional Info: 220 calories, 5g fat, 13g carbs, 20g protein

Cajun Spiced Salmon

Serves: 2 , Cooking Time: 8 minutes

Ingredients:
- 2 (6-oz.) salmon steaks
- 2 tbsp. Cajun seasoning

Directions:
1) Rub the salmon steaks with the Cajun seasoning evenly and set aside for about 10 minutes.
2) Arrange the "Cook & Crisp Basket" in the pot of Ninja Foodi.
3) Close the Ninja Foodi with crisping lid and select "Air Crisp".
4) Press "Start/Stop" to begin and set the temperature to 390 degrees F.
5) Set the time for 5 minutes to preheat.
6) Now, place the salmon steaks into "Cook & Crisp Basket".
7) Close the Ninja Foodi with crisping lid and select "Air Crisp".
8) Set the temperature to 390 degrees F for 4 minutes per side.
9) Press "Start/Stop" to begin. Open the lid and serve.

Nutrition Information:
Calories: 225; Carbohydrates: 0g; Protein: 33.1g; Fat: 10.5g; Sugar: 0g; Sodium: 225mg; Fiber: 0g

Wine Braised Salmon

Serves: 6 , Cooking Time: 1 hour

Ingredients:
- 1½ C. chicken broth
- ½ C. white wine
- 1 shallot, sliced thinly
- 4 (4-oz.) salmon fillets
- Salt and freshly ground black pepper, to taste

Directions:
1) In the pot of Ninja Foodi, mix together broth, shallot and lemon.
2) Arrange salmon fillets on top, skin side down and sprinkle with salt and black pepper.
3) Close the crisping lid and select "Slow Cooker".
4) Set on "Low" for about 45-60 minutes.
5) Press "Start/Stop" to begin.
6) Open the lid and serve hot.

Nutrition Information:
Calories: 192; Carbohydrates: 1.9g; Protein: 24g; Fat: 7.5g; Sugar: 0.5g; Sodium: 377mg; Fiber: 0g

Miso Glazed Salmon

Serves: 4, Cooking Time: 9 minutes

Ingredients:

- 4 (4-oz.) (1-inch thick) frozen skinless salmon fillets
- Salt, to taste
- 2 tbsp. butter, softened
- 2 tbsp. red miso paste
- 2 heads baby bok choy, stems on, cut in half

Directions:

1) In the pot of Ninja Foodi, place ½ C. of water. In the pot, arrange the reversible rack in higher position. Season the salmon fillets with salt evenly.
2) Place the salmon fillets over the rack. Cover the Ninja Foodi with the pressure lid and place the pressure valve to "Seal" position.
3) Select "Pressure" and set to "High" for about 2 minutes.
4) Press "Start/Stop" to begin. Switch the valve to "Vent" and do a "Quick" release.
5) Meanwhile, spray the bok choy with cooking spray evenly.
6) In a bowl, add the butter and miso paste and mix well. Once all the pressure is released, open the lid. With paper towels, pat dry the salmon fillets and then, coat them with butter mixture evenly.
7) Arrange the bok choy around the salmon fillets,
8) Now, close the Ninja Foodi with crisping lid and select "Broil".
9) Set time to 7 minutes and select "Start/Stop" to begin.
10) Open the lid and serve the salmon fillets alongside the bok choy.

Nutrition Information:

Calories: 210; Carbohydrates: 9g; Protein: 24.2g; Fat: 9g; Sugar: 5.5g; Sodium: 897mg; Fiber: 3.4g

French Salmon Meal

Serves: 6 , Cooking Time: 5 hours 55 minutes

Ingredients:

- ¾ C. green lentils
- 1 C. carrot, peeled and chopped
- 2 C. chicken broth
- Salt and freshly ground black pepper, to taste
- 6 (4-oz.) skinless, boneless salmon fillets

Directions:

1) In the pot of Ninja Foodi, place all ingredients except the salmon and stir to combine.
2) Close the crisping lid and select "Slow Cooker".
3) Set on "High" for about 5-5½ hours
4) Press "Start/Stop" to begin.
5) Open the lid and arrange a large parchment paper over lentil mixture.
6) Season the salmon fillets with salt and black pepper evenly.
7) Arrange the salmon fillets over parchment paper in a single layer.
8) Close the crisping lid and select "Slow Cooker".
9) Set on "High" for about 25 minutes.
10) Press "Start/Stop" to begin.
11) Open the lid and serve the salmon fillets with lentil mixture.

Nutrition Information:

Calories: 247; Carbohydrates: 16.5g; Protein: 33.3g; Fat: 4.8g; Sugar: 1.6g; Sodium: 336mg; Fiber: 7.8g__

Flavorsome Salmon

Serves: 2 , Cooking Time: 13 minutes

Ingredients:

- ¼ C. soy sauce
- ¼ C. honey
- 2 tsp. rice wine vinegar
- 1 tsp. water
- 2 (4-oz.) salmon fillets

Directions:

1) In a small bowl, mix together all ingredients except salmon.
2) In a small bowl, reserve about half of the mixture. Add the salmon in remaining mixture and coat well. Refrigerate, covered to marinate for about 2 hours.
3) Arrange the "Cook & Crisp Basket" in the pot of Ninja Foodi.
4) Close the Ninja Foodi with crisping lid and select "Air Crisp".
5) Press "Start/Stop" to begin and set the temperature to 355 degrees F.
6) Set the time for 5 minutes to preheat.
7) Now, place the salmon fillets into "Cook & Crisp Basket".
8) Close the Ninja Foodi with crisping lid and select "Air Crisp".
9) Set the temperature to 355 degrees F for 13 minutes.
10) Press "Start/Stop" to begin. After 8 minutes, flip the salmon fillets and coat with reserved marinade.

11) Open the lid and serve.

Nutrition Information:
Calories: 299; Carbohydrates: 37.4g; Protein: 24.1g; Fat: 7g; Sugar: 35.3g; Sodium: 1600mg; Fiber: 0.3g

Hearty Tilapia Bowl

Serves: 2, Cooking Time: 18 minutes

Ingredients:
- 3 C. chicken broth
- 1 C. stone ground grits
- 1 C. heavy cream
- Salt, to taste
- 2 (4-oz.) tilapia fillets

Directions:
1) In the pot of Ninja Foodi, place the chicken broth, grits, heavy cream and salt and stir to combine.
2) Cover the Ninja Foodi with the pressure lid and place the pressure valve to "Seal" position. Select "Pressure" and set to "High" for about 8 minutes.
3) Press "Start/Stop" to begin. Switch the valve to "Vent" and do a "Natural" release for about 10 minutes. Then do a "Quick" release.
4) Meanwhile, spray the tilapia fillets with cooking oil spray and then, season with salt evenly.
5) Once all the pressure is released, open the lid and stir the grits mixture.
6) Arrange a large piece of fil over grits mixture.
7) Arrange the tilapia fillets over foil in a single layer.
8) Now, close the Ninja Foodi with crisping lid and select "Air Crisp".
9) Set the temperature to 400 degrees F for 10 minutes.
10) Press "Start/Stop" to begin. Open the lid and serve the tilapia fillets with grits mixture.

Nutrition Information:
Calories: 679; Carbohydrates: 72g; Protein: 37.7g; Fat: 29.2g; Sugar: 1.1g; Sodium: 1300mg; Fiber: 6g

Buttered Halibut

Serves: 4 , Cooking Time: 30 minutes

Ingredients:
- 1 lb. halibut fillets
- 2 tbsp. ginger-garlic paste
- Salt and freshly ground black pepper, to taste
- 3 green chilies, chopped
- ¾ C. butter, chopped

Directions:
1) Select "Bake/Roast" of Ninja Foodi and set the temperature to 360 degrees F.
2) Press "Start/Stop" to begin and preheat the Ninja Foodi for about 10 minutes.
3) Coat the halibut fillets with ginger-garlic paste and then, season with salt and black pepper.
4) In the pot of Ninja Foodi, place the halibut fillets and top with green chilies, followed by the butter.
5) Close the Ninja Foodi with crisping lid and set the time for 30 minutes.
6) Press "Start/Stop" to begin. Open the lid and serve.

Nutrition Information:
Calories: 517; Carbohydrates: 2.4g; Protein: 31.5g; Fat: 41.6g; Sugar: 0.2g; Sodium: 364mg; Fiber: 0.1g

Well-Seasoned Catfish

Serves: 4, Cooking Time: 23 minutes

Ingredients:
- 4 (4-oz.) catfish fillets
- ¼ C. Louisiana fish fry seasoning
- 1 tbsp. olive oil
- 1 tbsp. fresh parsley, chopped

Directions:
1) Rub the fish filets with seasoning generously and then, coat with oil.
2) Arrange the "Cook & Crisp Basket" in the pot of Ninja Foodi.
3) Close the Ninja Foodi with crisping lid and select "Air Crisp".
4) Press "Start/Stop" to begin and set the temperature to 400 degrees F.
5) Set the time for 5 minutes to preheat.

6) Now, place the fish fillets into "Cook & Crisp Basket".
7) Close the Ninja Foodi with crisping lid and select "Air Crisp".
8) Set the temperature to 400 degrees F for 23 minutes.
9) Press "Start/Stop" to begin.
10) After 10 minutes, flip the fish fillets and again after 20 minutes.
11) Open the lid and serve with the garnishing of parsley.

Nutrition Information:

Calories: 206; Carbohydrates: 4.7g; Protein: 17.7g; Fat: 12.1g; Sugar: 0g; Sodium: 201mg; Fiber: 0.7g

Family Feast Shrimp

Serves: 4, Cooking Time: 20 minutes

Ingredients:
- 1 lb. shrimp, peeled and deveined
- Salt and freshly ground black pepper, to taste
- 8-oz. coconut milk
- ½ C. panko breadcrumbs
- ½ tsp. cayenne pepper

Directions:
1) In a shallow dish, mix together the coconut milk, salt and black pepper.
2) In another shallow dish, mix together breadcrumbs, cayenne pepper, salt and black pepper.
3) Dip the shrimp in coconut milk mixture and then coat with the breadcrumbs mixture. Arrange the "Cook & Crisp Basket" in the pot of Ninja Foodi.
4) Close the Ninja Foodi with crisping lid and select "Air Crisp".
5) Press "Start/Stop" to begin and set the temperature to 350 degrees F.
6) Set the time for 5 minutes to preheat.
7) Now, place the shrimp into "Cook & Crisp Basket". Close the Ninja Foodi with crisping lid and select "Air Crisp".
8) Set the temperature to 350 degrees F for 20 minutes.
9) Press "Start/Stop" to begin. Open the lid and serve.

Nutrition Information:

Calories: 301; Carbohydrates: 12.5g; Protein: 28.2g; Fat: 15.7g; Sugar: 2.2g; Sodium: 393mg; Fiber: 2.3g

Rosemary Scallops

Serves: 6, Cooking Time: 6 minutes

Ingredients:

- ½ C. butter
- 4 garlic cloves, minced
- 2 tbsp. fresh rosemary, chopped
- 2 lb. sea scallops
- Salt and freshly ground black pepper, to taste

Directions:

1) Select "Sauté/Sear" setting of Ninja Foodi and place the butter into the pot.
2) Press "Start/Stop" to begin and heat for about 2-3 minutes.
3) Add the garlic and rosemary and cook, uncovered for about 1 minute.
4) Stir in the scallops, salt and black pepper and cook for about 2 minutes.
5) Press "Start/Stop" to stop the cooking.
6) Now, close the Ninja Foodi with crisping lid and select "Air Crisp".
7) Set the temperature to 350 degrees F for 3 minutes.
8) Press "Start/Stop" to begin. Open the lid and serve.

Nutrition Information:

Calories: 275; Carbohydrates: 4.9g; Protein: 25.7g; Fat: 16.7g; Sugar: 0g; Sodium: 380mg; Fiber: 0.5g__

Chapter 7 Appetizers Recipes

Buffalo Chicken Soup

Servings: 4 servings, **Prep Time:** 10 minutes, **Cooking Time:** 20 minutes

Ingredients:
- 1 tsp olive oil
- ½ cup chopped onion
- ½ cup chopped celery
- 3 garlic cloves, minced
- 1 ½ cup chicken broth
- 1 cup shredded cooked chicken
- 1 Tbsp Buffalo Sauce
- 4 oz cream cheese
- 1/3 cup cream

Directions:
1. Press the saute button on your Ninja Foodi and then add the oil, onion and celery to the pot. Stir and cook until the veggies are soft, about 8 minutes.
2. Add the garlic and cook for one more minute.
3. Add the chicken, broth and buffalo sauce and stir everything together.
4. Place the lid on the Ninja Foodi and seal the pot. Use the pressure cooker function and cook on high pressure for 5 minutes. Once the timer goes off, let the pressure naturally release. Open the lid.
5. Add the cream cheese and cream to the pot and stir until it is melted into the soup. Enjoy while hot.

Nutritional Info:

Calories: 244g, Carbohydrates: 5g, Protein: 13g, Fat: 22g, Sugar: 3g, Sodium: 480mg

Mini Meatballs

Servings: 4 servings, **Prep Time:** 5 minutes, **Cooking Time:** 10 minutes

Ingredients:
- 1 tsp olive oil
- 3 cups low carb tomato sauce
- 1 ½ pounds ground beef
- 1 tbsp dried parsley
- ½ cup grated parmesan cheese
- ½ cup almond flour
- 2 eggs
- 1 tsp salt
- ½ tsp ground black pepper
- 1 tsp dried oregano
- ¼ cup water

Directions:

1. Mix the ground beef, parsley, parmesan cheese, almond flour, eggs, salt and pepper together in a bowl. Use your hands to shape into mini meatballs, about 1 inch in diameter.
2. Pour the olive oil in the bottom of the Ninja Foodi and press saute. Add the meatballs to the pot and sear for two minutes on each side to brown.
3. Add the tomato sauce to the pot and close the lid.

4. Use the pressure cooker function and cook on low pressure for 10 minutes. Once the timer goes off, let the pressure naturally release for 10 minutes then open the pot and serve hot with a toothpick.

Nutritional Info:
Calories: 639g, Carbohydrates: 6g, Protein: 60g, Fat: 38g, Sugar: 8g, Sodium: 198g

Artichoke Dip

Servings: 6 servings, **Prep Time:** 2 minutes, **Cooking Time:** 6 minutes

Ingredients:
- ¼ cup chicken broth
- 4 oz cream cheese
- 5 ounces chopped spinach
- 1 cup canned artichoke hearts
- ½ cup sour cream
- 1 clove garlic
- ½ tsp onion powder
- 6 ounces parmesan cheese, grated
- 6 ounces Swiss cheese

Directions:
1. Add all the ingredients to the Ninja Foodi Pot except the parmesan cheese and Swiss cheese.
2. Close the lid and set the steamer valve to seal. Use the pressure cooker function and cook the dip on high pressure for 4 minutes. Do a quick pressure release and open the pot.
3. Add the cheeses, reserving a small amount of each, and mix. Sprinkle the final cheese over the top of the dip and lower the crisper plate over the dip.
4. Use the broil function for 2 minutes to brown the cheese. Serve hot!

Nutritional Info:
Calories: 427g, Carbohydrates: 10g, Protein: 22g, Fat: 32g, Sugar: 2g, Sodium: 812mg

Buffalo Cauliflower Bites

Servings: 4 servings, **Prep Time:** 15 minutes, **Cooking Time:** 35 minutes

Ingredients:
- 6 cups Cauliflower florets
- 1 ½ cups water
- 1/3 cup hot sauce
- 1 ½ cups cornstarch
- ½ cup almond flour
- 2 tsp baking powder
- 1 tsp garlic powder
- 1 tsp salt
- ½ tsp black pepper
- 2 eggs

Directions:
1. Add the cauliflower and ½ cup of the water to the bowl of the Ninja Foodi. Place the lid on the machine and use the pressure cooker on low

pressure to cook the cauliflower for 2 minutes. Once the cooking is complete, do a quick pressure release, and remove the lid. Cool the cauliflower in the fridge.

2. In a small bowl, mix together the corn starch, almond flour, baking powder, garlic powder, salt, eggs and pepper. Add the remaining cup of water and mix until smooth.

3. Toss the chilled cauliflower in the batter then place the coated cauliflower on a separate tray and cool in the freezer for about 30 minutes.

4. Place the chilled cauliflower in the cook and crisp basket in one layer, try not to overlap.

5. Preheat the Ninja Foodi using the air crisp setting to 350 degrees.

6. Place the cauliflower basket into the Ninja Foodi and close the crisper lid. Set the timer to twenty minutes. Remove the cauliflower once cooked and toss with the hot sauce. Serve immediately.

Nutritional Info:
Calories: 72g, Carbohydrates: 5g, Protein: 5g, Fat: 4g, Sugar: 2g, Sodium: 1405mg

Loaded Nachos

Servings: 4 servings, **Prep Time:** 10 minutes, **Cooking Time:** 25 minutes

Ingredients:
- 2 chicken breasts, boneless and skinless
- 1 cup keto salsa
- 1 tsp salt
- 1 Tbso taco seasoning
- 4 cups grain free tortilla chips
- 1 cup shredded Mexican cheese blend
- 1 jalapeno, sliced

Directions:
1. Place the chicken and salsa in the Ninja Foodi and place the lid on as well. Set the pressure cooker steam valve to seal and cook on high pressure for 15 minutes. Do a quick pressure release and remove the lid. Use two forks to shred the chicken, mixing it into the sauce.

2. Add the taco seasoning and salt to the mix and stir to combine.

3. Place the tortilla chips on top of the chicken mix inside the pot. Sprinkle the shredded cheese and jalapenos over the top of the chips then close the crisper lid and set the temperature for 360 degrees for 5 minutes.

4. Remove the perfectly browned nachos and serve while warm!

Nutritional Info:
Calories: 198g, Carbohydrates: 3g, Protein:

20g, Fat: 10g, Sugar: 4g, Sodium: 1016mg

French Onion Soup

Servings: 4 servings, **Prep Time:** 10 minutes, **Cooking Time:** 35 minutes

Ingredients:

- 2 Tbsp butter
- 2 onions, sliced
- 1 tbsp tomato paste
- 1 tbsp soy sauce
- 1 tbsp Worcestershire sauce
- 3 cups beef stock
- 1 tsp salt
- ½ tsp pepper
- 2 cups mozzarella cheese

Directions:

1. Place the butter in the bottom of the Foodi pot and turn the machine on to sear. Add the onions after the butter has melted and stir together. Cook for about 10 minutes, stirring occasionally.
2. Add the Worcestershire sauce, tomato paste and soy sauce to the pot and mix. Cook for another 5 minutes then add the remaining ingredients except the mozzarella cheese.
3. Close the pressure cooker lid and set the steamer valve to seal. Cook the soup on high pressure for 10 minutes. Once cooked, do a quick pressure release and remove the lid.
4. Sprinkle the soup with the mozzarella cheese and put the crisper lid on top. Set the Ninja Foodi to broil and the timer for 6 minutes. Once the cheese has browned, serve immediately.

Nutritional Info:

Calories: 252g, Carbohydrates: 5g, Protein: 16g, Fat: 18g, Sugar: 4g, Sodium: 1604 mg

Almond Cheddar Cornbread

Servings: 6 servings,   **Prep Time:** 15 minutes, **Cooking Time:** 25 minutes

Ingredients:

- 1 ¼ cup almond flour
- ¾ cup coconut flour
- 2 Tbsp baking stevia
- 2 tsp baking powder
- 2 tsp salt
- 1 egg
- 1 cup whole milk
- ½ cup canned corn, drained
- ¼ cup coconut oil
- 1 cup cheddar cheese

Directions:

1. Pre heat the Ninja Foodi by closing the crisper lid and pressing the broil button, setting the timer for 10 minutes.
2. In a separate bowl, mix together all the dry ingredients. Then add the remaining wet ingredients and stir until the batter is smooth. Pour the

batter into a greased eight inch baking pan and set inside the preheated Ninja Foodi on top of the reversible rack.

3. Close the crisper lid again and use the bake function, set at 350 degrees, for 25 minutes. Once the

bread begins to turn golden brown, remove it from the Foodi and allow to cool before serving.

Nutritional Info:
Calories: 621g, Carbohydrates: 7g, Protein: 14g, Fat: 57g, Sugar: 8g, Sodium: 1022 mg

Jicama Fries

Servings: 4 servings,   **Prep Time:** 5 minutes,   **Cooking Time:** 10 minutes

Ingredients:
- 1 medium jicama
- 3 Tbsp olive oil
- ½ tsp salt
- ¼ tsp ground black pepper

Directions:
1. Peel the jicama and cup it into ¼ inch strips.
2. Toss the slices with the oil, salt and pepper.

3. Place the strips in the air crisp basket, put the basket into the Ninja Foodie and put the air crisp lid on the machine.
4. Set the temperature to 390 degrees F and the timer for 20 minutes. Toss the fries occasionally to brown evenly. Serve hot

Nutritional Info:
Calories: 101g, Carbohydrates: 3g, Protein: 0g, Fat: 10g, Sugar: 2g, Sodium: 583g

The Easy Watermelon Jerky

(Cooking Time: 12 hours 10 minutes | Serves: 1 cup)

Ingredients
- 1 c. seedless watermelon, cubed

Directions:
1. Arrange watermelon cubes in single layer in the Cook and Crisp basket
2. Place the basket in the pot and close the crisping lid

3. Press the Dehydrate button and let it dehydrate for 12 hours at 135 degrees F
4. Once the dehydrating is done, remove the basket from pot and transfer jerky to your Air Tight container, serve and enjoy!

Nutrition Information: 46 calories, 0g fat, 12g carbs, 1g protein

Unsupervised Dried Mango

(Cooking Time: 8 hours 10 minutes | Serves: 2)
Ingredients

- ½ mango, peeled, pitted and sliced

Directions:

1. Arrange mango slices in single layer in the Cook and Crisp basket
2. Place the basket in the pot and close the crisping lid
3. Press the Dehydrate button and let it dehydrate for 12 hours at 135 degrees F
4. Once the dehydrating is done, remove the basket from pot and transfer slices to your Air Tight container, serve and enjoy!

Nutritional Info: 167 calories, 0g fat, 18g carbs, 1g protein

Cool Beet Chips

(Cooking Time: 8 hours 10 mins | Serves: 8)
Ingredients

- ½ beet, peeled and sliced

Directions:

1. Arrange beet slices in single layer in the Cook and Crisp basket
2. Place the basket in the pot and close the crisping lid
3. Press the Dehydrate button and let it dehydrate for 8 hours at 135 degrees F
4. Once the dehydrating is done, remove the basket from pot and transfer slices to your Air Tight container, serve and enjoy!

Nutritional Info: 35 calories, 0g fat, 8g carbs, 1g protein

Elegant Mushroom Sautee

(Cooking Time: 25 minutes | Serves: 8)
Ingredients

- 1 lb. white button mushrooms, stems trimmed
- 2 tbsps. butter, unsalted
- ½ tsp. salt
- ¼ c. water

Directions:

1. Quarter medium mushrooms and cut any large mushrooms into eight
2. Put mushrooms, butter, and salt in your Foodi's inner pot
3. Add water and lock pressure lid, making sure to seal the valve
4. Cook on HIGH pressure for 5 minutes, quick release pressure once did
5. Once done, set your pot to Sauté mode on HIGH mode and bring the mix to a boil over 5 minutes until all the water evaporates
6. Once the butter/water has evaporated, stir for 1 minute until slightly browned
7. Enjoy!

Nutritional Info: 50 calories, 4g fat, 2g carbs, 2g protein

Eggs Stuffed with Avocado & Watercress

(Cooking Time: 15 minutes | Serves: 6)

Ingredients:

- ½ tbsp. fresh lemon juice
- 1 medium ripe avocado, peeled, pitted and chopped
- 6 organic eggs, boiled, peeled and halved
- Salt
- ½ c. freshly trimmed watercress

Directions:

1. Set a steamer basket to the bottom of the Ninja Foodi and pour water.
2. Put the watercress on the basket and lock the lid.
3. Set the Ninja Foodi to "Pressure" for about 3 minutes.
4. Release the pressure quickly and drain the watercress completely.
5. Remove the egg yolks and transfer into a bowl.
6. Add watercress, avocado, lemon juice and salt and mash with a fork completely.
7. Place the egg whites in a serving dish and fill the egg whites with watercress mixture.

Nutritional Info: 132 calories, 10.9g fat, 3.3g carbs, 6.3g protein

Cheese Casserole

(Cooking Time: 37 minutes | Serves: 6)

Ingredients:

- 16 oz. marinara sauce
- 10 oz. shredded parmesan
- 2 tbsps. olive oil
- 16 oz. shredded mozzarella cheese
- 2 lbs. scrambled sausages

Directions:

1. Grease the pot of Ninja Foodi with olive oil and arrange half of the scrambled sausages.
2. Layer with half of the marinara, followed by half of the mozzarella and Parmesan cheese.
3. Top with the remaining half of the scrambled sausages, marinara, mozzarella and Parmesan cheese.
4. Press "Bake/Roast" and set the timer to 20 minutes at 360 degrees F.
5. Remove from the Ninja Foodi after 20 minutes and dish out to serve.

Nutritional Info: 521 calories, 38.8g fat, 6g carbs, 35.4g protein

Avocado Chips

(Cooking Time: 20 minutes | Serves: 4)

Ingredients:

- 4 tbsps. butter
- 4 raw avocados, peeled and sliced
- Salt and black pepper

Directions:

1. Season the avocado slices with salt and black pepper.
2. Grease the pot of Ninja Foodi with butter and add avocado slices.
3. Press "Air Crisp" and set the timer to 10 minutes at 350 degrees F.
4. Remove from the Ninja Foodi and dish out to serve.

Nutritional Info: 391 calories, 38.2g fat, 15g carbs, 3.5g protein

Mixed Nuts

(Cooking Time: 20 minutes | Serves: 5)

Ingredients:

- 1 tbsp. melted butter
- ½ c. raw cashew nuts
- 1 c. raw almonds
- 1 c. raw peanuts
- Salt

Directions:

1. Place the nuts in the pot of Ninja Foodi and lock the lid.
2. Press "Air Crisp" and set the timer to 10 minutes at 350 degrees F.

3. Remove the nuts into a bowl and add melted butter and salt.

4. Toss to coat well and return the nuts mixture into the Ninja Foodi.

5. Press "Bake/Roast" and bake for about 5 minutes.

6. Dish out to serve.

Nutritional Info: 189 calories, 16.5g fat, 6.6g carbs, 6.8g protein

Asparagus Bites

(Cooking Time: 25 minutes | Serves: 3)
Ingredients:

- 1 c. asparagus
- ½ c. coconut, desiccated
- ½ c. feta cheese

Directions:

1. Place the coconut in a shallow dish and coat asparagus with coconut evenly.

2. Place coated asparagus in the pot of Ninja Foodi and top with feta cheese.

3. Press "Air Crisp" and set the timer to 10 minutes at 360 degrees F.

4. Remove from the Ninja Foodi and dish out to serve.

5. **Nutritional Info:** 135 calories, 10.3g fat, 5g carbs, 7g protein

Zucchini Cream Cheese Fries

(Cooking Time: 20 minutes | Serves: 4)
Ingredients:

- 1 lb. zucchini, sliced
- Salt
- 1 c. cream cheese
- 2 tbsps. olive oil

Directions:

1. Put zucchini in a colander and add salt and cream cheese.

2. Put oil and zucchini in the pot of Ninja Foodi and lock the lid.

3. Press "Air Crisp" and set the timer to 10 minutes at 365 degrees F.

4. Dish out from the Ninja Foodi and serve.

Nutritional Info: 374 calories, 36.6g fat, 7.1g carbs, 7.7g protein

Chapter 8 Soup Recipes

Beefy White Cream Soup

(Serving: 2,   Cooking time: 17 minutes)

Ingredients:
- ½ pounds stew meat
- 2 cups beef broth
- 1 1/2 tablespoons Worcestershire sauce
- ½ teaspoon Italian seasoning
- 1 teaspoon onion powder
- 1 teaspoons garlic powder
- 1/4 cup sour cream
- 3 ounces mushrooms, sliced
- Salt and pepper to taste
- 2 ounces short noodles, blanched

Directions:
1. Place the meat, broth, Worcestershire sauce, Italian seasoning, onion powder, garlic powder, sour cream, and mushrooms. Season with salt and pepper to taste.
2. Install pressure lid. Close Ninja Foodi, press the pressure button, choose high settings, and set time to 12 minutes.
3. Once done cooking, do a quick release. Open the lid and press the sauté button. Stir in the noodles and allow to simmer for 5 minutes.
4. Serve and enjoy.

Nutrition information:
Calories: 599 ; carbohydrates: 65g; protein: 39.6g; fat: 20.1g

Chili-Quinoa 'n Black Bean Soup

(Serving: 2, Cooking time: 20 minutes)

Ingredients:
- 1/2 bell pepper, diced
- 1 medium-sized sweet potatoes, peeled and diced
- 1/2 onion, diced
- 1 clove garlic, minced
- 1 stalk celery, chopped
- 1 1/3 cups vegetable broth
- 1 tablespoon tomato paste
- 1/3 cup diced tomatoes
- 1/3 can black beans, rinsed and drained
- 1 teaspoon each of paprika and cumin
- Salt to taste
- 2 tbsp quinoa
- 2 cups vegetable broth

Directions:
1. Place all ingredients in the Ninja Foodi. Give a good stir.
2. Install pressure lid.
3. Close Ninja Foodi, press the pressure button, choose high settings, and set time to 20 minutes.

4. Once done cooking, do a quick release.
5. Serve and enjoy.

Nutrition information:
Calories: 377; carbohydrates: 73.7g; protein: 18.1g; fat: 1.0g

Filling Cauli-Squash Chowder

Serving: 2, Cooking time: 12 minutes

Ingredients:
- 1 tablespoon oil
- 1/2 onion, diced
- 1 clove garlic, minced
- 1/2-pound frozen cauliflower
- 1/2-pound frozen butternut squash
- 1 cup vegetable broth
- 1/2 teaspoon paprika
- 1/2 teaspoon dried thyme
- Salt and pepper to taste
- 1/4 cup half-and-half

Directions:
1. Press the sauté button on the Ninja Foodi and heat oil.
2. Stir in the onions and garlic. Sauté until fragrant.
3. Add the rest of the ingredients.
4. Install pressure lid. Close Ninja Foodi, press the button, choose high settings, and set time to 10 minutes.
5. Once done cooking, do a quick release.
6. Open the lid and transfer the contents into a blender. Pulse until smooth. Serve with cheese on top if desired.
7. Serve and enjoy.

Nutrition information:
Calories: 103; carbohydrates:15.2 g; protein:1.9 g; fat: 3.8g

Sweet Potato 'n Garbanzo Soup

Serving: 2, Cooking time: 10 minutes

Ingredients:
- 1/2 yellow onion, chopped
- 1/2 tablespoon garlic, minced
- 1 can garbanzo beans, drained
- 1/2-pound sweet potatoes, peeled and chopped
- Salt and pepper to taste
- 1/2 teaspoon ground ginger
- 1/2 teaspoon ground cumin
- 1/2 teaspoon ground coriander
- 1/2 teaspoon ground cinnamon
- 2 cups vegetable broth
- 2 cups spinach, torn

Directions:
1. Place all ingredients in the Ninja Foodi except for the spinach.

2. Install pressure lid. Close Ninja Foodi, press the manual button, choose high settings, and set time to 10 minutes.
3. Once done cooking, do a quick release.

4. Open the lid and stir in the spinach. Press the sauté button and allow to simmer until the spinach wilts.
5. Serve and enjoy.

Nutrition information:
Calories: 165; carbohydrates: 32.3g; protein: 6.3g; fat: 1.1g

Vegan Approver Tortilla Soup

Serving: 2, Cooking time: 40 minutes

Ingredients:
- 1/2 cup diced onion
- 1/2 bell pepper, diced
- 1/2 jalapeno pepper, diced
- 1 1/4 cups vegetable broth
- 1/2 can tomato sauce
- 1/4 cup salsa verde
- 1/2 tablespoon tomato paste
- 1/2 can black beans, drained and rinsed
- 1/2 can pinto beans, drained and rinsed
- 1/2 cup fresh corn kernels
- ½ teaspoon chili powder
- ½ teaspoon garlic powder
- Salt and pepper to taste
- 2 tbsp heavy cream

Directions:
1. Place all ingredients in the Ninja Foodi except for the heavy cream and give a good stir.
2. Install pressure lid. Close Ninja Foodi, press the manual button, choose high settings, and set time to 20 minutes.
3. Once done cooking, do a quick release.
4. Open the lid and press the sauté button. Stir in the heavy cream and allow to simmer for 5 minutes.
5. Serve and enjoy.

Nutrition information:
Calories: 341; carbohydrates: 48.7g; protein: 8.6g; fat: 12.4g

Spiced Potato-Cauliflower Chowder

Serving: 2, Cooking time: 7 minutes

Ingredients:

- 1 head cauliflower, cut into florets
- 2 small red potatoes, peeled and sliced
- 4 cups vegetable stock
- 6 cloves of garlic, minced
- 1 onion, diced
- 1 cup heavy cream
- 2 bay leaves
- Salt and pepper to taste
- 2 stalks of green onions

Directions:

1. Place the cauliflower, potatoes, vegetable stock, garlic, onion, heavy cream, and bay leaves in the Ninja Foodi. Season with salt and pepper to taste.
2. Install pressure lid. Close Ninja Foodi, press the pressure button, choose high settings, and set time to 6 minutes.
3. Once done cooking, do a quick release.
4. Open the lid and stir in the green onions.
5. Serve and enjoy.

Nutrition information:

Calories: 448; carbohydrates: 47.7g; protein: 10.1g; fat: 24.1g

Healthy Celery 'n Kale Soup

Serving: 2, Cooking time: 35 minutes

Ingredients:

- 1 teaspoon olive oil
- 1/2 onion, diced
- 1 clove garlic, minced
- 1 stalk celery, chopped
- 1 carrot, peeled and chopped
- 1 small potato, peeled and diced
- 1 teaspoon herbs de provence
- 1/2 can diced tomatoes
- 2 cups vegetable broth
- 2 cups green lentils, soaked overnight
- Salt and pepper to taste
- 1 cup kale, torn

Directions:

1. Press the sauté button on the Ninja Foodi and heat the oil.
2. Sauté the onion, garlic, and celery until fragrant.
3. Stir in the carrots, potatoes, herbs, tomatoes, vegetable broth and lentils. Season with salt and pepper to taste.
4. Install pressure lid. Close Ninja Foodi, press the pressure button, choose high settings, and set time to 30 minutes.

5. Once done cooking, do a quick release. Open the lid and stir in the kale while still hot. Serve and enjoy.

Nutrition information:
Calories: 331; carbohydrates: 53g; protein: 23g; fat: 3g

Coconut, Apple 'n Squash Chowder

Serving: 2, Cooking time: 15 minutes

Ingredients:
- 3/4 cup vegetable stock
- 1 cloves of garlic, minced
- 1 small carrot, diced
- 1 granny smith apple, cored and diced
- 1/2 small squash, seeded and diced
- 1/2 onion, diced
- Salt and pepper to taste
- A pinch of ground cinnamon
- 1/4 cup canned coconut milk
- A pinch of paprika powder

Directions:
1. In the Ninja Foodi, put in the vegetable stock, garlic, carrots, apples, and squash. Season with salt and pepper to taste and sprinkle with cinnamon.
2. Install pressure lid.
3. Close Ninja Foodi, press the manual button, choose high settings, and set time to 15 minutes.
4. Once done cooking, do a quick release.
5. Open the lid and press the sauté button. Stir in the coconut milk.
6. Using an immersion blender, pulse until the mixture becomes smooth.
7. Sprinkle with paprika on top.
8. Serve and enjoy.

Nutrition information:
Calories: 89; carbohydrates: 9.7g; protein: 1.4g; fat: 4.9g

Chickpea and potato soup

Serving: 2, Cooking time: 15 minutes

Ingredients:
- 1 tablespoon olive oil
- ½ onion, chopped
- 3 cloves of garlic, minced
- ½ cup chopped tomato
- 1/8 teaspoon fennel space
- ½ teaspoon onion powder
- ¼ teaspoon garlic powder
- ½ teaspoon oregano
- ¼ teaspoon cinnamon
- ½ teaspoon thyme
- 1 large potato, peeled and cubed
- ¾ cup carrots, chopped
- 1 ½ cups cooked chickpeas
- 1 cup water
- 1 cup almond milk

- 1 cup kale, chopped
- Salt and pepper to taste

Directions:
1. Press the sauté button on the Ninja Foodi and sauté the onion and garlic until fragrant.
2. Stir in the tomatoes, fennel, onion powder, garlic powder, oregano, cinnamon, and thyme. Stir until well-combined.
3. Add the rest of the ingredients. Install pressure lid. Close Ninja Foodi, press the pressure button, choose high settings, and set time to 10 minutes.
4. Once done cooking, do a quick release. Serve and enjoy.

Nutrition information:
Calories: 543; carbohydrates: 91.0g; protein: 17.7g; fat: 12g

Deliciously Traditional Clam Chowder

Servings: 2, Cooking time: 17 minutes

Ingredients:
- 2 6.5-oz cans chopped clams (reserve the clam juice)
- Water
- 2 slices bacon, chopped
- 1 1/2 tbsp butter
- 1 onion, diced
- 1 stalks celery, diced
- 1 sprig fresh thyme
- 1 cloves garlic, pressed or finely minced
- 1/2 tsp kosher salt or more
- 1/4 tsp pepper
- ½-lb potatoes, diced
- 1/2 tsp sugar
- 1/2 cup half and half
- Chopped chives, for garnish

Directions:
1. Drain the clam juice into a 2-cup measuring cup. Add enough water to make 2 cups of liquid. Set the clams and juice/water aside.
2. Press sauté button and cook bacon for 3 minutes until fat has rendered out of it, but not crispy. Add the butter, onion, celery, and thyme. Cook for 5 minutes while frequently stirring. Add the garlic, salt, and pepper. Cook for 1 minute, stirring frequently.
3. Add the potatoes, sugar (if using) and clam juice/water mixture and deglaze pot. Press stop.
4. Close Ninja Foodi, press pressure cook button, choose high settings, and set time to 4 minutes. Once done cooking, do a natural release for 3 minutes and then do a quick release. Mash the potatoes. Stir in half and half and the clams. Mix well.
5. Serve and enjoy garnished with chives.

Nutrition information:
Calories: 381; carbohydrates: 32.8g; protein: 29.3g; fat: 14.7

Chapter 9 Dessert Recipes

Strawberry Cake

Servings: 6 servings, **Prep Time:** 15 minutes, **Cooking Time:** 25 minutes

Ingredients:

- 8 Tbsp butter
- ½ cup Baking Stevia
- 1 egg
- 1 tsp vanilla
- 2 cups almond flour
- 2 tsp baking powder
- 1 tsp salt
- 1 cup chopped strawberries
- ½ cup buttermilk

Directions:

1. Use an electric mixer to cream the butter and stevia together until they are light and fluffy.
2. Mix the vanilla and eggs in a small bowl then add to the mixer with the butter blend. Ix until just combined
3. In a separate bowl, toss the raspberries and ¼ cup almond flour to coat the berries.
4. Add the remaining dry ingredients to the mixer and fold together by hand. Add the buttermilk and mix until smooth.
5. Add the Strawberries to the batter and mix briefly.
6. Pour the cake batter into your Ninja Foodi and place the lid on.
7. Press the air crisp button and set the temperature to 350 degrees and program the timer to 25 minutes.
8. Once cooked, a toothpick should come out of the center of the cake cleanly. Allow to cool and serve.

Nutritional Info:

Calories: 216g, Carbohydrates: 3g , Protein: 4g, Fat: 21g, Sugar: 3g, Sodium: 538 g

Balsamic Roasted Strawberries

Servings: 4 servings, **Prep Time:** 5 minutes, **Cooking Time:** 10 minutes

Ingredients:

- 4 Cups whole Strawberries
- ½ cup balsamic vinegar
- 2 Tbsp stevia

Directions:

1. Place all the ingredients into the pot of the Ninja Foodi and close the crisper lid.
2. Press the air crisp button and set the temperature to 350 degrees and program the timer to 10 minutes.
3. Serve hot or chilled

Nutritional Info:

Calories: 172g, Carbohydrates: 21g, Protein: 0g, Fat: 0g, Sugar: 37g, Sodium: 20mg

Almond Cake

Servings: 8 servings, **Prep Time:** 15 minutes, **Cooking Time:** 25 minutes

Ingredients:

- 8 Tbsp butter
- ½ cup Baking Stevia
- 1 egg
- 1 tsp vanilla
- 2 cups almond flour
- 2 tsp baking powder
- 1 tsp salt
- 1 cup chopped Almonds
- ½ cup buttermilk

Directions:

1. Use an electric mixer to cream the butter and stevia together until they are light and fluffy.
2. Mix the vanilla and eggs in a small bowl then add to the mixer with the butter blend until just combined
3. Add the remaining dry ingredients to the mixer and fold together by hand. Add the buttermilk and mix until smooth.
4. Add the almonds to the batter and mix briefly.
5. Pour the cake batter into your Ninja Foodi and place the lid on.
6. Press the air crisp button and set the temperature to 350 degrees and program the timer to 25 minutes.
7. Once cooked, a toothpick should come out of the center of the cake cleanly. Allow to cool and serve.

Nutritional Info:

Calories: 295 g, Carbohydrates: 6g , Protein: 7g, Fat: 29 g, Sugar: 1g, Sodium: 165 mg

Key Lime Curd

Servings: 6 servings, **Prep Time:** 10 minutes, **Cooking Time:** 10 minutes

Ingredients:

- 3 oz butter
- ½ cup baking stevia
- 2 eggs
- 2 egg yolks
- 2/3 cup key lime juice
- 2 tsp lime zest

Directions:

1. Blend the butter and stevia then add in the eggs slowly, creating an emulsion.
2. Add the key lime juice and zest and the separate into mason jars
3. Add 1 ½ cups of water to the bottom of the Ninja Foodi and place the mason jars on top of the metal trivet inside the pot.
4. Place the pressure cooker lid on the pot and set the pressure cooker function to high pressure for 10 minutes. Let the pressure release naturally after the cooking time is completed.
5. Let cool and then enjoy.

Nutritional Info:

Calories: 151g, Carbohydrates: 3g, Protein: 3g, Fat: 15g, Sugar: 1g, Sodium: 109mg

Chocolate Cheese Cake

Servings: 6 servings, **Prep Time:** 15 minutes, **Cooking Time:** 20 minutes

Ingredients:

Crust: ¼ cup almond flour

- ¼ cup coconut flour
- 2 Tbsp stevia
- 2 Tbsp melted butter

Filling: 16 oz cream cheese

- ½ cup baking stevia
- 1/3 cup cocoa powder
- 1 egg and 2 egg yolks
- ¼ cup sour cream
- ¾ cup heavy cream
- 6 oz melted chocolate
- 1 tsp vanilla

Directions:

1. In a small bowl, mix all the ingredients for the crust together. Press the crust into a 7" spring form pan wrapped in foil. Set aside

2. Add the cream cheese, stevia and cocoa powder to a food processor and blend. Add the egg and yolks and blend again. Add remaining ingredients and mix just to combine. Pour cheesecake mix on top of the prepared crust.

3. Place the pan in the Ninja Foodi bowl on top of the metal trivet. Add 2 cups of water to the bowl under the cake. Place the pressure cooker lid on and set it to high pressure for 20 minutes. Allow the pot to naturally release the pressure once he cooking time is done. Chill and then serve.

Nutritional Info:

Calories: 474 g, Carbohydrates: 10g , Protein: 8g, Fat: 46 g, Sugar: 4g, Sodium: 338 g

Lemon Ricotta Cake

Servings: 6 servings, **Prep Time:** 15 minutes, **Cooking Time:** 20 minutes

Ingredients:

Crust: ¼ cup almond flour

- ¼ cup coconut flour
- 2 Tbsp stevia
- 2 Tbsp melted butter

Filling: 8 oz cream cheese

- ½ cup baking stevia
- 8 ounces ricotta
- 1 egg and 2 egg yolks
- ¼ cup sour cream
- ¾ cup heavy cream
- 2 Tsp lemon zest
- 1 tsp vanilla

Directions:

1. In a small bowl, mix all the ingredients for the crust together. Press the crust into a 7" spring form pan wrapped in foil. Set aside

2. Add the cream cheese, stevia and ricotta to a food processor and blend. Add the egg and yolks and blend again. Add remaining ingredients and mix just to combine. Pour cheesecake mix on top of the prepared crust.

3. Place the pan in the Ninja Foodi bowl on top of the metal trivet. Add 2 cups of water to the bowl under the cake.

Place the pressure cooker lid on and set it to high pressure for 20 minutes. Allow the pot to naturally release the pressure once he cooking time is done. Chill and then serve.

Nutritional Info:
Calories: 483 g, Carbohydrates: 10g , Protein: 7g, Fat: 36 g, Sugar: 4g, Sodium: 338g

Almond Cheese Cake

Servings: 6 servings, **Prep Time:** 15 minutes, **Cooking Time:** 20 minutes

Ingredients:

Crust: ½ cup almond flour

- 2 Tbsp stevia
- 2 Tbsp melted butter

Filling: 16 oz cream cheese

- ½ cup baking stevia
- 1 egg
- 2 egg yolks
- ¼ cup sour cream
- ¾ cup heavy cream
- 1 tsp almond extract

Directions:

1. In a small bowl, mix all the ingredients for the crust together. Press the crust into a 7" spring form pan wrapped in foil. Set aside

2. Add the cream cheese, stevia and cocoa powder to a food processor and blend. Add the egg and yolks and blend again. Add remaining ingredients and mix just to combine. Pour cheesecake mix on top of the prepared crust.

3. Place the pan in the Ninja Foodi bowl on top of the metal trivet. Add 2 cups of water to the bowl under the cake. Place the pressure cooker lid on and set it to high pressure for 20 minutes. Allow the pot to naturally release the pressure once he cooking time is done. Chill and then serve.

Nutritional Info:
Calories: 474g, Carbohydrates: 10g, Protein:8g, Fat: 46g, Sugar: 4g, Sodium: 338g

Raspberry Mug Cake

Servings: 2 servings, **Prep Time:** 5 minutes, **Cooking Time:** 10 minutes

Ingredients:

- 2/3 cup almond flour
- 2 eggs
- 2 Tbsp maple syrup
- 1 tsp vanilla
- 1/8 tsp salt
- 1 cup fresh raspberries

Directions:

1. Mix all the ingredients together except the raspberries. Fold well to ensure no lumps.
2. Fold in raspberries
3. Pour the batter into two 8 oz mason jars and cover the jars with foil.
4. Place the metal trivet into the Ninja Foodi and add 1 cup of water to the bowl.
5. Place the two mason jars on top of the trivet and close the pressure cooker top. Seal the steamer valve and set the timer to 10 minutes
6. Let the pressure naturally release and then open the lid and enjoy the warm cake.

Nutritional Info:

Calories: 215g, Carbohydrates: 10g, Protein: 9g, Fat: 10g, Sugar: 16g, Sodium: 82m

Strawberry Chocolate Chip Mug Cake

Servings: 2 servings, **Prep Time:** 5 minutes, **Cooking Time:** 10 minutes

Ingredients:

- 2/3 cup almond flour
- 2 eggs
- 2 Tbsp maple syrup
- 1 tsp vanilla
- 1/8 tsp salt
- ½ cup chopped strawberries
- ¼ cup dark chocolate chips

Directions:

1. Mix all the ingredients together except the strawberries and chocolate chips. Fold well to ensure no lumps.
2. Fold in strawberries and chocolate chips.
3. Pour the batter into two 8 oz mason jars and cover the jars with foil.
4. Place the metal trivet into the Ninja Foodi and add 1 cup of water to the bowl.
5. Place the two mason jars on top of the trivet and close the pressure cooker top. Seal the steamer valve and set the timer to 10 minutes
6. Let the pressure naturally release and then open the lid and enjoy the warm cake.

Nutritional Info:

Calories: 326g, Carbohydrates: 35g, Protein: 8g, Fat: 18g, Sugar: 26g, Sodium: 228mg

Chocolate Mug Cake

Servings: 2 servings, **Prep Time:** 5 minutes, **Cooking Time:** 10 minutes

Ingredients:

- 2/3 cup almond flour
- ¼ cup cocoa powder
- 2 eggs
- 2 Tbsp maple syrup
- 1 tsp vanilla
- ¼ tsp salt

Directions:

1. Mix all the ingredients together. Fold well to ensure no lumps.
2. Pour the batter into two 8 oz mason jars and cover the jars with foil.
3. Place the metal trivet into the Ninja Foodi and add 1 cup of water to the bowl.
4. Place the two mason jars on top of the trivet and close the pressure cooker top. Seal the steamer valve and set the timer to 10 minutes
5. Let the pressure naturally release and then open the lid and enjoy the warm cake.

Nutritional Info:

Calories: 208g, Carbohydrates: 22g, Protein: 10g, Fat: 11g, Sugar: 16g, Sodium: 1238mg

Coconut Cake

Servings: 6 servings, **Prep Time:** 15 minutes, **Cooking Time:** 25 minutes

Ingredients:

- 8 Tbsp butter
- ½ cup Baking Stevia
- 1 egg
- 1 tsp vanilla
- 1 cup coconut flour
- ½ cup almond flour
- ½ cup shredded coconut, unsweetened
- 2 tsp baking powder
- 1 tsp salt
- 1 cup chopped strawberries
- ½ cup buttermilk

Directions:

1. Use an electric mixer to cream the butter and stevia together until they are light and fluffy.
2. Mix the vanilla and eggs in a small bowl then add to the mixer with the butter blend until just combined
3. Add the remaining dry ingredients to the mixer and fold together by hand. Add the buttermilk and mix until smooth.
4. Pour the cake batter into your Ninja Foodi and place the lid on.
5. Press the air crisp button and set the temperature to 350 degrees and program the timer to 25 minutes.

6. Once cooked, a toothpick should come out of the center of the cake cleanly. Allow to cool and serve.

Nutritional Info:
Calories: 197 g, Carbohydrates: 6g , Protein: 3g, Fat: 18 g, Sugar: 2g, Sodium: 559 mg

Carrot Pecan

Servings: 6 servings, **Prep Time:** 15 minutes, **Cooking Time:** 25 minutes

Ingredients:
- 8 Tbsp butter
- ½ cup Baking Stevia
- 1 egg
- 1 tsp vanilla
- 1 cup almond flour
- 1 cup pecan flour
- 1 cup shredded carrots
- 2 tsp baking powder
- 1 tsp salt
- ¼ cup buttermilk

Directions:
1. Use an electric mixer to cream the butter and stevia together until they are light and fluffy.
2. Mix the vanilla and eggs in a small bowl then add to the mixer with the butter blend until just combined
3. Add the remaining dry ingredients to the mixer and fold together by hand. Add the buttermilk and mix until smooth.
4. Pour the cake batter into your Ninja Foodi and place the lid on.
5. Press the air crisp button and set the temperature to 350 degrees and program the timer to 25 minutes.
6. Once cooked, a toothpick should come out of the center of the cake cleanly. Allow to cool and serve.

Nutritional Info:
Calories: 334 g, Carbohydrates: 17g , Protein: 5g, Fat: 29 g, Sugar: 5g, Sodium: 722 mg

Crunchy Cinnamon Topped Peaches

Servings: 2, Cooking time: 30 minutes

Ingredients:
- 2 cups sliced peaches, frozen
- 1 1/2 tablespoons sugar
- 1 tablespoon flour, white
- 1/2 teaspoon sugar, white
- 2 tbsp flour, white
- 3 tbsp oats, dry rolled
- 1 1/2 tablespoons butter, unsalted
- 1/2 teaspoons cinnamon
- 1 ½ tablespoons pecans, chopped

Directions:
1) Lightly grease the pot of Ninja Foodi with cooking spray. Mix in a tsp cinnamon, 2 tbsp flour, 3 tbsp sugar, and peaches.
2) For 20 minutes, bake on 300°F.

3) Mix the rest of the ingredients: in a bowl. Pour over peaches.
4) Bake for 10 minutes more at 330°F.
5) Serve and enjoy.

Nutrition information:
Calories: 435; carbs: 74.1g; protein: 4.3g; fat: 13.4g

Nutty Cinnamon   'n cranberry Cake

Servings: 2, Cooking time: 25 minutes

Ingredients:

- 2 tbsp cashew milk (or use any dairy or non-dairy milk you prefer)
- 1 medium egg
- 1/2 tsp vanilla extract
- 1/2 cup almond flour
- 2 tbsp monk fruit (or use your preferred sweetener)
- 1/4 tsp baking powder
- 1/4 tsp cinnamon
- 1/8 tsp salt
- 3 tbsp fresh cranberries
- 2 tbsp cup chopped pecans

Directions:

1) In blender, add all wet ingredients: and mix well. Add all dry ingredients: except for cranberries and pecans. Blend well until smooth.
2) Lightly grease baking pot of Ninja Foodi with cooking spray. Pour in batter. Drizzle cranberries on top and then followed by pecans.
3) For 20 minutes, cook on 330°F.
4) Let stand for 5 minutes.
5) Serve and enjoy.

Nutrition information:
Calories: 98; carbs: 11.7g; protein: 1.7g; fat: 4.9g

Fruity and Tasty Vegan Crumble

Servings: 2, Cooking time: 15 minutes

Ingredients:

- 1 medium apple, finely diced
- ½ cup frozen blueberries, strawberries, or peaches
- ¼ cup plus 1 tablespoon sear button rice flour
- 2 tablespoons sugar
- ½ teaspoon ground cinnamon
- 2 tablespoons nondairy butter

Directions:

1) Lightly grease pot of Ninja Foodi with cooking spray.
2) Spread frozen blueberries and apple slices on bottom of pot.
3) In a bowl, whisk well butter, cinnamon, sugar, and flour. Sprinkle over fruit. If needed, sprinkle extra flour to cover exposed fruit.
4) For 15 minutes, bake at 350°F

5) Serve and enjoy.

Nutrition information:

Calories: 281; carbs: 40.1g; protein: 2.0g; fat: 12.5g

Choco-Coffee Cake

Servings: 2, Cooking time: 25 minutes

Ingredients:
- 4 tbsp granulated sweetener
- 3 small eggs
- 1/8 teaspoon salt
- 2 tbsp almond flour
- 1 1/4 tablespoons unsweetened cocoa powder
- 1/2 teaspoon vanilla extract
- 1 tablespoon instant coffee crystals
- 2 tbsp heavy cream
- 1-ounce unsweetened chocolate
- 1/4 cup butter
- Coconut oil spray

Directions:
1. Grease sides and bottom of Ninja Foodi with cooking spray.
2. Press sauté button. Add butter and chocolate. Mix well. Make sure to mix constantly so as the bottom doesn' t burn. Once fully incorporated, press stop to keep warm.
3. Meanwhile, in a small bowl whisk well vanilla, coffee crystals, and heavy cream.
4. In another bowl, mix well salt, almond flour, and cocoa powder.
5. In a mixing bowl, beat eggs until thick and pale, around 5 minutes while slowly stirring in sweetener.
6. While beating, slowly drizzle and mix in melted butter mixture.
7. Mix in the almond flour mixture and mix well.
8. Add the coffee mixture and beat until fully incorporated.
9. Pour batter into Ninja Foodi.
10. Cover pot, press bake button, and bake for 20 minutes at 350°F.

Nutrition information:
Calories: 407; carbohydrates: 27.9g; protein: 3.6g; fat: 31.2g

Chocolatey 'n Peanut Butter Cakes

Servings: 2, Cooking time: 15 minutes

Ingredients:

- 1/2 can black beans, drained and rinsed
- 1/4 cup cocoa powder, unsweetened
- 1/4 cup egg whites
- 2 tbsp canned pumpkin
- 2 tbsp unsweetened applesauce
- 2 tbsp sear button sugar
- 1/2 teaspoon vanilla extract
- ¾ teaspoon baking powder
- ¼ teaspoon salt
- 1 1/2 tablespoon peanut butter baking chips

Directions:

1. Place all the ingredients except the peanut butter chips inside a food processor. Process until smooth.

2. Add the peanut butter chips and fold until evenly distributed within the batter.
3. Place the batter in a ramekin sprayed with cooking oil.
4. Place a steam rack in the Ninja Foodi and add 1 cup water.
5. Place the ramekins with the batter onto the steamer rack.
6. Install pressure lid. Close the lid and press the manual button. Cook on high for 10 minutes.
7. Do natural pressure release.
8. Serve chilled.

Nutrition information:
Calories: 246; carbohydrates: 34.9g; protein: 12.0g; fat: 6.5

Easy Peasy Applesauce

Servings: 2, Cooking time: 8 minutes

Ingredients:

- 2 medium apples, peeled and cored
- 1 cup water
- 2 teaspoons cinnamon, ground

Directions:

1. Place the apples in the Ninja Foodi. Pour in the water.
2. Install pressure lid. Close the lid and press the manual button. Cook on high for 8 minutes.

3. Do natural pressure release and open the lid.
4. Remove the excess water. Place the apples in a blender and process until smooth.
5. Add the rest of the ingredients.
6. Serve chilled.

Nutrition information:
Calories: 108; carbohydrates: 25.7g; protein: 0.5g; fat: 0.3g

Scrumptiously Molten Lava Cake

Servings: 3, Cooking time: 6 minutes

Ingredients:
- 1 egg
- 4 tablespoon sugar
- 2 tablespoon olive oil
- 4 tablespoon milk
- 4 tablespoon all-purpose flour
- 1 tablespoon cacao powder
- ½ teaspoon baking powder
- Pinch of salt
- Powdered sugar for dusting

Directions:
1. Grease two ramekins with butter or oil. Set aside
2. Pour 1 cup of water in the Ninja Foodi and place the steamer rack.
3. In a medium bowl, mix all the ingredients except the powdered sugar. Blend until well combined.
4. Pour in the ramekins. Place the ramekins in the Ninja Foodi.
5. Install pressure lid and close. Press the pressure button and cook on high for 6 minutes.
6. Once the Ninja Foodi beeps, remove the ramekin.
7. Sprinkle powdered sugar once cooled.
8. Serve and enjoy.

Nutrition information:
Calories: 290; carbohydrates: 30.0g; protein: 5.2g; fat: 16.6g

Sweet Sticky Coco-Rice

Servings: 2, Cooking time: 20 minutes

Ingredients:
- 1/2 cup Thai sweet rice
- ¾ cup water
- 1/2 can full fat coconut milk
- A pinch of salt
- 2 tablespoons pure sugar
- 1/4 teaspoon cornstarch + 1 tablespoon water
- 1 small mango, sliced
- Sesame seeds for garnish

Directions:
1. Place rice and water in the Ninja Foodi.
2. Install pressure lid. Close the lid and press the pressure button. Cook on high for 5 minutes.
3. Turn off the Ninja Foodi and do natural pressure release for 10 minutes.
4. While the rice is cooking, place the coconut milk, salt, and sugar in a saucepan. Heat over medium heat for 10 minutes while stirring constantly.

5. Once the Ninja Foodi lid can be open, add the coconut milk mixture. Stir well. Place a clean kitchen towel over the opening of the lid and let it rest for 10 minutes.
6. Meanwhile, mix cornstarch with water and add to the rice. Press the sauté button and mix until the rice becomes creamy and thick.
7. Serve with mango slices and sesame seeds.

Nutrition information:

Calories: 318; carbohydrates: 36.5g; protein: 3.5g; fat: 17.5g

Orange-Cranberry Pudding

Servings: 2, Cooking time: 20 minutes

Ingredients:
- 1/3 cup cranberries
- 1 tablespoon butter, softened
- 1/3 cup sugar
- 1/4 tablespoon vanilla
- 1 orange, juiced and zested
- 1 cup half and half
- 1 1/2 cups brioche, cube
- 2 egg yolks

Directions:
1. In a 6-inch square baking dish, mix well vanilla extract, half & half, orange juice, zest, juice, cranberries, and eggs. Mix thoroughly.
2. Add cubed brioche and toss well to coat in egg mixture. Let it soak for ten minutes. Cover the top with foil.
3. Prepare the Ninja Foodi by placing the inner pot inside.
4. Place wire rack inside and add 2 cups of water.
5. Place baking dish on wire rack.
6. Install pressure lid. Cover and lock lid. Press steam button. Set the timer to 15 minutes.
7. Once done cooking, press stop, and do a quick release.
8. Let it cool completely before serving.

Nutrition information:

Calories: 326; carbohydrates: 48.6g; protein: 5.9g; fat: 12.0g

Coconutty-Blueberry Cake

Servings: 2, Cooking time: 10 minutes

Ingredients:
- 1/4 cup coconut flour
- 2 large eggs
- 1/2 teaspoon baking soda
- 1/4 cup coconut milk
- 1/4 teaspoon lemon zest

Directions:
1. Combine all ingredients in a mixing bowl.

2. Pour into two mugs. Cover top of mugs securely with foil.
3. Place a steam rack in the Ninja Foodi and pour a cup of water.
4. Place the mug on the steam rack.
5. Install pressure lid. Close the lid, press the steam button, and adjust the time to 10 minutes.
6. Do a natural pressure release.

Nutrition information:
Calories: 259; carbohydrates: 10.3g; protein: 7.2g; fat: 20.9g

Surprising Campfire S' mores

(Cooking Time: 14 minutes | Serves: 4)
Ingredients
- 4 Graham Crackers
- 4 marshmallows
- 2 (1½ oz. each) chocolate bars

Directions:
1. Place Cook and Crisp basket in the pot, close crisping lid
2. Pre-heat your pot by setting it to 350 degrees F on Air Crisp mode, for 5 minutes
3. Break graham crackers into half and place half of the chocolate bar on one half of Graham Cracker
4. Add marshmallow and top with remaining graham cracker half
5. Repeat with remaining ingredients to create the S' Mores
6. Use aluminum foil to wrap each S' More individually, place all 4 foil-wrapped S' Mores in your pre-heated Cook and Crisp Basket
7. Place Crisping Lid and select the Air Crisp mode, cook for 4 minutes at 350 degrees F
8. Carefully unwrap the S' mores, serve and enjoy!

Nutritional Info: 152 Calories, 7g fat, 24g carbs, 1g protein

Excellent Strawberry Toast Pastries

(Cooking Time: 30 minutes | Serves: 8)
Ingredients
- 1 refrigerated pie crust, at room temperature
- ¼ c. simple strawberry jam
- Vanilla icing
- Rainbow sprinkles

Directions:
1. Place Cook and Crisp basket in the pot and close the crisping lead, pre-heat at 350 degrees F on Air Crisp mode for 5 minutes

2. Roll out pie crust on a lightly floured surface, shaping it into a large rectangle, cut dough into 8 rectangles
3. Spoon a tablespoon of jam to the center of each of 4 dough rectangles, leaving ½ inch border
4. Brush edges of filled dough with water, top each with the other 4 dough rectangles and gently press edges to seal
5. Place pastries in your pre-heated basket and coat with cooking spray
6. Arrange pastries in the Cook and Crisp basket in a single layer
7. Close crisping lid and Air Crisp for 10 minutes at 350 degrees F
8. Repeat until all pastries are done, frost pastries with vanilla icing and top with sprinkles
9. Enjoy!

Nutritional Info: 363 calories, 15g fat, 55g carbs, 2g protein

Chocolate Peanut Butter Cups

Cooking Time: 40 minutes | Serves: 3
Ingredients:

- 1 c. butter
- ¼ c. heavy cream
- 2 oz. chocolate, unsweetened
- ¼ c. peanut butter, separated
- 4 packets stevia

Directions:

1. Melt the peanut butter and butter in a bowl and stir in unsweetened chocolate, stevia and heavy cream.
2. Mix thoroughly and pour the mixture in a baking mold.
3. Put the baking mold in the Ninja Foodi and press "Bake/Roast".
4. Set the timer for about 30 minutes at 360 degrees F and dish out to serve.

Nutritional Info: 479 calories, 51.5g fat, 7.7g carbs, 5.2g protein

Crème Brûlée

(Cooking Time: 25 minutes | Serves: 4)
Ingredients:

- 1 c. heavy cream
- ½ tbsp. vanilla extract
- 3 egg yolks
- 1 pinch salt
- ¼ c. stevia

Directions:

1. Mix together egg yolks, vanilla extract, heavy cream and salt in a bowl and beat until combined.

2. Divide the mixture into 4 greased ramekins evenly and transfer the ramekins in the basket of Ninja Foodi.
3. Press "Bake/Roast" and set the timer for about 15 minutes at 365 degrees F.

4. Remove from the Ninja Foodi and cover the ramekins with a plastic wrap.
5. Refrigerate to chill for about 3 hours and serve chilled.

Nutritional Info: 149 calories, 14.5g fat, 1.6g carbs, 2.6g protein

Flourless Chocolate Brownies

(Cooking Time: 42 minutes | Serves: 4)
Ingredients:
- 3 eggs
- ½ c. butter
- ½ c. chocolate chips, sugar-free
- 2 scoops stevia
- 1 tsp. vanilla extract

Directions:
1. Whisk together eggs, stevia and vanilla extract.
2. Transfer this mixture in the blender and blend until frothy.
3. Put the butter and chocolate in the pot of Ninja Foodi and press "Sauté".
4. Sauté for about 2 minutes until the chocolate is melted.
5. Add the melted chocolate mixture to the egg mixture.
6. Pour the mixture in the baking mold and transfer the baking mold in the Ninja Foodi.
7. Press "Bake/Roast" and set the timer for about 30 minutes at 360 degrees F.
8. Bake for about 30 minutes and dish out.
9. Cut into equal square pieces and serve with whipped cream.

Nutritional Info: 266 calories, 26.9g fat, 2.5g carbs, 4.5g protein

Cream Crepes

(Cooking Time: 26 minutes | Serves: 6)
Ingredients:
- 1½ tsps. Splenda
- 3 organic eggs
- 3 tbsps. coconut flour
- ½ cup heavy cream
- 3 tbsps. melted coconut oil, divided

Directions:

1. Mix together 1½ tablespoons of coconut oil, Splenda, eggs and salt in a bowl and beat until well combined.
2. Add the coconut flour slowly and continuously beat.
3. Stir in the heavy cream and beat continuously until well combined.

4. Press "Sauté" on Ninja Foodi and pour about ¼ of the mixture in the pot.
5. Sauté for about 2 minutes on each side and dish out.

6. Repeat with the remaining mixture in batches and serve.

Nutritional Info: 145 calories, 13.1g fat, 4g carbs, 3.5g protein

Nut Porridge

Cooking Time: 20 minutes | Serves: 4
Ingredients:
- 4 tsps. melted coconut oil
- 1 c. halved pecans
- 2 c. water
- 2 tbsps. stevia
- 1 c. raw cashew nuts, unsalted

Directions:
1. Put the cashew nuts and pecans in the food processor and pulse until chunked.

2. Put the nuts mixture into the pot and stir in water, coconut oil and stevia.
3. Press "Sauté" on Ninja Foodi and cook for about 15 minutes.
4. Dish out and serve immediately.

Nutritional Info: 260 calories, 22.9g fat, 12.7g carbs, 5.6g protein

Lemon Mousse

(Cooking Time: 22 minutes | Serves: 2)
Ingredients:
- 1 oz. softened cream cheese
- ½ c. heavy cream
- 1/8 c. fresh lemon juice
- ½ tsp. lemon liquid stevia
- 2 pinches salt

Directions:
1. Mix together cream cheese, heavy cream, lemon juice, salt and stevia in a bowl.

2. Pour into the ramekins and transfer the ramekins in the pot of Ninja Foodi.
3. Press "Bake/Roast" and bake for about 12 minutes at 350 degrees F.
4. Pour into the serving glasses and refrigerate for at least 3 hours before serving.

Nutritional Info: 305 calories, 31g fat, 2.7g carbs, 5g protein

Chocolate Cheese Cake

Cooking Time: 25 minutes | Serves: 6

Ingredients:

- 2 c. softened cream cheese
- 2 eggs
- 2 tbsps. cocoa powder
- 1 tsp. pure vanilla extract
- ½ c. swerve

Directions:

1. Place eggs, cocoa powder, vanilla extract, swerve and cream cheese in an immersion blender and blend until smooth.
2. Pulse to mix well and transfer the mixture evenly into mason jars.
3. Put the mason jars in the insert of Ninja Foodi and lock the lid.
4. Press "Bake/Roast" and bake for about 15 minutes at 360 degrees F.
5. Place in the refrigerator for 2 hours before serving and serve chilled.

Nutritional Info: 244 calories, 24.8g fat, 2.1g carbs, 4g protein

Vanilla Yogurt

(Cooking Time: 3 hours 20 minutes | Serves: 2)

Ingredients:

- ½ c. full-fat milk
- ¼ c. yogurt starter
- 1 c. heavy cream
- ½ tbsp. pure vanilla extract
- 2 scoops stevia

Directions:

1. Pour milk in the pot of Ninja Foodi and stir in heavy cream, vanilla extract and stevia.
2. Allow the yogurt to sit and press "Slow Cooker" and cook on Low for about 3 hours.
3. Add the yogurt starter in 1 cup of milk and return this mixture to the pot.
4. Lock the lid and wrap the Ninja Foodi in two small towels.
5. Let sit for about 9 hours and allow the yogurt to culture.
6. Dish out in a serving bowl or refrigerate to serve.

Nutritional Info: 292 calories, 26.2g fat, 8.2g carbs, 5.2g protein

Fudge Divine

(Cooking Time: 6 hours 20 minutes | Serves: 24)

Ingredients:

- ½ tsp. organic vanilla extract
- 1 c. heavy whipping cream
- 2 oz. softened butter
- 2 oz. chopped 70% dark chocolate

Directions:

1- Press "Sauté" and "Md:Hi" on Ninja Foodi and add vanilla and heavy cream.
2- Sauté for about 5 minutes and select "Lo".
3- Sauté for about 10 minutes and add butter and chocolate.
4- Sauté for about 2 minutes and transfer this mixture in a serving dish.
5- Refrigerate it for few hours and serve chilled.

Nutritional Info: 292 calories, 26.2g fat, 8.2g carbs, 5.2g protein

Chapter 10 Pressure Cooked Recipes

Pressure Cooker Pork Carnitas

Serving: 4,   Cooking time: 60 minutes

Ingredients

- 2 pounds pork butt, chopped into large cubes
- 1 teaspoon salt
- ½ teaspoon oregano
- ½ teaspoon cumin
- 1 orange, cut in half and juiced
- 6 cloves of garlic, peeled and crushed
- 1 cup chicken broth

Directions:

1. Place the ceramic pot in the Ninja Foodi base and place all ingredients.
2. Put the pressure lid and make sure that the vent is on the SEAL position.
3. Press the Pressure button.
4. Adjust the cooking time for 60 minutes.
5. Once cooked, take the pork out and shred using forks.
6. Serve with the sauce.

Nutrition information:

Calories: 321; Carbohydrates: 8g; Protein: 43g; Fat: 13g; Sugar: 4g; Sodium: 838mg

Spicy Pressure Cooker Short Ribs

Serving: 4,   Cooking time: 45 minutes

Ingredients

- 1 habanero pepper, minced
- 1 ½ teaspoons black pepper
- 1 teaspoon paprika
- ½ teaspoon ground cumin
- 2 pounds beef short ribs
- 1 can cola
- 2 tablespoons apple cider vinegar
- 1 tablespoon raspberry jam
- 1 tablespoon Worcestershire sauce
- 1 tablespoon brown sugar
- 2 teaspoons canola oil
- ½ onion, diced
- 4 cloves of garlic, minced
- 2 tablespoons water
- 2 tablespoons cornstarch

1. In a Ziploc bag, place the habanero, black pepper, paprika, cumin, beef short ribs, cola, apple cider vinegar, raspberry jam, Worcestershire sauce, and sugar. Marinate for at least 2 hours in the fridge.
2. Press the Sear/Sauté button and press the START button.
3. Heat the olive oil and sauté the onion and garlic until fragrant. Stir in the marinated beef (liquid included) and adjust the moisture.
4. Place the pressure lid and set the vent to the SEAL position. Press the Pressure button.
5. Adjust the cooking time to 45 minutes.

Directions:

6. Once cooking is done, do natural pressure release to open the lid.
7. Open the lid and press the Sear/Sauté button and stir in the cornstarch slurry.
8. Allow to simmer until the sauce thickens.

Nutrition information:
Calories: 582; Carbohydrates: 24.1g; Protein: 22g; Fat: 44.1g; Sugar: 10.4g; Sodium: 224mg

Mexican Beef and Vegetable Stew

Serving: 6,   Cooking time: 30 minutes

Ingredients

- 3 tablespoons vegetable oil
- ½ onion, chopped
- 2 cloves of garlic, minced
- 2 pounds beef chuck roast, cut into chunks
- ½ teaspoon paprika
- ½ teaspoon salt
- ¼ teaspoon pepper
- ¼ teaspoon cumin
- ¼ teaspoon dried Mexican oregano
- 2 cans Hunts Diced Tomatoes
- 1 quart beef broth
- 2 bay leaves
- ½ teaspoon crushed red pepper flakes
- 3 large potatoes, peeled and quartered
- 2 carrots, peeled and sliced
- 2 cups frozen corn

Directions:

1. Place the ceramic pot in the Ninja Foodi base and press the Sear/Sauté button. Press the START button.
2. Heat the oil and sauté the onions and garlic until fragrant. Stir in the beef chuck roast and continue stirring for 3 minutes. Season with paprika, salt, pepper, cumin, and oregano. Add in the tomatoes and the rest of the ingredients.
3. Place the pressure lid and make sure that the vent is set to the SEAL position. Press the Pressure button. Cook for 30 minutes.

Nutrition information:
Calories: 419; Carbohydrates: 25.3g; Protein: 28.6g; Fat: 22.5g; Sugar: 6.4g; Sodium: 1238mg

Easy Ninja Foodi Pot Roast

Serving:6,   Cooking time: 60 minutes

Ingredients

- 2 tablespoons vegetable oil
- 3 pounds boneless beef chuck roast, trimmed
- 1 tablespoon onion powder
- 1 can beef broth
- 1 ½ tablespoons Worcestershire sauce
- 1 onion, cut into wedges
- 4 carrots, peeled and sliced
- 4 large potatoes, peeled and cut into bite-sized pieces
- Salt and pepper to taste

Directions:

1. Press the Sear/Sauté button on the Ninja Foodi. Press the START button.

2. Heat the oil and sear the beef chuck roast for 2 minutes on each side. Season with salt, pepper, and onion powder.

3. Once golden, stir in the rest of the ingredients.

4. Close the pressure lid and set the vent to SEAL position. Press the Pressure button and adjust the cooking time to 60 minutes.

5. Press the START button and cook until done.

Nutrition information:

Calories: 450; Carbohydrates: 38.3g; Protein: 25.1g; Fat: 21.8g; Sugar: 10.2g; Sodium: 311mg

Filipino-Style Bistek Tagalog

Serving: 4,   Cooking time: 33 minutes

Ingredients

- 2 tablespoons vegetable oil
- 3 cloves of garlic, minced
- 1 onion, chopped finely
- 2 pounds flank steak, cut into thin strips
- 1 cup chicken broth
- Juice from 1 lemon
- ¼ cup soy sauce
- 1 laurel leaf
- 3 tablespoons sugar
- Black pepper to taste
- 1 red onion, cut into rings
- 2 tablespoons cornstarch
- 3 tablespoons water

Directions:

1. Press the Sear/Sauté button and then the START button.

2. Heat the oil and sauté the garlic and onion until fragrant.

3. Stir in the beef until lightly golden and stir in the chicken stock, lemon juice, soy sauce, bay leaf, sugar, and black pepper.

4. Close the pressure lid and set the vent to SEAL.

5. Press the Pressure button and adjust the cooking time to 30 minutes.

6. Once done, do quick pressure release to open the lid.
7. Once the lid is open, press the Sear/Sauté button and add in the onion rings and cornstarch slurry.
8. Allow to simmer until the sauce thickens.

Nutrition information:
Calories: 486; Carbohydrates: 24.3g; Protein: 33.2g; Fat: 28.4g; Sugar: 10.8g; Sodium: 891mg

Ninja Foodi Chili

Serving:4 Cooking time: 30 minutes

Ingredients

- 2 tablespoons olive oil
- 1 onion, chopped
- 2 cloves of garlic, minced
- 2 pound ground beef
- 1 green bell pepper, chopped
- 1 jalapeno pepper, chopped
- 2 cans red kidney beans, rinsed and drained
- 2 cans diced tomatoes, undrained
- 3 tablespoons tomato paste
- 1 tablespoon sugar
- 2 teaspoons unsweetened cocoa powder
- ¼ teaspoon crushed red pepper flakes
- 2 tablespoons chili powder
- 2 teaspoons ground cumin
- ½ teaspoon salt
- 2 cups water

Directions:

1. Press the Sear/Sauté button and then the START button.
2. Heat the oil and sauté the garlic and onion until fragrant.
3. Stir in the ground beef and cook for another 2 minutes.
4. Add in the rest of the ingredients.
5. Close the pressure lid and set the vent to SEAL.
6. Press the Pressure button and adjust the cooking time to 30 minutes.

Nutrition information:
Calories: 285; Carbohydrates: 35.3g; Protein: 22.3g; Fat: 14.9g; Sugar: 13.8g; Sodium: 790mg

Simple Pot Roast and Potatoes

Serving: 6,   Cooking time: 50 minutes

Ingredients

- 3 pounds beef rump roast
- 1/3 cup all-purpose flour
- ¼ cup olive oil
- 2 packages dry onion soup mix
- 2 ½ cups water
- 3 onions, peeled and cut into wedges
- 8 potatoes, peeled and halved
- Salt and pepper to taste

Directions:

1. Season the beef with salt and pepper. Dredge in flour.
2. Press the Sear/Sauté button and then the START button.
3. Heat the oil and sear the beef on all sides for at least 2 minutes.
4. Add the rest of the ingredients.
5. Close the pressure lid and set the vent to SEAL.
6. Press the Pressure button and adjust the cooking time to 50 minutes.

Nutrition information:

Calories: 700; Carbohydrates: 71.3g; Protein: 47.6g; Fat: 24.9g; Sugar: 21.7g; Sodium: 935mg

Pressure Cooker Bone-In Pork Chops with Vegetables

Serving:4, Cooking time: 30 minutes

Ingredients

- 4 ¾ -inch bone-in pork chops
- Salt and pepper to taste
- ¼ cup butter, divided
- 1 cup baby carrots
- 4 whole potatoes, peeled and halved
- 1 onion, chopped
- 1 cup vegetable broth
- 3 tablespoons Worcestershire sauce

Directions:

1. Season the beef with salt and pepper. Dredge in flour.
2. Press the Sear/Sauté button and then the START button.
3. Season the pork with salt and pepper to taste.
4. Put half of the butter in the pot and sear the pork for at least 2 minutes on both sides.
5. Stir in the carrots, potatoes, onions, vegetable broth, and Worcestershire sauce.
6. Close the pressure lid and set the vent to SEAL.
7. Press the Pressure button and adjust the cooking time to 30 minutes.
8. Do natural pressure release.
9. Once the lid is open, stir in the remaining butter.

Nutrition information:

Calories: 577; Carbohydrates: 60.3g; Protein: 34.6g; Fat: 21.9g; Sugar: 20.6g; Sodium: 404mg

Bangladeshi Beef Curry

Serving: 4 Cooking time: 45 minutes

Ingredients

- 3 tablespoons olive oil
- 1 onion, chopped
- 6 cloves of garlic, minced
- 5 green chili peppers, sliced
- 1 teaspoon ginger paste
- 3 whole cardamom seeds
- 2 whole cloves
- 1 ½ inch cinnamon sticks
- 1 teaspoon ground cumin
- 1 teaspoon ground coriander
- 1 teaspoon ground turmeric
- 1 teaspoon garlic powder
- 2 pounds boneless beef chuck, cut into chunks
- 1 cup water
- Salt and pepper to taste

Directions:

1. Season the beef with salt and pepper. Dredge in flour.
2. Press the Sear/Sauté button and then the START button.
3. Heat the oil and sauté the onion and garlic until fragrant. Stir in the rest of the ingredients except for the beef and water.
4. Keep stirring for 3 minutes until the toasted.
5. Stir in the beef and cook for 2 minutes. Pour in water and season with salt and pepper to taste. Close the pressure lid and set the vent to SEAL.
6. Press the Pressure button and adjust the cooking time to 45 minutes.

Nutrition information:

Calories: 322; Carbohydrates: 8.8g; Protein: 19.5g; Fat: 23.1g; Sugar: 0.8g; Sodium: 50mg

Pressure Cooker Red Beans and Sausages

Serving: 4 Cooking time: 40 minutes

Ingredients

- ½ pound smoked sausages, sliced
- 2 cloves of garlic, minced
- 1 stalk celery, chopped
- ½ green bell pepper, chopped
- 1 pound dried red beans, rinsed
- 1 bay leaf
- 2 tablespoons Cajun seasoning
- 1 teaspoon dried parsley
- ¼ teaspoon ground cumin
- 5 cups water
- Salt and pepper to taste

Directions:

1. Season the beef with salt and pepper. Dredge in flour.
2. Press the Sear/Sauté button and then the START button.
3. Place the sausage in the pot and allow fat to render.
4. Sauté the onion and celery until fragrant.
5. Stir in the rest of the ingredients.
6. Close the pressure lid and set the vent to SEAL.
7. Press the Pressure button and adjust the cooking time to 40 minutes.

Nutrition information:
Calories: 298; Carbohydrates: 16g; Protein: 17g; Fat: 18.4g; Sugar: 6.3g; Sodium: 1511mg

Pressure Cooker Pasta Stew

Serving:6 Cooking time: 20 minutes

Ingredients

- 1 pound lean ground beef
- 1 cloves of garlic, minced
- 1 onion, chopped
- 1 package bow tie pasta
- 1 can tomato sauce
- 1 can stewed tomatoes
- 1 teaspoon oregano
- 1 teaspoon Italian seasoning
- 1 cup mozzarella cheese
- 1 cup ricotta cheese
- Salt and pepper to taste

Directions:

1. Season the beef with salt and pepper. Dredge in flour.
2. Press the Sear/Sauté button and then the START button.
3. Sauté the beef until some of the fat has rendered. Stir in the garlic and onions until fragrant.
4. Add in the pasta, tomatoes, oregano, and Italian seasoning. Season with salt and pepper to taste. Stir in the rest of the ingredients.
5. Close the pressure lid and set the vent to SEAL.
6. Press the Pressure button and adjust the cooking time to 10 minutes.
7. Do quick pressure release.
8. Once the lid is open, press the Sear/Sauté button then the START button.
9. Stir in the cheese and allow to simmer for another 5 minutes.

Nutrition information:
Calories: 469; Carbohydrates: 53g; Protein: 29.3g; Fat: 15.5g; Sugar: 24.3g; Sodium: 567mg

Ninja Foodie Pressure Cooked Adobo

Serving: 4 Cooking time: 30 minutes

Ingredients

- 2 pounds chicken breasts and thighs, bones removed
- ½ cup soy sauce
- ¼ cup rice vinegar
- 2 tablespoons brown sugar
- 1 bay leaf
- 8 hard-boiled egg, peeled
- Salt and pepper to taste

Directions:

1. Place all ingredients in the pot except for the hard-boiled eggs.
2. Close the pressure lid and set the vent to SEAL.
3. Press the Pressure button and adjust the cooking time to 30 minutes.
4. Do natural release.
5. Before serving, place the hard-boiled eggs.

Nutrition information:
Calories: 489; Carbohydrates: 21.3g; Protein:

54.5g; Fat: 20.6g; Sugar: 14g; Sodium: 979mg

Ninja Foodi Pressure Cooked Barbecue Chicken

Serving: 4 Cooking time:　20 minutes

Ingredients

- 2 pounds boneless chicken thighs
- 1 teaspoon ground paprika
- 1 onion, minced
- ½ cup chili sauce
- ½ cup water
- 2 tablespoons vinegar
- Salt and pepper to taste

Directions:

1. Place all ingredients in the pot except for the hard-boiled eggs.
2. Close the pressure lid and set the vent to SEAL.
3. Press the Pressure button and adjust the cooking time to 20 minutes.
4. Do natural release.

Nutrition information:
Calories: 215; Carbohydrates: 7g; Protein: 19.8g; Fat: 11.9g; Sugar: 1.2g; Sodium: 313mg

Pressure Cooker Pork Tenderloin

Serving:3 Cooking time:　40 minutes

Ingredients

- ¼ cup fresh cilantro leaves
- ¼ cup lime juice
- 2 cloves of garlic
- ½ teaspoon red pepper flakes
- ¼ teaspoon salt
- 1 pound pork tenderloin
- ¾ cup chicken broth
- ¼ cup lemon juice

Directions:

1. Place all ingredients in the pot except for the hard-boiled eggs.
2. Close the pressure lid and set the vent to SEAL.
3. Press the Pressure button and adjust the cooking time to 40 minutes.
4. Do natural pressure release.

Nutrition information:
Calories: 231; Carbohydrates: 4.9g; Protein: 40.3g; Fat: 5.5g; Sugar: 1.3g; Sodium: 480mg

Amazing Beef Sauerbraten

Serving: 4 Cooking time: 40 minutes

Ingredients

- 2 tablespoons shortening or olive oil
- 2 pounds beef stew meat
- 5 cups water
- 1 cup white vinegar
- 3 bay eaves
- 3 tablespoons cornstarch
- 4 tablespoons all-purpose flour
- Salt and pepper to taste

Directions:

1. Press the Sear/Sauté button and then the START button.
2. Heat the oil and brown the beef stew meat on all sides for at least 3 minutes.
3. Close the pressure lid and set the vent to SEAL.
4. Press the Pressure button and adjust the cooking time to 40 minutes.
5. Do natural pressure release to open the lid.
6. Once the lid is open, press the Sear/Sauté button and stir in the cornstarch slurry.
7. Allow to simmer until the sauce thickens.

Nutrition information:

Calories: 746; Carbohydrates: 3.1g; Protein: 59.2g; Fat: 55.2g; Sugar: 0.5g; Sodium: 150m

Ninja Foodie Short Ribs

Serving: 8 Cooking time: 60 minutes

Ingredients

- 1 bottle (750mL) red wine
- 4 pounds beef short ribs
- 3 tablespoons unsalted butter
- 1 ½ cups onion, chopped
- 3 cloves of garlic, minced
- 1 cup minced carrots
- 2 sprigs fresh rosemary
- 2 cups chicken stock
- Salt and pepper to taste

Directions:

1. Place all ingredients in the pot except for the hard-boiled eggs.
2. Close the pressure lid and set the vent to SEAL.
3. Press the Pressure button and adjust the cooking time to 60 minutes.
4. Do natural pressure release.

Nutrition information:

Calories: 436; Carbohydrates: 13.2g; Protein: 15.9g; Fat: 35.5g; Sugar: 5.8g; Sodium: 277mg

Ninja Foodi Caveman Stew

Serving:4 Cooking time: 20 minutes

Ingredients

- 2 pound ground beef
- 5 carrots, sliced
- 4 potatoes, peeled and cut into wedges
- 1 onion, quartered
- 1 can tomato soup
- 1 cup water
- Salt and pepper to taste

Directions:

1. Press the Sear/Sauté button and then the START button.
2. Place the beef in the pot and stir until the fat slightly renders.
3. Add in the rest of the ingredients.
4. Close the pressure lid and set the vent to SEAL.
5. Press the Pressure button and adjust the cooking time to 20 minutes.

Nutrition information:

Calories: 487; Carbohydrates: 61.2g; Protein: 26.1g; Fat: 15.3g; Sugar: 8.3g; Sodium: 567mg

Greek Style Stew

Serving: 5 Cooking time: 53 minutes

Ingredients

- 1 tablespoon olive oil
- 2 pound beef stew meat, cubed
- 1 onion, chopped
- 2 cloves of garlic, chopped
- Salt and pepper to taste
- ¼ cup red wine
- ½ cup beef broth
- 1 tablespoon tomato paste
- ½ teaspoon dried rosemary
- ½ teaspoon dried oregano
- 2 bay leaves
- 1/8 teaspoon ground cinnamon
- 1 pinch ground cloves
- 1 ½ teaspoons brown sugar
- 1 can plum tomatoes
- ½ cup water
- 2 potatoes, peeled and chopped

Directions:

1. Press the Sear/Sauté button and then the START button.
2. Heat the oil in the inner pot and stir in the meat, onion, and garlic. Season with salt and pepper to taste. Keep stirring for at least 3 minutes.
3. Add in the rest of the ingredients and give a good stir.
4. Close the pressure lid and set the vent to SEAL.
5. Press the Pressure button and adjust the cooking time to 50 minutes.

Nutrition information:

Calories: 288; Carbohydrates: 26.8g; Protein: 15.9g; Fat: 13g; Sugar: 10.2g; Sodium: 367mg

Ninja Foodi Chinese Ribs

Serving:13 Cooking time: 35 minutes

Ingredients

- 3 tablespoons paprika
- 1 tablespoon garlic powder
- ½ teaspoon ground black pepper
- ½ teaspoon salt
- 6 ½ pounds pork ribs
- 2 tablespoons vegetable oil
- 3 cups water
- ¾ cup ketchup
- ¼ cup brown sugar
- ¼ cup Chinese vinegar

Directions:

1. In a bowl, combine the paprika, garlic powder, black pepper, and salt.
2. Sprinkle on to the pork ribs and rub to coat everything with the spices.
3. Press the Sear/Sauté button and then the START button.
4. Heat the oil and stir in the pork ribs. Allow to brown for 5 minutes.
5. Stir in the rest of the ingredients.
6. Close the pressure lid and set the vent to SEAL.
7. Press the Pressure button and adjust the cooking time to 30 minutes.

Nutrition information:

Calories: 768; Carbohydrates: 31.9g; Protein: 56.9g; Fat: 45.8g; Sugar: 14.6g; Sodium: 889mg

Pressure Cooker Lamb Stew

Serving: 6 Cooking time: 75 minutes

Ingredients

- 2 tablespoons olive oil
- 2 cloves of garlic, minced
- 2 ½ pounds lamb, cut into cubes
- 1 tablespoon dried marjoram
- 1 tablespoon dried parsley
- 1 teaspoon dried chives
- 1 tablespoon all spice powder
- 2 cups water
- 1 bay leaf
- 16 baby carrots
- 8 potatoes, cut into chunks
- Salt and pepper to taste

Directions:

1. Press the Sear/Sauté button and then the START button.
2. Heat the oil and sauté the garlic until fragrant.
3. Add in the lamb and stir in the marjoram, parsley, chives, and all spice. Season with salt and pepper to taste.
4. Stir in the rest of the ingredients.
5. Close the pressure lid and set the vent to SEAL.
6. Press the Pressure button and adjust the cooking time to 75 minutes.

Nutrition information:

Calories: 480; Carbohydrates: 29.8g; Protein: 32.7g; Fat: 25.5g; Sugar: 5.8g; Sodium: 644mg

MakhaniDaal (Butterfly Lentils)

Serving: 5 Cooking time: 43 minutes

Ingredients

- 2 teaspoons vegetable oil
- 1 onion, finely chopped
- 2 cloves of garlic, minced
- 1 teaspoon cumin seeds
- 2 teaspoons ground coriander
- 1 teaspoon garam masala
- ½ teaspoon chili powder
- ½ teaspoon ground turmeric
- 2 tomatoes, chopped
- 1 cup dry black lentils, soaked overnight
- ¼ cup split chickpeas, soaked overnight
- ¼ cup red kidney beans, soaked overnight
- 3 cups water
- Salt and pepper to taste
- 2 teaspoons butter
- 2 teaspoons yogurt

Directions:

1. Press the Sear/Sauté button and then the START button.
2. Heat the oil and sauté the onion and garlic until fragrant.
3. Stir in the cumin, coriander, garam masala, chili powder, and turmeric. Stir for 2 minutes until lightly toasted.
4. Stir in the tomatoes. Add the beans and water. Season with salt and pepper to taste.
5. Close the pressure lid and set the vent to SEAL.
6. Press the Pressure button and adjust the cooking time to 40 minutes.
7. Do quick pressure release. Once open, stir in butter and yogurt before serving.

Nutrition information:
Calories: 341; Carbohydrates: 51.7g; Protein: 19g; Fat: 6.4g; Sugar: 10.8g; Sodium: 71mg

Mexican Pork in Annatto Sauce

Serving: 10 Cooking time: 75 minutes

Ingredients

- 3 ounces achiote paste or annatto powder
- 1 white onion, chopped
- 2 cloves of garlic, minced
- 2 cups orange juice
- ½ cup lemon juice
- ¼ cup white vinegar
- 2 tablespoons salt
- 1 tablespoon ground black pepper
- 1 tablespoon Mexican oregano
- 5 pounds pork shoulder roast

Directions:

1. Place all ingredients in the Ninja Foodi Pot.
2. Close the pressure lid and set the vent to SEAL.
3. Press the Pressure button and adjust the cooking time to 75 minutes.
4. Do natural pressure release.

Nutrition information:
Calories: 414; Carbohydrates: 8.3g; Protein: 37.6g; Fat: 25.6g; Sugar: 4.9g; Sodium: 122mg

Spicy Short Ribs

Serving: 4 Cooking time: 60 minutes

Ingredients

- 2 teaspoons canola oil
- 1 onion, diced
- 4 cloves of garlic, minced
- 2 pounds beef short ribs
- 1 teaspoon paprika
- 1 teaspoon cumin
- 2 tablespoons apple cider vinegar
- 1 can cola
- 1 tablespoon raspberry jam
- 1 tablespoon Worcestershire sauce
- 1 tablespoon sugar
- 2 tablespoons cornstarch
- 2 tablespoons water
- Salt and pepper to taste

Directions:

1. Press the Sear/Sauté button and then the START button. Heat the oil and sauté the onion and garlic until fragrant.
2. Stir in the beef short ribs and season with salt, pepper, paprika, and cumin.
3. Stir until all sides are lightly golden.
4. Add in the apple cider vinegar, cola, raspberry jam, Worcestershire sauce, and sugar.
5. Close the pressure lid and set the vent to SEAL.
6. Press the Pressure button and adjust the cooking time to 60 minutes.
7. Do quick pressure release. Once the lid is open, press the Sear/Sauté button and stir in the cornstarch slurry. Allow to simmer until the sauce thickens.

Nutrition information:

Calories: 471; Carbohydrates: 45.1g; Protein: 22g; Fat: 22.5g; Sugar: 21.9g; Sodium: 624mg

Red Wine Braised Short Ribs

Serving:10 Cooking time: 60 minutes

Ingredients

- 5 pounds beef short ribs, cut into chunks
- 2/3 cup all-purpose flour
- 2 tablespoons olive oil
- 2 onions, chopped
- 2 cloves of garlic, minced
- 2 stalks of celery, chopped
- 2 tablespoons tomato paste
- 3 carrots, peeled and sliced
- 4 cup beef stock
- 1 cup dry red wine
- Salt and pepper to taste

Directions:

1. Season the ribs with salt and pepper.
2. Dredge the meat on all-purpose flour.
3. Press the Sear/Sauté button and then the START button.
4. Heat the oil and sear the meat on all sides for at least 3 minutes.
5. Sauté the onion and garlic until fragrant. Stir in the celery until wilted.
6. Add the rest of the ingredients.

7. Close the pressure lid and set the vent to SEAL.
8. Press the Pressure button and adjust the cooking time to 60 minutes.

Nutrition information:
Calories: 592; Carbohydrates: 23.2g; Protein: 51.1g; Fat: 32.7g; Sugar: 15.9g; Sodium: 986mg

Pressure Cooker Fenugreek Chicken

Serving: 8 Cooking time: 30 minutes

Ingredients
- 2 tablespoons cooking oil
- 6 pounds whole chicken, cut into 8 pieces
- Salt and pepper to taste
- ½ teaspoon garam masala
- 1 teaspoon cumin seeds
- 1 cinnamon stick
- 1 black cardamom pod
- 4 whole cloves
- 1 onion, sliced
- 4 green chili pepper, halved
- 1 cup water
- ½ cup fenugreek leaves

Directions:
1. Press the Sear/Sauté button and then the START button.
2. Heat the oil and sear the chicken on all sides.
3. Season with salt, pepper, garam masala and cumin seeds.
4. Add in the rest of the ingredients except for the fenugreek leaves.
5. Close the pressure lid and set the vent to SEAL.
6. Press the Pressure button and adjust the cooking time to 25minutes.
7. Do quick pressure release.
8. Once the lid is open, add the fenugreek leaves last.

Nutrition information:
Calories: 305; Carbohydrates: 8g; Protein: 36.7g; Fat: 14g; Sugar: 2g; Sodium: 395mg

Chapter 11 Steamed Recipes

Easy-Steam Lobster Tails

Serving: 4. Cooking time: 10 minutes

Ingredients

- 4 6-ounces lobster tails
- Salt and pepper to taste
- ½ cup butter

Directions:

1. Place the Foodi™ Cook &Crisp™ reversible rack inside the ceramic pot.
2. Pour a cup of water in the pot.
3. Season the lobster tails with salt and pepper to taste.
4. Place the seasoned lobster tails on the reversible rack.
5. Close the pressure lid and set the vent to SEAL.
6. Press the Steam button and adjust the cooking time to 10 minutes.
7. Do quick pressure release.
8. Once the lid is open, take the lobster tail out and serve with butter on top.

Nutrition information:

Calories: 353; Carbohydrates: 0.9g; Protein: 32.2g; Fat: 24.5g; Sugar: 0.2g; Sodium: 1987mg

Flaky Fish with Ginger

Serving: 2 Cooking time: 15minutes

Ingredients

- 1 pound halibut fillet, skin removed
- 1 teaspoon salt to taste
- 1 tablespoon fresh ginger, sliced thinly
- 3 tablespoons green onion
- 1 tablespoon dark soy sauce
- 1 tablespoon peanut oil
- 2 teaspoons sesame oil

Directions:

1. Place the Foodi™ Cook &Crisp™ reversible rack inside the ceramic pot.
2. Pour a cup of water in the pot.
3. Season the halibut fillets with salt to taste.
4. Place in a heat-proof ceramic dish. Drizzle with the rest of the ingredients.
5. Place the ceramic dish with the fish inside on the reversible rack.
6. Close the pressure lid and set the vent to SEAL.
7. Press the Steam button and adjust the cooking time to 15 minutes.
8. Do quick pressure release.

Nutrition information:

Calories: 352; Carbohydrates: 2g; Protein: 48.1g; Fat: 16.8g; Sugar: 0.2g; Sodium: 1908mg

Spicy 'n Steamy Shrimps

Serving: 2 Cooking time: 10 minutes

Ingredients

- pound tiger prawns with shell
- 1 packet Old Bay seasoning
- 1 jar cocktail sauce

Directions:

1. Place the Foodi™ Cook &Crisp™ reversible rack inside the ceramic pot.
2. Pour a cup of water in the pot.
3. Season the prawns with Old Bay seasoning.
4. Place the shrimps on the reversible rack.
5. Close the pressure lid and set the vent to SEAL.
6. Press the Steam button and adjust the cooking time to 10 minutes.
7. Do quick pressure release.
8. Serve with cocktail sauce

Nutrition information:

Calories: 360; Carbohydrates: 38.8g; Protein: 41.1g; Fat: 4.4g; Sugar: 10.9g; Sodium: 1250mg

Cajun Style Blue Crabs

Serving: 6 Cooking time: 10 minutes

Ingredients

- 1 cup beer
- ¼ cup vinegar
- 12 medium-sized blue crabs
- 1 tablespoon Old Bay seasoning

Directions:

1. Place the Foodi™ Cook &Crisp™ reversible rack inside the ceramic pot.
2. Pour the beer and vinegar in the pot.
3. Season the crabs with Old Bay seasoning.
4. Place the crabs on the reversible rack.
5. Close the pressure lid and set the vent to SEAL.
6. Press the Steam button and adjust the cooking time to 10 minutes.
7. Do quick pressure release.
8. Discard the beer and vinegar mixture.

Nutrition information:

Calories: 118; Carbohydrates: 2.3g; Protein: 21.5g; Fat: 2.5g; Sugar: 0.8g; Sodium: 954mg

Chinese Steamed Fish

Serving: 2 Cooking time: 10 minutes

Ingredients

- 1 pound red snapper fillets
- 1 tablespoon grated ginger
- 1 tablespoon soy sauce
- 2 tablespoons sesame oil
- 2 shiitake mushrooms, sliced thinly
- 1 tomato, quartered
- ½ fresh red chili pepper, chopped
- 2 sprigs of cilantro, chopped
- Salt and pepper to taste

Directions:

1. Place the Foodi™ Cook &Crisp™ reversible rack inside the ceramic pot.
2. Pour a cup of water in the pot.
3. One a heat-proof ceramic bowl, place the fish and season with salt, pepper, ginger, and soy sauce.
4. Pour over sesame oil and add mushrooms, tomatoes, and red chili on top.
5. Place the ceramic dish with the fish on the reversible rack.
6. Close the pressure lid and set the vent to SEAL.
7. Press the Steam button and adjust the cooking time to 10 minutes.
8. Do quick pressure release.
9. Serve with chopped cilantro

Nutrition information:

Calories: 290; Carbohydrates: 5.9g; Protein: 48.3g; Fat: 8.1g; Sugar: 0.8g; Sodium: 1187mg

Ginger-Soy on Tuna Fish

Serving: 4 Cooking time: 20 minutes

Ingredients

- 2 pounds fresh tuna steaks
- ½ cup soy sauce
- ½ cup sherry
- ½ cup vegetable oil
- 1 bunch green onions, chopped
- ½ cup minced ginger root
- 3 cloves garlic, minced
- Salt and pepper to taste

Directions:

1. Marinate the tuna steaks in soy sauce, sherry and vegetable oil. Allow to marinate in the fridge for at least 2 hours.
2. Place the Foodi™ Cook & Crisp™ reversible rack inside the ceramic pot.
3. Pour the marinade into the pot.
4. In a large foil, place the tuna in the middle and top with green onions, ginger, and garlic. Season with more salt and pepper if desired.
5. Close the foil and place the tuna steak packets on the reversible rack.
6. Close the pressure lid and set the vent to SEAL.
7. Press the Steam button and adjust the cooking time to 20 minutes.
8. Do quick pressure release.
9. Once the lid is open, remove the tuna packets and the reversible rack.

10. Press the Sear/Sauté button and allow the sauce the simmer until reduced.
11. Brush the tuna steaks with the reduced sauce.

Nutrition information:
Calories: 275; Carbohydrates: 7.1g; Protein: 28.3g; Fat: 14.8g; Sugar: 1.4g; Sodium: 1330mg

Steamed Egg Chawan Mushi

Serving: 2 Cooking time: 20 minutes

Ingredients

- 2 eggs
- 1 cup cool chicken stock
- 1 dash sake
- ½ teaspoon soy sauce
- ½ cup chicken meat, chopped
- 1 shiitake mushroom, sliced
- 2 sprigs parsley, chopped

Directions:

1. Place the Foodi™ Cook &Crisp™ reversible rack inside the ceramic pot.
2. Pour a cup of water in the pot.
3. In a mixing bowl, whisk together the eggs, chicken stock, sake, and soy sauce until well-combined.
4. Pour into heat-proof ramekins.
5. Top each egg mixture with chicken and mushroom slices.
6. Place on the reversible rack
7. Close the pressure lid and set the vent to SEAL.
8. Press the Steam button and adjust the cooking time to 20 minutes.
9. Once cooked, garnish with chopped parsley.

Nutrition information:
Calories: 156; Carbohydrates: 3.3g; Protein: 17.3g; Fat: 8.1g; Sugar: 1.4g; Sodium: 527mg

Butter-Lemon on Walleye Pickerel

Serving: 8 Cooking time: 20 minutes

Ingredients

- 8 fillets walleye pickerel
- ¼ cup clarified butter
- ¼ cup lemon juice
- 1 large onion, sliced into rings
- Salt and pepper to taste

Directions:

1. Place the Foodi™ Cook &Crisp™ reversible rack inside the ceramic pot.
2. Pour a cup of water in the pot.
3. On a large aluminum foil, place the pickerel and pour over the butter, lemon juice, salt and pepper.
4. Garnish with onion rings on top.
5. Close the aluminum foil and crimp the edges.
6. Place on the reversible rack.
7. Close the pressure lid and set the vent to SEAL.
8. Press the Steam button and adjust the cooking time to 20 minutes.

Nutrition information:

Calories: 336; Carbohydrates: 4.8g; Protein: 43.9g; Fat: 15.6g; Sugar: 2.8g; Sodium: 118mg

Steamed Brisket in Guinness

Serving: 8 Cooking time: 50 minutes

Ingredients

- 3 ½ cups Irish stout beer (Guinness)
- 2 bay leaves
- 1 tablespoon salt
- 1 tablespoon ground black pepper
- 2 teaspoons paprika
- 1 teaspoon dried basil
- 1 teaspoon dried oregano
- 1 teaspoon garlic powder
- 1 teaspoon onion powder
- 4 pounds beef brisket
- 2 large onions, sliced
- 2 tablespoons cornstarch
- 3 tablespoons water

Directions:

1. Place the Foodi™ Cook &Crisp™ reversible rack inside the ceramic pot.
2. Pour the Guinness in the pot. Stir in the bay leaves.
3. In a small bowl, combine the salt, black pepper, paprika, dried basil, oregano, garlic powder, and onion powder. This will be the dry rub.
4. Season the beef brisket with the dry rub. Place the beef brisket on the reversible rack.
5. Close the pressure lid and set the vent to SEAL.
6. Press the Steam button and adjust the cooking time to 50 minutes.

7. Do quick pressure release. Once the lid is open, remove the beef. Take out the basket as well. Press the Sear/Sauté button and allow the sauce to simmer.
8. Stir in the onions and cornstarch until the sauce thickens.
9. Pour the sauce over the steamed beef.

Nutrition information:
Calories: 714; Carbohydrates: 83.4g; Protein: 46.2g; Fat: 21.7g; Sugar: 0.9g; Sodium: 693mg

Scrumptious Sausage Dinner

Serving: 10 Cooking time: 15 minutes
Ingredients

- 2 ½ pounds smoked sausage, sliced
- 2 pounds hammocks, sliced
- 4 large potatoes, peeled and cut into large chunks
- 6 turnips, peeled and cut into chunks
- 6 carrots, peeled and cut into chunks
- 2 onions, cut into large chunks
- 1 large cabbage, quartered
- 1 teaspoon salt

Directions:

1. Place the Foodi™ Cook &Crisp™ reversible rack inside the ceramic pot.
2. Pour water into the pot.
3. Arrange all ingredients on the reversible rack and season with salt to taste.
4. Close the pressure lid and set the vent to SEAL.
5. Press the Steam button and adjust the cooking time to 15 minutes.

Nutrition information:
Calories: 625; Carbohydrates: 42.5g; Protein: 31.4g; Fat: 36.6g; Sugar:8.3 g; Sodium: 1536mg

Vegetable and Tilapia Dinner

Serving: 6 Cooking time: 15 minutes

Ingredients

- 1 teaspoon olive oil
- 6 tilapia fillets
- 1 pinch Greek seasoning
- 4 stalks celery, halved
- 1 cup fresh baby carrots
- 1 bell pepper, cut into chunks
- ½ onion, sliced
- Salt and pepper to taste

Directions:

1. Place the Foodi™ Cook &Crisp™ reversible rack inside the ceramic pot.
2. Pour water into the pot.
3. Brush oil on to the tilapia fillets.
4. Season with Greek seasoning, salt and pepper.
5. Place the tilapia fillets on the basket.
6. Layer the vegetables on top.
7. Close the pressure lid and set the vent to SEAL.
8. Press the Steam button and adjust the cooking time to 15 minutes.

Nutrition information:

Calories: 134; Carbohydrates: 4.4g; Protein: 23.6g; Fat: 2.4g; Sugar: 0.8g; Sodium: 126mg

Juicy Corned Beef

Serving: 4 Cooking time: 15 minutes

Ingredients

- 1 can corned beef
- ¼ green bell pepper, chopped
- ¼ onion, chopped
- 1 teaspoon vegetable oil
- 2 teaspoons tomato paste
- ¼ teaspoon dried thyme
- Salt and pepper to taste

Directions:

1. Place the Foodi™ Cook &Crisp™ reversible rack inside the ceramic pot.
2. Pour water into the pot.
3. Place in a heat-proof dish the rest of the ingredients. Stir to combine.
4. Place the dish on the reversible rack.
5. Close the pressure lid and set the vent to SEAL.
6. Press the Steam button and adjust the cooking time to 15 minutes.

Nutrition information:

Calories: 223; Carbohydrates: 1.7g; Protein: 23.1g; Fat: 13.7g; Sugar: 0.4g; Sodium: 869mg

Lemony Steamed Fish

Serving: 6 Cooking time: 15 minutes

Ingredients

- 6 halibut fillets
- 1 tablespoon dried dill weed
- 1 tablespoon onion powder
- 2 teaspoons dried parsley
- ¼ teaspoon paprika
- A pinch of salt
- 1 pinch lemon pepper
- 1 pinch garlic powder
- 2 tablespoons lemon juice

Directions:

1. Place the Foodi™ Cook &Crisp™ reversible rack inside the ceramic pot.
2. Pour water into the pot.
3. Season the halibut fillets with dill weed, onion powder, dried parsley, paprika, salt, pepper, garlic powder, and lemon juice.
4. Place the seasoned fish fillets on the reversible rack.
5. Close the pressure lid and set the vent to SEAL.
6. Press the Steam button and adjust the cooking time to 15 minutes.

Nutrition information:

Calories: 137; Carbohydrates: 1.9g; Protein: 29.7g; Fat: 1.1g; Sugar: 0.2g; Sodium: 184mg

Chinese Steamed Buns

Serving: 8 Cooking time: 30 minutes

Ingredients

- 1 tablespoon active dry yeast
- 1 teaspoon white sugar
- ¼ cup all-purpose flour
- ¼ cup warm water
- ½ cup water
- 1 ½ cups all-purpose flour
- ¼ teaspoon salt
- 2 tablespoons white sugar
- 1 tablespoon vegetable oil
- ½ teaspoon baking powder

Directions:

1. Place the Foodi™ Cook &Crisp™ reversible rack inside the ceramic pot. Pour water into the pot.
2. In a mixing bowl, mix together the dry yeast, white sugar, ¼ cup all-purpose flour, and ¼ cup water. Allow the yeast to activate for 10 minutes. This is evident with bubbles forming on top.
3. In another bowl, combine ½ cup water, 1 ½ cups all-purpose flour, salt, white sugar, vegetable oil, and baking powder. Add in the activated yeast mixture.
4. Fold the mixture until you form a dough.
5. On a floured surface, pour the dough and knead for at least 10 minutes using your hands until it becomes springy. Cover the bowl with warm towel and allow to rest for 2 hours.
6. Once risen, knead the dough and cut into 8 equal parts. Cover with warm towel and allow to rest for another 2 hours.

7. Place on the reversible rack. Close the pressure lid and set the vent to SEAL.
8. Press the Steam button and adjust the cooking time to 30 minutes.

Nutrition information:

Calories: 44; Carbohydrates: 8.4g; Protein: 1.1g; Fat:0.6 g; Sugar:1.4 g; Sodium: 35mg

Fragrant Steamed Pork

Serving: 2 Cooking time: 45 minutes

Ingredients

- 2 boneless pork chops
- 2 tablespoons fresh orange juice
- 2 cups water
- ¼ teaspoon ground cloves
- ¼ teaspoon ground coriander
- ¼ teaspoon ground cinnamon
- 1 pinch cayenne pepper

Directions:

1. Place all ingredients in a Ziploc bag and marinate in the fridge for at least 2 hours.
2. Place the Foodi™ Cook &Crisp™ reversible rack inside the ceramic pot.
3. Pour water into the pot.
4. Place the marinated meat on the reversible rack.
5. Close the pressure lid and set the vent to SEAL.
6. Press the Steam button and adjust the cooking time to 45 minutes.

Nutrition information:

Calories: 104; Carbohydrates: 2.2g; Protein: 12.7g; Fat: 4.6g; Sugar: 0.3g; Sodium: 33mg

Steamed Garlic Prawn Chinese Style

Serving:10   Cooking time: 20 minutes

Ingredients

- 20 large tiger prawns, shells not removed
- 2 tablespoons soy sauce
- 5 cloves of garlic, minced
- 1 tablespoon brandy

Directions:

1. Place all ingredients in a Ziploc bag and marinate in the fridge for at least 2 hours.
2. Place the Foodi™ Cook &Crisp™ reversible rack inside the ceramic pot.
3. Pour water into the pot.
4. Place the marinated shrimps on the reversible rack.
5. Close the pressure lid and set the vent to SEAL.
6. Press the Steam button and adjust the cooking time to 20 minutes.

Nutrition information:

Calories: 67; Carbohydrates: 1.8g; Protein: 12.1g; Fat: 1.8g; Sugar: 0.5g; Sodium: 574mg

Juicy Asian Steamed Chicken

Serving: 4 Cooking time: 45 minutes

Ingredients

- 4 bone-in chicken thighs
- 1 teaspoon salt
- 1 piece fresh ginger, sliced
- 3 green onions, sliced
- 2 cloves of garlic, minced
- 1 ½ tablespoons fish sauce
- 1 tablespoon vinegar
- 1 tablespoon lime juice
- 4 Thai green chilies, chopped
- 5 sprigs, cilantro, chopped
- 1 teaspoon sugar

Directions:

1. Place all ingredients in a Ziploc bag and allow to marinate in the fridge for at least 2 hours.
2. Place the Foodi™ Cook &Crisp™ reversible rack inside the ceramic pot.
3. Pour water into the pot.
4. Place the marinated chicken on the reversible rack.
5. Close the pressure lid and set the vent to SEAL.
6. Press the Steam button and adjust the cooking time to 45 minutes.

Nutrition information:

Calories: 314; Carbohydrates: 19.2g; Protein: 19.9g; Fat:17.3 g; Sugar: 10.5g; Sodium: 93

Chinese Style Steamed Fish

Serving: 3 Cooking time: 25 minutes

Ingredients

- 1 ½ pounds halibut, cut into 4 pieces
- 3 green onions, chopped
- 2 fresh mushrooms, sliced
- 6 leaves napa cabbage, slice
- 2 slices fresh ginger root, chopped
- 2 clove of garlic, chopped
- ¼ cup soy sauce
- 1/8 cup water
- ¼ cup crushed red pepper flakes
- ½ cup fresh cilantro sprigs for garnish

Directions:

1. Place the Foodi™ Cook &Crisp™ reversible rack inside the ceramic pot.
2. Pour water into the pot.
3. In a big aluminum foil, place the halibut and arrange the rest of the ingredients on top of the halibuts.
4. Fold the aluminum foil and crimp the edges.
5. Place on the reversible rack.
6. Close the pressure lid and set the vent to SEAL.
7. Press the Steam button and adjust the cooking time to 25 minutes.

Nutrition information:

Calories: 210; Carbohydrates: 5.2g; Protein: 37.7g; Fat: 4.2g; Sugar: 2.1g; Sodium: 636mg

Steamed Lemon Grass Crab Legs

Serving: 4 Cooking time: 25 minutes

Ingredients

- 2 tablespoons vegetable oil
- 3 cloves of garlic, minced
- 1 piece fresh ginger root, crushed
- 1 stalk lemon grass, crushed
- 2 tablespoons fish sauce
- 1 tablespoon oyster sauce
- 2 pounds frozen Alaskan king crab
- Salt and pepper to taste

Directions:

1. Place the Foodi™ Cook &Crisp™ reversible rack inside the ceramic pot.
2. Pour water into the pot.
3. Combine all ingredients in a big Ziploc bag and marinate for at least 30 minutes.
4. Place the crabs on the reversible rack.
5. Close the pressure lid and set the vent to SEAL.
6. Press the Steam button and adjust the cooking time to 25 minutes.

Nutrition information:

Calories: 564; Carbohydrates: 5.3g; Protein: 89.1g; Fat: 20.7g; Sugar: 2.2g; Sodium: 1023mg

Sole Steamed with Tomatoes And Leaks

Serving: 2 Cooking time: 25 minutes

Ingredients

- 2 fillets of sole
- 1 tablespoon olive oil
- 1cup chopped leeks
- ½ teaspoon minced garlic
- ½ cup dry white wine
- 3 tomatoes, chopped
- ½ teaspoon dried thyme
- 1 teaspoon dill weed

Directions:

1. Place the Foodi™ Cook &Crisp™ reversible rack inside the ceramic pot
2. Pour water into the pot.
3. Get a big aluminum foil and place the sole fillets in the middle.
4. Add in the rest of the ingredients and season with salt and pepper to taste.
5. Fold the aluminum foil and crimp the edges.
6. Place on the reversible rack.
7. Close the pressure lid and set the vent to SEAL.
8. Press the Steam button and adjust the cooking time to 25 minutes.

Nutrition information:

Calories: 285; Carbohydrates: 15.9g; Protein: 34.2g; Fat: 9.3g; Sugar: 2.4g; Sodium: 161mg

Steamed Mussels with Fennel and Tomatoes

Serving: 8 Cooking time: 15 minutes

Ingredients

- 2 shallots, chopped
- 4 cloves of garlic, chopped
- 1 bulb fennel, sliced
- 1 tomato, cubed
- ½ cup white wine
- ½ cup heavy cream
- 4 pounds mussels, cleaned
- 1/3 cup basil leaves, torn
- Salt to taste

Directions:

1. Place everything in a large Ziploc bag and allow the mussels to soak in the marinade.
2. Place the Foodi™ Cook &Crisp™ reversible rack inside the ceramic pot.
3. Pour water into the pot.
4. Place the mussels and the vegetables (except the marinade) on the reversible rack.
5. Close the pressure lid and set the vent to SEAL.
6. Press the Steam button and adjust the cooking time to 15 minutes.
7. Meanwhile, pour the marinade on a saucepan and heat over medium flame until the sauce thickens.
8. Serve the sauce over the clams.

Nutrition information:

Calories: 270; Carbohydrates: 15.7g; Protein: 16.3g; Fat: 15.7g; Sugar: ,4.7g; Sodium: 245mg

Orange Lobster Tail

Serving: 2 Cooking time: 25 minutes

Ingredients

- ¼ cup wine
- 1 cup orange juice
- 2 lobster tails, shells removed
- 6 cubes of butter
- Salt to taste

Directions:

1. Place the wine, orange juice, and lobster tails in a Ziploc bag. Allow to marinate in the fridge.
2. Place the Foodi™ Cook &Crisp™ reversible rack inside the ceramic pot.
3. Pour the marinade in the pot and place the lobster tails on the reversible rack.
4. Close the pressure lid and set the vent to SEAL.
5. Press the Steam button and adjust the cooking time to 20 minutes.
6. Do quick pressure release.
7. Once the lid is open, take out the lobster tails and the reversible rack.
8. Press the Sear/Sauté button and heat the marinade until it thickens. This will be the sauce.
9. Once the sauce thickens, pour over on to the lobster tails.
10. Garnish with butter cubes.

Nutrition information:

Calories: 517; Carbohydrates: 15.4g; Protein: 26.5g; Fat: 38.8g; Sugar: 7.9g; Sodium: 770mg

Steamed Broccoli and Carrots with Lemon

Serving: 3 Cooking time: 8 minutes

Ingredients

- 1 cup broccoli florets
- ½ cup carrots, julienned
- 2 tablespoons lemon juice
- Salt and pepper to taste

Directions:

1. Place the Foodi™ Cook &Crisp™ reversible rack inside the ceramic pot.
2. Pour water into the pot.
3. Toss everything in a mixing bowl and combine.
4. Place the vegetables on the reversible rack.
5. Close the pressure lid and set the vent to SEAL.
6. Press the Steam button and adjust the cooking time to 10 minutes.
7. Do quick pressure release.

Nutrition information:

Calories: 35; Carbohydrates: 8.1g; Protein: 1.7g; Fat: 0.3g; Sugar: 0.7g; Sodium: 497mg

Portuguese Steamed Clams

Serving: 12 Cooking time: 15 minutes

Ingredients

- 1 can diced tomatoes
- 1 large onion, cut into wedges
- 1 ½ pounds chorizo, sliced into chunks
- 5 pounds clams, shells scrubbed
- 2 cups white wine
- ¼ cup olive oil
- Salt and pepper to taste

Directions:

1. Place the tomatoes at the bottom of the ceramic bowl.
2. Add the large onions and the chorizo on top.
3. Put on top the clams.
4. Pour over the white wine and season with salt and pepper to taste.
5. Close the pressure lid and set the vent to SEAL.
6. Press the Steam button and adjust the cooking time to 15 minutes.
7. Do quick pressure release.
8. Drizzle the clams with olive oil before serving.

Nutrition information:

Calories: 630; Carbohydrates: 9.1g; Protein: 29.9g; Fat: 52.6g; Sugar: 3.6g; Sodium: 1567 mg

Hard Steamed Eggs

Serving: 12 Cooking time: 15 minutes

Ingredients

12 eggs

Directions:

1. Place the Foodi™ Cook &Crisp™ reversible rack inside the ceramic pot.
2. Pour water into the pot.
3. Place the eggs gently on the baking insert.
4. Close the pressure lid and set the vent to SEAL.
5. Press the Steam button and adjust the cooking time to 10 minutes.
6. Do quick pressure release.
7. Place the eggs in iced water for about 20 minutes to easily peel off the shell.

Nutrition information:

Calories: 72; Carbohydrates: 0.4g; Protein: 6.3g; Fat: 5g; Sugar: 0g; Sodium: 70mg

Chapter 12 Air Crisped Recipes

Buffalo Air Fried Chicken

Serving:2   Cooking time: 30 minutes

Ingredients

- ½ cup plain fat-free Greek yogurt
- 1 egg, beaten
- 1 tablespoon hot sauce
- 1 cup panko bread crumbs
- 1 tablespoon paprika
- 1 tablespoon garlic pepper seasoning
- 1 tablespoon cayenne pepper
- 1 pound skinless chicken breasts, cut into strips

Directions:

1. Place the Foodi™ Cook &Crisp™ basket in the ceramic pot.
2. In a bowl, combine together the yogurt, eggs, and hot sauce. Set aside.
3. Mix the bread crumbs, paprika, garlic pepper seasoning, and cayenne pepper. Set aside.
4. Dip the chicken in the egg mixture before dredging in the breadcrumb mixture.
5. Place the chicken pieces in the basket.
6. Close the crisping lid and press the Air Crisp button before pressing the START button.
7. Adjust the cooking time to 30 minutes.
8. Open the lid halfway through the cooking time to flip the chicken for even cooking.

Nutrition information:

Calories: 255; Carbohydrates: 22.1g; Protein: 31.2g; Fat: 4.6g; Sugar: 6.9g; Sodium: 696mg

Crispy Fried Crumbed Fish

Serving per recipe:4 Cooking time: 20 minutes

Ingredients

- 4 flounder fillets
- 1 egg, beaten
- 1 cup dry bread crumbs
- ¼ cup vegetable oil
- 1 lemon, sliced
- Salt and pepper

Directions:

1. Place in the ceramic pot the Foodi™ Cook &Crisp™ basket.
2. Season the flounder fillet with salt and pepper.
3. Dip in egg and dredge in flour.
4. Carefully place in the basket and brush generously with oil.
5. Close the crisping lid and press the Air Crisp button before pressing the START button.
6. Adjust the cooking time to 20 minutes.
7. Serve with sliced lemons.

26.9g; Fat: 17.7g; Sugar: 4.2g; Sodium: 309mg

Calories: 357; Carbohydrates: 22.5g; Protein:

Crunchy Onion Rings

Serving:2 Cooking time: 10 minutes

Ingredients

- ¾ cup all-purpose flour
- ½ cup cornstarch
- 2 teaspoons baking powder
- 1 teaspoon salt
- 1 large onion, cut into rings
- 1 cup milk
- 1 egg, beaten
- 1 cup bread crumbs
- A dash of garlic powder
- A dash of paprika
- Cooking spray

Directions:

1. Place in the ceramic pot the Foodi™ Cook &Crisp™ basket.
2. In a large bowl, toss together all-purpose flour, cornstarch, baking powder, salt, and onion rings. Toss until the onion rings have been coated with flour.
3. In another bowl, mix the milk and egg. Set aside.
4. In another bowl, mix the breadcrumbs, garlic powder and paprika. Set aside.
5. Dip each floured onion ring in the milk mixture before dredging in the breadcrumbs.
6. Place the onion rings in the basket.
7. Close the crisping lid and press the Air Crisp button before pressing the START button.
8. Adjust the cooking time to 10 minutes.
9. Be sure to flip the onion rings halfway through the cooking time for even cooking.

Nutrition information:

Calories: 319; Carbohydrates: 59.7g; Protein: 10.2g; Fat: 4.3g; Sugar: 10.5g; Sodium: 1069mg

Spiced Chickpeas with a Crunch

Serving: 2 Cooking time: 15 minutes

Ingredients

- 1 can chickpeas, rinsed and drained
- 1 tablespoon nutritional yeast
- 1 tablespoon olive oil
- 1 teaspoon smoked paprika
- 1 teaspoon garlic
- ½ teaspoon salt
- 1 pinch cumin

Directions:

1. Place in the ceramic pot the Foodi™ Cook & Crisp™ basket.
2. Toss all ingredients in a bowl until well-combined.

3. Place the seasoned chickpeas in the basket.
4. Close the crisping lid and press the Air Crisp button before pressing the START button.

5. Adjust the cooking time to 15 minutes.

Nutrition information:
Calories: 128; Carbohydrates: 17.4g; Protein: 4.7g; Fat: 4.4g; Sugar: 3.2g; Sodium: 501mg

Cheesy Mozzarella Sticks

Serving:1 Cooking time: 15 minutes
Ingredients
- ½ cup water
- ¼ cup all-purpose flour
- 5 tablespoons cornstarch
- 1 tablespoon cornmeal
- 1 teaspoon garlic salt
- ½ teaspoon salt
- 1 cup panko bread crumbs
- 1 tablespoon Italian seasoning blend
- 5 ounce mozzarella cheese, cut into strips
- 1 tablespoon all-purpose flour
- Cooking spray

Directions:

1. Place in the ceramic pot the Foodi™ Cook &Crisp™ basket.
2. In a mixing bowl, combine the water, ¼ cup all-purpose flour, cornstarch, cornmeal, garlic salt, and salt. Mix until well-blended. Set aside.
3. In another bowl, mix the bread crumbs and Italian seasoning mix. Set aside.
4. Dust the mozzarella cheese with 1 tablespoon all-purpose flour.
5. Dip the dusted mozzarella cheese in the egg mixture before dredging in the flour mixture.
6. Place gently inside the basket.
7. Close the crisping lid and press the Air Crisp button before pressing the START button.
8. Adjust the cooking time to 15 minutes.
9. Halfway through the cooking time, open the lid and give the basket a shake.

Nutrition information:
Calories: 270; Carbohydrates: 39.2g; Protein: 12.9g; Fat: 6.8g; Sugar: 13.7g; Sodium: 936mg

Tasty Asparagus Fries

Serving:6 Cooking time: 10 minutes

Ingredients

- 1 large egg
- 1 teaspoon honey
- 1 cup panko bread crumbs
- ½ cup grated parmesan cheese
- 12 asparagus spears, cleaned and trimmed
- ¼ cup stone-ground mustard
- ¼ cup Greek yogurt
- A pinch of cayenne pepper

Directions:

1. Place in the ceramic pot the Foodi™ Cook &Crisp™ basket.
2. Mix in a bowl the egg and honey. Whisk until well combined. Set aside.
3. In another bowl, combine the bread crumbs and parmesan cheese. Set aside.
4. Dip the asparagus spears in the egg mixture before dredging in the breadcrumbs.
5. Place in the basket.
6. Close the crisping lid and press the Air Crisp button before pressing the START button.
7. Adjust the cooking time to 10 minutes.
8. While the spears are cooking, combine the mustard, yogurt and cayenne pepper. This will be the dipping sauce.
9. Serve the asparagus with the dipping sauce.

Nutrition information:

Calories: 140; Carbohydrates: 18g; Protein: 7.5g; Fat: 4.2g; Sugar: 2.4g; Sodium: 356m

Celery Root Fried Crisped

Serving:2 Cooking time: 10 minutes

Ingredients

- ½ celeriac or celery root, cut into sticks
- 3 cups of water
- 1 tablespoon lime juice
- 1/3 cup mayonnaise
- 1 tablespoon mustard
- 1 teaspoon powdered horseradish
- 1 tablespoon olive oil
- Salt and pepper to taste

Directions:

1. Place in the ceramic pot the Foodi™ Cook &Crisp™ basket.
2. Place the celery root slices in water and lime juice. Allow to soak for 1 hour.
3. Drain the celery roots and pat dry with a paper towel. Season with salt and pepper to taste.
4. Place in the basket.
5. Close the crisping lid and press the Air Crisp button before pressing the START button.
6. Adjust the cooking time to 10 minutes.
7. Give the basket a shake halfway through the cooking time.

8. While the celery roots are frying, mix the rest of the ingredients in a bowl. This will be the dipping sauce.
9. Serve the celery roots with the dipping sauce.

Nutrition information:
Calories: 176; Carbohydrates: 13g; Protein: 1.8g; Fat: 12.9g; Sugar: 2.1g; Sodium: 259mg

Easy   'n Crispy Egg Rolls

Serving:12 Cooking time: 10 minutes

Ingredients
- 2 cups frozen corn, thawed
- 1 can black beans, rinsed and drained
- 1 can spinach, drained
- 1 ½ cups shredded jalapeno Jack cheese
- 1 cup sharp cheddar cheese, shredded
- 1 can diced green chilies, drained
- 4 green onions, sliced
- 1 teaspoon salt
- 1 teaspoon ground cumin
- 1 teaspoon chili powder
- 1 package egg roll wrapper
- Cooking spray

Directions:
1. Place in the ceramic pot the Foodi™ Cook &Crisp™ basket.
2. In a mixing bowl, combine all the ingredients except for the egg roll wrapper and cooking spray. Mix to combine.
3. Place an egg roll wrapper on a flat surface. Place ¼ cup of the filling in the center of the wrapper. Moisten the edges of the wrapper with water and fold then roll to create the spring roll. Do the same thing with the other egg wrappers.
4. Place the spring rolls in the basket and brush with oil.
5. Close the crisping lid and press the Air Crisp button before pressing the START button.
6. Adjust the cooking time to 10 minutes.
7. Open the crisping lid and flip the spring rolls to cook evenly.

Nutrition information:
Calories: 220; Carbohydrates: 27g; Protein: 10.6g; Fat: 7.7g; Sugar: 7.4g; Sodium: 632mg

Fried Meatballs with Tomato Sauce

Serving:2 Cooking time: 20 minutes

Ingredients

- 1 small onion
- 1 pound minced beef
- 1 tablespoon chopped parsley
- 1 tablespoon chopped thyme leaves
- 1 egg, beaten
- 3 tablespoons bread crumbs
- ¾ cup of your favorite tomato sauce
- Salt and pepper to tast

Directions:

1. Place in the ceramic pot the Foodi™ Cook &Crisp™ basket.
2. In a mixing bowl, combine all ingredients except for the tomato sauce.
3. Form small balls using your hands.
4. Place the balls in the basket.
5. Close the crisping lid and press the Air Crisp button before pressing the START button.
6. Adjust the cooking time to 20 minutes.
7. Give the basket a shape halfway through the cooking time to evenly cook the food.
8. Once cooked, pour over your favorite tomato sauce on top.

Nutrition information:

Calories: 231; Carbohydrates: 12.1g; Protein: 15.1g; Fat: 13.5g; Sugar: 5.3g; Sodium:267 mg

Crusty Sweet Potato Hash

Serving: 4 Cooking time: 10 minutes

Ingredients

- 2 large sweet potatoes, cut into small cubes
- 2 slices of bacon, cut into small pieces
- 2 tablespoons olive oil
- 1 tablespoon smoked paprika
- 1 teaspoon salt
- 1 teaspoon ground black pepper
- 1 teaspoon dill weed

Directions:

1. Place in the ceramic pot the Foodi™ Cook &Crisp™ basket.
2. Combine all ingredients in a bowl and give a good stir.
3. Form small patties using your hands.
4. Place the patties in the basket.
5. Close the crisping lid and press the Air Crisp button before pressing the START button.
6. Adjust the cooking time to 10 minutes.
7. Flip the patties halfway through the cooking time for even cooking.

Nutrition information:

Calories: 195; Carbohydrates: 31.4g; Protein: 3.7g; Fat: 6g; Sugar: 15.9g; Sodium: 446mg

Sumptuous Breakfast Frittata

Serving: 2 Cooking time: 15 minutes

Ingredients

- ¼ pounds breakfast sausage, cooked and crumbled
- 4 eggs, beaten
- ½ cup Mexican cheese blend of your choice
- 2 tablespoons red bell pepper, diced
- 1 green onion, chopped
- A pinch of cayenne pepper

Directions:

1. Into the ceramic pot, place all ingredients until well-combined.
2. Close the crisping lid and press the Air Crisp button before pressing the START button.
3. Adjust the cooking time to 20 minutes.

Nutrition information:

Calories: 383; Carbohydrates: 2.9g; Protein: 31.2g; Fat: 27.4g; Sugar: 0.2g; Sodium:443 mg

Air Fried Zucchini Chips

Serving: 3 Cooking time: 15 minutes

Ingredients

- 1 cup panko bread crumbs
- ¾ cup grated Parmesan cheese
- 1 medium zucchini, sliced thinly
- 1 large egg, beaten

Directions:

1. Place in the ceramic pot the Foodi™ Cook &Crisp™ basket.
2. Mix the panko bread crumbs and parmesan cheese. Set aside.
3. Dip the zucchini in egg before dredging in the panko mixture.
4. Place the dredged zucchini in the basket.
5. Close the crisping lid and press the Air Crisp button before pressing the START button.
6. Adjust the cooking time to 15 minutes.

Nutrition information:

Calories: 187; Carbohydrates: 21.1g; Protein: 10.8g; Fat: 6.6g; Sugar: 4.9g; Sodium: 384mg

Crispy 'n Tasty Cauliflower Bites

Serving: 4 Cooking time: 10 minutes

Ingredients

- 3 cloves of garlic, minced
- 1 tablespoon olive oil
- ½ teaspoon salt
- ½ teaspoon smoked paprika
- 4 cups cauliflower florets

Directions:

1. Place in the ceramic pot the Foodi™ Cook &Crisp™ basket.
2. Place all ingredients in a bowl and toss to combine.
3. Place the seasoned cauliflower florets in the basket.
4. Close the crisping lid and press the Air Crisp button before pressing the START button.
5. Adjust the cooking time to 10 minutes.
6. Give the basket a shake for even cooking

Nutrition information:

Calories: 130; Carbohydrates: 12.4g; Protein: 4.3g; Fat: 7g; Sugar: 0.7g; Sodium: 642mg

Tiger Shrimp A La Bang Bang

Serving: 2 Cooking time: 15 minutes

Ingredients

- ½ cup mayonnaise
- ¼ cup sweet chili oil
- 1 pound raw shrimps, peeled and deveined
- ¼ cup all-purpose flour
- 1 cup panko bread crumbs
- 1 head loose leaf lettuce
- 2 green onions, chopped

Directions:

1. Place in the ceramic pot the Foodi™ Cook &Crisp™ basket.
2. In a bowl, combine the mayonnaise and sweet chili oil. Reserve half of it as dipping sauce.
3. Dust the shrimps with all-purpose flour and dip in half of the mayonnaise mixture.
4. Dredge the shrimps in panko bread crumbs.
5. Close the crisping lid and press the Air Crisp button before pressing the START button.
6. Adjust the cooking time to 15 minutes.
7. Serve on top of lettuce and garnish with green onions.

Nutrition information:

Calories: 442; Carbohydrates: 32.7g; Protein: 23.9g; Fat: 23.9g; Sugar: 10.8g; Sodium: 894mg

Olive-Brined Air Fryer Turkey Breasts

Serving: 7 Cooking time: 45 minutes

Ingredients

- ½ cup salt
- 6 cups water
- ½ cup butter milk
- 3 ½ pounds boneless turkey breasts
- 1 sprig rosemary
- 2 sprigs thyme

Directions:

1. Place all ingredients in a large bowl or stock pot and allow the turkey to soak in the brine for at least 24 hours.
2. Rinse the turkey and pat dry.
3. Place in the ceramic pot the Foodi™ Cook & Crisp™ basket
4. Place the turkey breasts in the basket.
5. Close the crisping lid and press the Air Crisp button before pressing the START button.
6. Adjust the cooking time to 45 minutes.

Nutrition information:

Calories: 135; Carbohydrates: 1.4g; Protein: 30.2g; Fat: 0.9g; Sugar:0 g; Sodium: 62mg

Chapter 13 Baked/Roasted Recipes

Baked Teriyaki Chicken

Serving:12 ,   Cooking time: 40 minutes

Ingredients

- 1 tablespoon cornstarch
- 1 tablespoon cold water
- ½ cup white sugar
- ½ cup soy sauce
- ¼ cup apple cider vinegar
- 1 clove of garlic, minced
- ½ teaspoon ground ginger
- ¼ teaspoon ground black pepper
- 12 skinless chicken thighs

Directions:

1. Mix together the cornstarch, cold water, white sugar, soy sauce, apple cider vinegar, garlic, ground ginger, and black pepper.
2. Place the mixture in a saucepan and simmer on low heat until the sauce thickens.
3. Season the chicken with salt and pepper.
4. Place in the ceramic pot the Foodi™ Cook & Crisp™ reversible rack.
5. Place the chicken on the reversible tray and brush the chicken with the sauce.
6. Close the crisping lid and press the Bake/Roast button before pressing the START button.
7. Adjust the cooking time to 40 minutes.

Nutrition information:

Calories: 267; Carbohydrates: 19.9g; Protein: 24.7g; Fat: 9.8g; Sugar: 15.2g; Sodium: 1282mg

Cheesy   'n Milky Haddock

Serving: 4,   Cooking time: 20 minutes

Ingredients

- 4 haddock fillets
- ¾ cup milk
- 2 teaspoons salt
- ¾ cup bread crumbs
- ¼ cup grated Parmesan cheese
- ¼ teaspoon ground dried thyme
- ¼ cup butter, melted

Directions:

1. Place in the ceramic pot the Foodi™ Cook &Crisp™ reversible rack.
2. Dip the haddock fillets in milk then season with salt.   Set aside.
3. In a mixing bowl, combine the bread crumbs, parmesan cheese, and ground thyme.

4. Dredge the fillets in the bread crumbs mixture.
5. Place the fish on the reversible rack.
6. Brush with butter on all sides.
7. Close the crisping lid and press the Bake/Roast button before pressing the START button.
8. Adjust the cooking time to 20 minutes.

Nutrition information:
Calories: 321; Carbohydrates: 17g; Protein: 27.7g; Fat: 15.7g; Sugar: 8.4g; Sodium: 1546mg

Easy Foiled Baked Salmon

Serving:2, Cooking time: 20 minutes
Ingredients
- 2 salmon fillets
- 2 cloves of garlic, minced
- 6 tablespoons olive oil
- 1 teaspoon dried basil
- 1 teaspoon salt
- 1 teaspoon ground black pepper
- 1 tablespoon lemon juice
- 1 tablespoon fresh parsley, chopped

Directions:
1. Place in the ceramic pot the Foodi™ Cook &Crisp™ reversible rack.
2. On a large foil, place the salmon fillets and season with the rest of the ingredients.
3. Do not fold the aluminum foil.
4. Place the foil - fish and all - on the reversible tray.
5. Close the crisping lid and press the Bake/Roast button before pressing the START button.
6. Adjust the cooking time to 20 minutes or until the fish is flaky.

Nutrition information:
Calories: 619; Carbohydrates: 2.9g; Protein: 36.3g; Fat: 51.3g; Sugar: 0.3g; Sodium: 1235mg

Hearty Egg and Sausage Bake

Serving:6 , Cooking time: 30 minutes
Ingredients
- 1 ½ pounds bulk pork sausages, sliced
- 1 ½ cups milk
- 8 eggs, beaten
- ¾ teaspoon dry mustard
- 1 can condensed cream of mushroom soup
- 8 slices of bread, torn into small squares
- 2 cups shredded mozzarella cheese

Directions:
1. Place the ceramic tray in the Ninja Foodi.
2. Place the sausages in the pot.

3. In a bowl, combine the milk, eggs, mustard and mushroom soup.
4. Pour the egg mixture into the ceramic pot and add the bread pieces.
5. Top with mozzarella cheese.
6. Close the crisping lid and press the Bake/Roast button before pressing the START button.
7. Adjust the cooking time to 30 minutes.

Nutrition information:
Calories: 159; Carbohydrates: 14.7g; Protein: 20.5g; Fat: 22g; Sugar: 7.3g; Sodium: 976mg

Appetizing Baked Pompano

Serving: 3 Cooking time: 40 minutes
Ingredients
- 1 cup soy sauce
- ½ cup rice cooking wine
- 5 tablespoons olive oil, divided
- 2 teaspoons hoisin sauce
- 2 teaspoons fish sauce
- 2 teaspoons oyster sauce
- 1 lime, halved
- 1 shallot, died
- 1 piece ginger, grated
- 1 ½ pounds whole pompano fish, gutted and cleaned
- 1 teaspoon dill
- 2 cups Napa cabbage leaves
- Salt and pepper to taste

Directions:
1. Place in the ceramic pot the Foodi™ Cook &Crisp™ reversible rack.
2. In a big dish, place soy sauce, wine, half of the olive oil, hoisin sauce, fish sauce, oyster sauce, lime, shallot, and ginger.
3. Place the pompano fish in the dish and brush with the marinade. Allow to marinate in the fridge for at least 2 hours.
4. Take the fish out and place on the rack. Brush with the remaining half of the oil and season with dill, salt, and pepper.
5. Close the crisping lid and press the Bake/Roast button before pressing the START button. Adjust the cooking time to 40 minutes.
6. Once cooked, place the fish on a bed of napa cabbage.

Nutrition information:
Calories: 501; Carbohydrates: 13.4g; Protein: 36.8g; Fat: 33.3g; Sugar:4.6 g; Sodium: 998mg

Mouthwatering Baked Brisket

Serving: 14 Cooking time: 60 minutes

Ingredients

- 20 cloves of garlic, minced
- 2 bunches of cilantro, chopped
- 1 ¼ cup red wine vinegar
- 3 onions, sliced thinly
- 8 pounds beef brisket

Directions:

1. Place in the ceramic pot the Foodi™ Cook &Crisp™ reversible rack.
2. In a blender, place the garlic, cilantro, red wine, and onions. Pulse until smooth.
3. Place the mixture in a Ziploc bag and add in the beef brisket. Season with salt and pepper to taste. Allow to marinate in the fridge for at least 2 hours.
4. Place the marinated brisket on the rack.
5. Close the crisping lid and press the Bake/Roast button before pressing the START button.
6. Adjust the cooking time to 60 minutes.
7. Meanwhile, place the marinade in a saucepan and bring to a simmer until the sauce is reduced.
8. Use the sauce to brush on the beef brisket halfway through the cooking time.

Nutrition information:

Calories: 483; Carbohydrates: 3.4g; Protein: 26.7g; Fat: 40.2g; Sugar: 0.9g; Sodium: 100mg

Healthy Asparagus Bake

Serving: 8,   Cooking time: 25 minutes

Ingredients

- 4 cups asparagus spears, trimmed
- 12 dinner rolls
- 1 ½ cup diced cheese
- 2 ½ cups cooked ham
- 6 eggs, beaten
- 3 cups milk
- 3 tablespoons minced onion
- Salt and pepper to taste

Directions:

1. Place the ceramic pot in the Ninja Foodi.
2. Place the asparagus spears in the ceramic pot.
3. Add in a layer of dinner rolls, cheese, and ham.
4. In a bowl, combine the eggs and milk. Whisk until well-combined.
5. Pour the egg mixture over the layer of the ingredients.
6. Stir in the onion and season with salt and pepper to taste.
7. Close the crisping lid and press the Bake/Roast button before pressing the START button.
8. Adjust the cooking time to 25 minutes.

Nutrition information:

Calories: 239; Carbohydrates: 15.1g; Protein: 15.3g; Fat: 13g; Sugar: 6.7g; Sodium: 825mg

Ninja Foodi Baked Fudge

Serving:6   Cooking time: 50 minutes

Ingredients

- 2 cups white sugar
- ½ cup all-purpose flour
- ½ cup cocoa powder
- 4 eggs, beaten
- 1 cup butter, melted
- 2 teaspoons vanilla extract
- 1 cup chopped pecans

Directions:

1. Place in the ceramic pot the Foodi™ Cook &Crisp™ reversible rack.
2. Close the crisping lid and press the Broil button before pressing the START button to preheat the Ninja Foodi.
3. In a bowl, sift together the sugar, flour, and cocoa. Add in eggs, melted butter, vanilla, and pecans. Mix to combine everything.
4. Pour the batter into a baking pan that will fit inside the Ninja Foodi.
5. Place in the preheated Ninja Foodi and close the crisping lid.
6. Press the Bake/Roast button before pressing the START button.
7. Adjust the cooking time to 50 minutes.

Nutrition information:

Calories: 397; Carbohydrates: 40.7g; Protein: 4.3g; Fat: 24.1g; Sugar: 25.3g; Sodium: 159mg

Flavorsome Baked Bananas

Serving:4,   Cooking time: 10 minutes

Ingredients

- 4 firm bananas, peeled and halved
- ¼ cup maple syrup
- 1 tablespoons ground cinnamon
- 1 piece fresh ginger, grated
- 1 ½ teaspoon nutmeg

Directions:

1. Place in the ceramic pot the Foodi™ Cook &Crisp™ reversible rack.
2. In a bowl, season the bananas with maple syrup, ground cinnamon, ginger, and nutmeg.
3. Place the bananas on the rack.
4. Close the crisping lid and press the Bake/Roast button before pressing the START button. Adjust the cooking time to 10 minutes.

Nutrition information:

Calories: 183; Carbohydrates: 42.2g; Protein:1.4 g; Fat: 0.9g; Sugar: 24.7g; Sodium: 3mg

Herb Roasted Pork

Serving: 10 Cooking time: 2 hours

Ingredients

- 1 teaspoon sage
- ½ teaspoon salt
- ¼ teaspoon pepper
- 1 clove of garlic, crushed
- 5 pounds boneless pork loin, scored
- ½ cup sugar
- 1 tablespoon cornstarch
- ¼ cup vinegar
- ¼ cup water
- 2 tablespoons soy sauce

Directions:

1. Place in the ceramic pot the Foodi™ Cook &Crisp™ reversible rack.
2. In a bowl, combine the sage, salt, pepper, and garlic.
3. Rub all over the pork and place the pork on the reversible rack.
4. Close the crisping lid and press the Bake/Roast button before pressing the START button.
5. Adjust the cooking time to 2 hours.
6. Meanwhile, place the remaining ingredients in a saucepan and heat until the sauce thickens.
7. Serve the roasted pork with the sauce.

Nutrition information:

Calories: 461; Carbohydrates: 13.9g; Protein: 45.8g; Fat: 24.6g; Sugar: 4.3g; Sodium: 470m

Savory Roasted Vegetables

Serving: 16 Cooking time: 20 minutes

Ingredients

- 8 zucchinis, peeled and chopped
- 1 eggplant, diced
- 8 carrots, peeled and diced
- 16 cherry tomatoes, halved
- 2 red onions, sliced
- 1 red bell pepper, sliced
- 1 yellow bell pepper, sliced
- ½ cup olive oil
- 1 teaspoon dried rosemary
- 1 teaspoon dried thyme
- 2 bay leaves, crushed
- 1 teaspoon dried oregano
- 2 cloves of garlic, minced
- 2 tablespoons fresh lemon juice
- 1 teaspoon grated lemon zest
- Salt and pepper to taste

Directions:

1. Place in the ceramic pot the Foodi™ Cook &Crisp™ basket insert.
2. Toss all ingredients in a mixing bowl.
3. Place in the basket insert.
4. Close the crisping lid and press the Bake/Roast button before pressing the START button.
5. Adjust the cooking time to 20 minutes.
6. Give the basket a shake to evenly roast the vegetables.

Nutrition information:

Calories: 78; Carbohydrates: 7.3g; Protein: 1.5g; Fat:4.7 g; Sugar: 0.6g; Sodium: 11mg

Spiced Roasted Broccoli

Serving:2,   Cooking time: 20 minutes

Ingredients

- 2 cups broccoli florets
- 1 yellow bell pepper, sliced
- 1 teaspoon garlic powder
- 1 tablespoon steak seasoning
- 2 teaspoons chili powder
- 1 tablespoon extra-virgin olive oil
- Salt and pepper to taste

Directions:

1. Place in the ceramic pot the Foodi™ Cook &Crisp™ basket insert.
2. Toss all ingredients in a mixing bowl.
3. Place the vegetables in the basket.
4. Close the crisping lid and press the Bake/Roast button before pressing the START button.
5. Adjust the cooking time to 20 minutes.
6. Give the basket a shake to roast the vegetables evenly

Nutrition information:

Calories: 76; Carbohydrates. 8g; Protein: 2.1g; Fat: 3.9g; Sugar: 0.6g; Sodium: 718mg

Coffee-Flavored Chuck Roast

Serving:8 Cooking time: 2 hours

Ingredients

- 2 tablespoons butter
- 4 pounds chuck roast
- 1 tablespoon butter
- 1 onion, chopped finely
- 6 cups brewed coffee
- Salt and pepper to taste

Directions:

1. Place all ingredients in a bowl and allow the chuck roast to marinate for at least overnight in the fridge.
2. Place in the ceramic pot the Foodi™ Cook & Crisp™ basket insert.
3. Place the marinated roast on the basket insert.
4. Close the crisping lid and press the Bake/Roast button before pressing the START button.
5. Adjust the cooking time to 2 hours.

Nutrition information:

Calories: 690; Carbohydrates: 8g; Protein: 59.7g; Fat: 46.5g; Sugar: 2.4g; Sodium: 501mg

Simple Yet Tasty Beef Roast

Serving: 4,   Cooking time: 2 hours

Ingredients

- ½ cup salt
- 10 cups water
- 2 pounds beef roast
- 1 sprig of thyme
- 1 teaspoon oregano

Directions:

1. Place in the ceramic pot the Foodi™ Cook &Crisp™ basket insert.
2. Make the brine by combining the salt and water.
3. Soak the beef roast and add the thyme and oregano.
4. Allow the beef to soak in the brine for at least overnight.
5. Place the beef in the basket insert.
6. Close the crisping lid and press the Bake/Roast button before pressing the START button.
7. Adjust the cooking time to 2 hours.

Nutrition information:

Calories: 348; Carbohydrates: 2g; Protein: 31.1g; Fat: 23.9g; Sugar: 0g; Sodium: 1529mg

Simple Beer-Marinated Pork Roast

Serving: 8 Cooking time: 2 hours

Ingredients

- 4 pounds pork shoulder roast, scored
- 2 cans beer
- 2 bay leaves
- 3 sprigs fresh rosemary
- Salt and pepper to taste

Directions:

1. Place in the ceramic pot the Foodi™ Cook &Crisp™ basket insert.
2. In a large bowl, mix all ingredients and allow the pork to marinate in the fridge for at least overnight.
3. Place the marinated pork in the basket.
4. Close the crisping lid and press the Bake/Roast button before pressing the START button.
5. Adjust the cooking time to 2 hours.

Nutrition information:

Calories: 476; Carbohydrates: 38.5g; Protein: 30.8g; Fat: 22g; Sugar: 15.8g; Sodium: 931mg

Herb Roasted Pork Loin with Potatoes

Serving: 8 Cooking time: 2 hours

Ingredients

- 4 pounds pork loin, fat trimmed
- 2 tablespoons olive oil
- ½ teaspoon dried thyme
- ½ teaspoon garlic powder
- Salt and pepper to taste
- 6 medium potatoes, peeled and quartered
- 1 ½ teaspoons chopped fresh chives

Directions:

1. Place in the ceramic pot the Foodi™ Cook & Crisp™ basket insert.
2. Season the pork loin with olive oil, thyme, garlic powder, salt and pepper.
3. Place in the basket insert and place the potatoes on the side. Season with salt and pepper and garnish with fresh chives.
4. Close the crisping lid and press the Bake/Roast button before pressing the START button.
5. Adjust the cooking time to 2 hours.

Nutrition information:

Calories: 345; Carbohydrates: 29.5g; Protein: 28.9g; Fat: 12.3g; Sugar: 6.6g; Sodium: 53mg

Ninja Foodi Cola Roast

Serving: 8,   Cooking time: 2 hours

Ingredients

- 4 pounds beef sirloin roast
- 1 can cola
- 3 cups water
- 1 clove of garlic, minced
- 1 bay leaf
- Salt and pepper to taste

Directions:

1. Place in the ceramic pot the Foodi™ Cook &Crisp™ basket insert.
2. Place all ingredients in a bowl and allow the beef to soak in the cola for at least overnight.
3. Place the marinated beef in the basket insert.
4. Close the crisping lid and press the Bake/Roast button before pressing the START button.
5. Adjust the cooking time to 2 hours.

Nutrition information:

Calories: 416; Carbohydrates: 12.7g; Protein: 38.8g; Fat: 23.3g; Sugar: 6.9g; Sodium: 736mg

Apple Butter Pork Loin

Serving: 4 Cooking time: 1 hour and 30 minutes

Ingredients

- 2 pounds boneless pork loin roast
- 2 cups apple juice
- ½ cup apple butter
- ¼ cup brown sugar
- 2 tablespoons water
- ¼ teaspoon ground cinnamon
- ¼ teaspoon ground cloves
- Salt and pepper to taste

Directions:

1. Place in the ceramic pot the Foodi™ Cook &Crisp™ basket insert.
2. Season the pork loin with salt and pepper.
3. Place the pork in a roasting pan that will fit inside the basket insert.
4. Pour over the apple juice and cover with aluminum foil.
5. Close the crisping lid and press the Bake/Roast button before pressing the START button.
6. Adjust the cooking time to 1hour and 30 minutes.
7. Meanwhile, place the apple butter, sugar, water, cinnamon, and cloves in a saucepan until it thickens.
8. Halfway through the cooking time, brush the pork loin with the sauce.

Nutrition information:

Calories: 591; Carbohydrates: 25.7g; Protein: 64.9g; Fat: 25.4g; Sugar: 16.4g; Sodium: 151mg

Roasted Whole Chicken

Serving:4 Cooking time: 60 minutes

Ingredients

- ½ cup salt
- 10 cups water
- 2 pounds whole rotisserie chicken
- 1 sprig rosemary
- 1 tablespoon sage

Directions:

1. Dissolve the salt in water to make a brine in a deep bowl or stock pot.
2. Soak the chicken and put in the rosemary and sage.
3. Allow the chicken to marinate in the brine for overnight.
4. Place in the ceramic pot the Foodi™ Cook & Crisp™ reversible rack.
5. Place the chicken on the rack.
6. Close the crisping lid and press the Bake/Roast button before pressing the START button.
7. Adjust the cooking time to 1hour.

Nutrition information:

Calories: 406; Carbohydrates: 0.9g; Protein: 34.2g; Fat: 29.5g; Sugar: 0g; Sodium: 899mg

Broiled Cranberry Pork

Serving: 6 Cooking time: 1 hour and 30 minutes

Ingredients

- 3 pounds boneless pork loin roast
- 1 can cranberry sauce
- 1/3 cup French salad dressing
- 1 onion, sliced

Directions:

1. Place in the ceramic pot the pork loin roast and pour the cranberry sauce and French salad dress. Top with onions.

2. Close the crisping lid and press the Bake/Roast button before pressing the START button.

3. Adjust the cooking time to 1hour and 30 minutes.

Nutrition information:

Calories: 375; Carbohydrates: 32.9g; Protein: 26.8g; Fat: 15.1g; Sugar: 19.8g; Sodium: 184mg

Spicy Honey Mustard Pork Roast

Serving: 6 Cooking time: 1 hour and 30 minutes

Ingredients

- 3 pounds pork roast
- ¼ cup honey
- 2 tablespoons Dijon mustard
- 2 tablespoons black pepper
- ½ teaspoon salt
- ½ teaspoon dried thyme

Directions:

1. Place in the ceramic pot the Foodi™ Cook & Crisp™ reversible rack.

2. Score the pork roast with a knife and place on a circular baking dish that will fit in the Ninja Foodi.

3. In a mixing bowl, mix together the rest of the ingredients until well-blended.

4. Brush the pork with the spice rub.

5. Place the pork in a baking dish on the rack.

6. Close the crisping lid and press the Bake/Roast button before pressing the START button.

7. Adjust the cooking time to 1hour and 30 minutes.

Nutrition information:

Calories: 242; Carbohydrates: 14.1g; Protein: 26.5g; Fat: 8.8g; Sugar: 7.9g; Sodium: 366mg

Herbed Pork Rump Roast

Serving: 4 Cooking time: 1 hour and 30 minutes

Ingredients

- 2 tablespoons olive oil
- ½ teaspoon thyme
- ½ teaspoon garlic powder
- 1 ½ teaspoons chopped chives
- 2 pounds pork rump
- Salt and pepper to taste

Directions:

1. Place in the ceramic pot the Foodi™ Cook & Crisp™ reversible rack.
2. In a bowl, mix together olive oil, thyme, garlic powder, chives, salt, and pepper. This will be the seasoning.
3. Rub the pork rump with the seasoning.
4. Close the crisping lid and press the Bake/Roast button before pressing the START button.
5. Adjust the cooking time to 1 hour and 30 minutes.

Nutrition information:

Calories: 518; Carbohydrates: 0.9g; Protein: 47.3g; Fat: 36.1g; Sugar: 0g; Sodium: 852mg

Balsamic Roasted Pork Loin

Serving: 4 Cooking time: 1 hour and 30 minutes

Ingredients

- 2 tablespoons steak seasoning rub
- ½ cup balsamic vinegar
- ½ cup olive oil
- 2 pounds boneless pork loin roast

Directions:

1. Place in the ceramic pot the Foodi™ Cook &Crisp™ reversible rack.
2. Mix the steak seasoning rub, balsamic vinegar, and olive oil.
3. Rub the pork loin roast with the seasoning.
4. Close the crisping lid and press the Bake/Roast button before pressing the START button.
5. Adjust the cooking time to 1 hour and 30 minutes.

Nutrition information:

Calories: 297; Carbohydrates: 3.1g; Protein: 18.3g; Fat: 23.4g; Sugar: 0.8g; Sodium:732 mg

Chinese Pork Roast

Serving: 8 Cooking time: 1 hour and 30 minutes

Ingredients

- 4 pounds pork roast, trimmed
- ¾ cup soy sauce
- ½ cup dry sherry
- 1/3 cup honey
- 2 cloves of garlic, minced
- ½ teaspoon ground ginger

Directions:

1. Place in the ceramic pot the Foodi™ Cook &Crisp™ reversible rack.
2. Place all ingredients in a bowl and allow the meat to marinate in the fridge for at least 12 hours.
3. Place the marinated meat on the rack.
4. Close the crisping lid and press the Bake/Roast button before pressing the START button.
5. Adjust the cooking time to 1 hour and 30 minutes.
6. Meanwhile, put the marinade in a saucepan and bring to a simmer until the sauce has reduced.
7. Halfway through the cooking time, baste the pork with sauce.

Nutrition information:

Calories: 345; Carbohydrates: 15.1g; Protein: 22.3g; Fat: 21.5g; Sugar: 8.6g; Sodium: 1310mg

Salt-Encrusted Prime Rib Roast

Serving: 8 Cooking time: 45 minutes

Ingredients

- 2 cups salt
- 4 pounds prime rib roast
- 1 tablespoon black pepper

Directions:

1. Place in the ceramic pot the Foodi™ Cook &Crisp™ reversible rack.
2. In a roasting pan that will fit in the Ninja Foodi, place the salt. Place the roast on top of the bed of salt. Season the pork with black pepper.
3. Place the pan with the meat on the rack.
4. Close the crisping lid and press the Bake/Roast button before pressing the START button.
5. Adjust the cooking time to 45 minutes.

Nutrition information:

Calories: 382; Carbohydrates: 1.2g; Protein: 36.1g; Fat: 25.8g; Sugar: 0g; Sodium: 3092mg

Chapter 14 Broiled Recipes

Broiled & Buttered Scallops

Serving: 3,   Cooking time: 20 minutes

Ingredients

- 1 ½ pounds bay scallops, removed from shells
- 1 tablespoon garlic salt
- 2 tablespoons melted butter
- 2 tablespoon lemon juice

Directions:

1. Place in the ceramic pot the Foodi™ Cook &Crisp™ basket insert.
2. In a mixing bowl, combine all ingredients until the scallops are coated with the seasoning.
3. Place in the basket insert.
4. Close the crisping lid and press the Broil button before pressing the START button.
5. Adjust the cooking time to 20 minutes.

Nutrition information:

Calories: 265; Carbohydrates: 6.8g; Protein: 38.3g; Fat: 9.4g; Sugar: 2.3g; Sodium: 2232mg

Easy Broiled Lobster Tails

Serving per recipe:2   Cooking time: 20 minutes

Ingredients

- 2 ounces fresh lobster tails
- 1 tablespoon olive oil
- 1 teaspoon lemon pepper seasoning

Directions:

1. Place in the ceramic pot the Foodi™ Cook & Crisp™ reversible tray.
2. Season the lobster tails with olive oil and lemon-pepper seasoning.
3. Place the lobster tails on the tray.
4. Close the crisping lid and press the Broil button before pressing the START button.
5. Adjust the cooking time to 20 minutes.

Nutrition information:

Calories: 208; Carbohydrates: 1.1g; Protein: 32g; Fat: 8.3g; Sugar: 0.4g; Sodium: 734mg

Broiled Short Ribs

Serving:8   Cooking time: 45 minutes

Ingredients

- 4 pounds boneless beef short ribs
- Salt and pepper to taste
- 1/3 cup molasses
- 2/3 ketchup
- ¼ cup fresh lemon juice
- 1 tablespoon dry mustard
- ½ teaspoon chili powder
- ½ teaspoon garlic powder

Directions:

1. Place in the ceramic pot the Foodi™ Cook & Crisp™ reversible tray.
2. Combine all ingredients in a mixing bowl and allow to marinate in the fridge for at least 12 hours.
3. Close the crisping lid and press the Broil button before pressing the START button.
4. Adjust the cooking time to 45 minutes.

Nutrition information:

Calories: 357; Carbohydrates: 16.4g; Protein: 31.2g; Fat: 18.5g; Sugar:8.3 g; Sodium: 287mg

Easy Garlic Broiled Chicken

Serving: 6 Cooking time: 30 minutes

Ingredients

- ½ cup butter
- 3 tablespoons minced garlic
- ¼ teaspoon black pepper
- 1 tablespoon dried parsley
- 6 boneless chicken thighs
- Dried parsley

Directions:

1. Place in the ceramic pot the Foodi™ Cook &Crisp™ reversible tray.
2. Place all ingredients in a Ziploc bag and allow to marinate in the fridge for at least 3 hours.
3. Close the crisping lid and press the Broil button before pressing the START button.
4. Adjust the cooking time to 30 minutes.

Nutrition information:

Calories: 284; Carbohydrates: 2.3g; Protein: 16.8g; Fat: 23g; Sugar: 0.7g; Sodium: 615mg

Flaky Broiled Salmon

Serving:4   Cooking time: 20 minutes

Ingredients

- 1 clove of garlic, chopped
- 2 tablespoons olive oil
- 4 salmon fillets
- ½ cup butter
- 2 tablespoons Worcestershire sauce
- 2 tablespoons lemon juice
- ¼ cup white wine
- 1 teaspoon ground black pepper
- 1 teaspoon garlic salt
- 1 ½ teaspoon fines herbs
- ¼ cup fresh dill

Directions:

1. Place in the ceramic pot the Foodi™ Cook &Crisp™ reversible tray.

2. In a Ziploc bag, combine all ingredients and allow the salmon to marinate in the fridge for at least 2 hours.

3. Place the salmon fillets on the reversible tray.

4. Close the crisping lid and press the Broil button before pressing the START button.

5. Adjust the cooking time to 20 minutes.

Nutrition information:

Calories: 519; Carbohydrates: 4g; Protein: 36.4g; Fat: 39.7g; Sugar: 1.2g; Sodium: 772m

Chapter 15 Dehydrated Recipes

Dehydrated Beet Chips

Serving: 5, Cooking time: 8 hours

Ingredients

- 3 large beets, peeled and sliced
- ¼ cup water
- ¼ cup apple cider vinegar
- 1 tablespoon olive oil
- A dash of salt flakes

Directions:

1. Place in the ceramic pot the Foodi™ Cook & Crisp™ dehydrating tray.
2. Soak the beets in water and apple cider vinegar.
3. Let it sit for a few hours in the fridge.
4. Drain the beets and pat dry using a paper towel.
5. Season the beets with oil and salt flakes.
6. Close the crisping lid and press the Dehydrate button before pressing the START button.
7. Adjust the cooking time to 8 hours.

Nutrition information:

Calories: 117; Carbohydrates: 17.9g; Protein: 3g; Fat: 3.7g; Sugar: 2.4g; Sodium: 14466mg

Spicy Salmon Jerky

Serving: 6, Cooking time: 12 hours

Ingredients

- 3 pounds salmon fillets, skin removed
- 1 cup soy sauce
- 2 tablespoons molasses
- 2 tablespoons white sugar
- 2 tablespoons Worcestershire sauce
- 2 tablespoons lemon juice
- 1 ½ tablespoons ground black pepper
- 2 teaspoons liquid smoke seasoning
- 12 dashes of hot sauce

Directions:

1. Place in the ceramic pot the Foodi™ Cook & Crisp™ dehydrating tray.
2. Mix all ingredients in a mixing bowl and allow to marinate in the fridge for at least 2 hours.
3. Place the marinated salmon fillets on the dehydrating tray.
4. Close the crisping lid and press the Dehydrate button before pressing the START button.
5. Adjust the cooking time to 12 hours.

Nutrition information:

Calories: 227; Carbohydrates: 7.5g; Protein: 25.6g; Fat: 10.5g; Sugar: 3.2g; Sodium: 1317mg

Low-Carb Zucchini Chips

Serving: 4, Cooking time: 12 hours

Ingredients

- 2 large zucchinis, thinly sliced
- 1 tablespoon olive oil
- Salt to taste

Directions:

1. Place in the ceramic pot the Foodi™ Cook & Crisp™ dehydrating tray.
2. Season the zucchini with olive oil, salt and taste.
3. Place the zucchini on the dehydrating tray.
4. Close the crisping lid and press the Dehydrate button before pressing the START button.
5. Adjust the cooking time to 12 hours.

Nutrition information:

Calories: 130; Carbohydrates: 10.8g; Protein: 3.9g; Fat: 7.9g; Sugar: 0.2g; Sodium: 192mg

Dad's Beef Jerky

Serving: 4, Cooking time: 12 hours

Ingredients

- ½ cup soy sauce
- ¼ cup Worcestershire sauce
- ½ teaspoon liquid seasoning
- 1 teaspoon hot pepper sauce
- 1 teaspoon garlic powder
- 1 teaspoon onion powder
- ½ teaspoon black pepper
- ½ cup brown sugar
- 2 pounds beef sirloin, cut into strips

Directions:

1. Place in the ceramic pot the Foodi™ Cook &Crisp™ dehydrating tray.
2. Mix all ingredients in a mixing bowl and allow to marinate in the fridge for at least 2 hours.
3. Place the marinated beef slices on the dehydrating tray.
4. Close the crisping lid and press the Dehydrate button before pressing the START button.
5. Adjust the cooking time to 12 hours.

Nutrition information:

Calories: 216; Carbohydrates: 6.9g; Protein: 34.2g; Fat: 5.7g; Sugar: 2.4g; Sodium: 993mg

Deliciously Dehydrated Apple Chips

Serving: 4

Cooking time: 12 hours

Ingredients

- 2 Golden Delicious apples, cored and sliced
- 1 ½ teaspoons white sugar
- ½ teaspoon ground cinnamon

Directions:

1. Place in the ceramic pot the Foodi™ Cook &Crisp™ dehydrating tray.
2. Season the apples with white sugar and cinnamon
3. Place the apples on the dehydrating tray.
4. Close the crisping lid and press the Dehydrate button before pressing the START button.
5. Adjust the cooking time to 12 hours.

Nutrition information:

Calories: 28; Carbohydrates: 6.9g; Protein: 0.1g; Fat: 0g; Sugar: 3.6g; Sodium: 1mg

Made in the USA
Lexington, KY
23 January 2019